Violent Differences

Violent Differences

THE IMPORTANCE OF RACE IN SEXUAL ASSAULT AGAINST QUEER MEN

Doug Meyer

UNIVERSITY OF CALIFORNIA PRESS

University of California Press
Oakland, California

Library of Congress Cataloging-in-Publication Data

Names: Meyer, Doug, 1980- author.
Title: Violent differences : the importance of race in sexual assault
    against queer men / Doug Meyer.
Description: Oakland, California : University of California Press, [2022]
    | Includes bibliographical references and index.
Identifiers: LCCN 2022006816 (print) | LCCN 2022006817 (ebook) |
    ISBN 9780520384699 (cloth) | ISBN 9780520384705 (paperback) |
    ISBN 9780520384712 (epub)
Subjects: LCSH: Male rape victims—United States—21st century. |
    Gays—Violence against.
Classification: LCC HV6250.4.H66 M495 2022 (print) | LCC HV6250.4.H66
    (ebook) | DDC 362.88392086/64—dc23/eng/20220525
LC record available at https://lccn.loc.gov/2022006816
LC ebook record available at https://lccn.loc.gov/2022006817

31 30 29 28 27 26 25 24 23 22
10 9 8 7 6 5 4 3 2 1

Contents

Acknowledgments

My deepest thanks go to the men who spoke with me for this book. I learned a great deal from each and every participant I interviewed, and conducting this research, although sometimes difficult, was ultimately very rewarding. The men I spoke with were extremely generous with their time, thoughts, and emotions. I hope they got something out of the interviews as well and that I have reflected their voices and experiences throughout this book. I would also like to thank the organizations that allowed me to place my flyers up in their space, either in person or online. They did not have to do so, and it helped me tremendously in being able to conduct this research.

Friends and colleagues at multiple institutions helped improve this project. First, I would like the thank Bailey Troia, who served as my research assistant and helped improve this project tremendously. This book would not be where it is now without her thoughtful and helpful feedback at multiple stages of the project. For all of the comments she gave me and for all of the conversations we had, I thank her. Several students helped me with transcribing the interview files—in this regard, I would like to thank Dhanya Chittaranjan, Chloe Cook, Maria DeHart, Blake Hesson, and Jordan Moorefield. Several of you planted helpful seeds in my head when I was at the very beginning of this project, just through our conversations in my office. Early on, Valerie Jenness, Mimi Schippers, and Barbara Katz Rothman provided very useful feedback for me on some of my earliest writing, which ultimately led to my first publication based on this project. I thank them for pushing me in productive directions.

My colleagues at the University of Virginia in the Women, Gender and Sexuality Department have been extraordinarily supportive—I would like to thank Lanice Avery, André Cavalcante, Matthew Chin, Kat Cosby, Cori Field, Bonnie Hagerman, Domale Keys, Tiffany King, Brittany Leach, Farzaneh Milani, Charlotte Patterson, Allison Pugh, Lisa Speidel, and Denise Walsh. It makes a tremendous difference to me to have such wonderful and supportive colleagues. Bridget Murphy helped me numerous times throughout my writing of this book—my deepest appreciation for her help. Special thanks to Feyza Burak-Adli, Geeta Patel, Sabrina Pendergrass, Victoria Pitts-Taylor, Mitra Rastegar, Amy Steinbugler, and Kath Weston as well. Hearing others give presentations and ask productive questions at conferences over the years was also helpful for me in advancing this project. I would like to thank Jamal Brooks-Hawkins, Ada Cheng, Cati Connell, Heather Hlavka, Simone Kolysh, Mignon Moore, Amber Powell, Brandon Andrew Robinson, Amy Stone, Paige Sweet, and Jane Ward for their comments and questions that I received as I was working on this book. My dear friends Kara Van Cleaf and Julie Lavelle helped this project more than they probably realize.

This research was supported by several summer stipend awards for Arts, Humanities, and Social Sciences Faculty at the University of Virginia. This support, along with a sabbatical while being on the tenure track, was tremendously helpful and allowed me to complete this research in a timely manner. Special thanks to students in my Violence against Sexual Minorities class over the years, as their comments and questions helped me with thinking through this project many times. Although I have written *Violent Differences* to be more accessible to a general audience, some of the material in this book has previously appeared in academic journals. Part of chapter 2 appeared in the *Journal of Contemporary Criminal Justice* as "'So Much for Protect and Serve': Queer Male Survivors' Perceptions of Negative Police Experiences" (2020, 36(2):228–250). Part of chapter 4 appeared in *Social Problems* as "Racializing Emasculation: An Intersectional Analysis of Queer Men's Evaluations of Sexual Assault"

(2022, 69(1):39–57). Finally, part of chapter 5 is forthcoming in the journal *Sexualities* as "Constructing Hierarchies of Victimhood: Queer Male Survivors' Evaluations of Sexual Assault Survivors" (published online, ahead of print, doi: 10.1177/13634607211060502). I thank the editors and reviewers at these journals for their extremely useful feedback—the comments I received helped with shaping this book.

Naomi Schneider, my editor here at the University of California Press, helped this project along by providing support and encouragement. The anonymous reviewers pushed me in productive directions and helped me with improving this text. Special thanks to Summer Farah for her assistance, which helped me a lot. I especially thank my parents, A. J. Meyer and Howard Meyer, as well as my stepmother, Sharron Meyer. I would also like to thank my family members, Patricio McKelligan Barreda, María de Jesús Hernández Escobedo, Patricio McKelligan Hernández, Gabriela McKelligan Hernández, Cosme Tapia Uribe, Daniel Tapia McKelligan, and Alejandra Tapia McKelligan. Most of all, I would like to thank my spouse, Alberto McKelligan Hernández, for all of his love and support. Everything I hold dear in this world is wrapped up in my world with him, and he has helped this book in numerous ways. For reading many parts of this project and for answering all of my questions, I cannot thank him enough.

Introduction

UNDERSTANDING SEXUAL ASSAULT
AGAINST QUEER MEN THROUGH
THE LENS OF INTERSECTIONALITY

Most scholarly analyses of sexual assault have focused on women survivors, as many researchers examining this violence against men have
noted.[1] Scholars employing intersectionality—a feminist approach that
examines the overlapping effects of multiple systems of oppression—have
also pointed out that representations of survivors have often focused on
the experiences of white, implicitly heterosexual, women.[2] This emphasis
on white women does not reflect the group that experiences a preponderance of sexual assault, as research shows that Black and Latinx women,
and possibly even some men of color, experience this violence at higher
rates.[3] Tommy Curry, in an article focusing on Black men's assaultive experiences, has pointed to some nationally representative data in the U.S.
showing that Black men "have rates of sexual victimization higher than
white women."[4] While I have written this text in the spirit of solidarity for
survivors across the lines of race, gender, and sexuality, I also argue that
sexual assault scholarship and advocacy would benefit by continuing to
account for the experiences of survivors who are marginalized in multiple
ways—for example, based on race *and* gender or race *and* sexuality—
rather than based on only one of these power relations.

In *Violent Differences*, I build on intersectional work that has examined sexual assault against women of color, yet I focus on another marginalized group—queer men—and draw particular attention to the experiences of Black queer male survivors. This research, based on interviews with sixty queer men who have experienced sexual assault, is the first book-length, intersectional analysis of this group of men.[5] Participants in this study identified in a variety of ways; *queer men* is used as an umbrella term throughout to refer to men who do not identify as heterosexual. A majority of these respondents, thirty-seven, self-identified as Black or African American.

BACKGROUND ON INTERSECTIONALITY AND CURRENT STUDY

A considerable amount of intersectional scholarship has revealed the limitations of approaches that focus on one form of inequality such as a gender-only or race-only analysis.[6] These approaches have been critiqued for failing to address the more holistic and interdependent ways that inequalities operate, as systems of oppression such as racism and sexism overlap to such an extent that addressing one of them ends up being less productive for reducing structural inequities than tackling both of them simultaneously.[7] Moreover, challenges to one system of oppression may reinforce other forms of inequality. Challenging sexism, for example, by underscoring the experiences of white heterosexual women may reinforce the privileging of whiteness and heterosexuality, further harming women who are not white or heterosexual. Indeed, intersectionality developed in part in response to theories that reduced sexism to the experiences of white women and racism to the experiences of Black men, which effectively rendered invisible Black women's simultaneous experiences of racism and sexism.[8] Intersectional work in lesbian, gay, bisexual, transgender, and queer (LGBTQ) studies has also emphasized that the mainstream gay-rights movement has often focused sole attention on sexuality, which privileges white gay men's challenges and marginalizes LGBTQ people of color's experiences of structural oppression.[9] In short, intersectional approaches reject assumptions that one form of inequality should be privileged and instead focus on multiple forms of inequality simultaneously.

With regard to sexual assault, the harmful consequences of not attending to racial inequality can be seen with a history of US-based lynching that has involved false charges of rape against Black men.[10] In the United States, attempts to combat sexual assault have often reinforced racial inequality and relied on a racializing of "the rapist"—what Angela Davis has referred to as the "myth of the Black rapist."[11] These racialized notions have also helped to conceal more privileged white male assailants' assaultive acts, given that they have been distanced from dominant understandings of who commits this violence.[12]

Along with a racializing of assailants, an emphasis on white women survivors has obscured more marginalized survivors' experiences, as scholars examining sexual assault against women of color have argued.[13] In one of the most foundational intersectional texts, Kimberlé Crenshaw revealed that advocacy devoted to violence against women has frequently privileged gender and focused primarily on the concerns of middle-class white women; simultaneously, some racial justice groups have excluded from their agenda issues such as sexual assault that disproportionately affect Black women.[14] As a result, Black women have been marginalized from both of these arenas.[15] These exclusions have persisted in other ways as well. Although the phrase *MeToo* was first used by activist Tarana Burke, a Black woman, on social media in 2006, the intersectional history of this activism is in danger of being forgotten or whitewashed. The cases that have become most synonymous with #MeToo have involved Hollywood actresses, disproportionately white and usually wealthy, as survivors.[16]

Although intersectionality has been employed in many studies of women survivors, less scholarship on male survivors has adopted an intersectional approach, despite some notable exceptions to the contrary.[17] Further, a few scholars have noted that media representations of male survivors have disproportionately focused on white, implicitly gay, men.[18] For instance, *The Hunting Ground*, a well-known documentary exploring sexual assault on college campuses, does not focus only on women survivors but also on men who have experienced this violence.[19] The male survivors who appear in the film—disproportionately white and feminine—are never identified as gay or bisexual, yet cultural understandings that link white male femininity with homosexuality likely construct these men as implicitly gay for many viewers. Such representations contribute to notions of male survivors as primarily white and may reproduce associations of white gay male femininity with victimhood or vulnerability.

In this text, I argue that inequalities based on race, gender, and sexuality have prevented significant attention to Black queer men's assaultive experiences, as this group has not figured as frequently as white or heterosexual survivors into representations of sexual assault. Instead, I argue for an analysis of sexual violence that decenters whiteness and considers racial inequality as central to many survivors' experiences. Given that racial inequality plays an important role in structuring oppression based on gender and sexuality, I contend that approaches devoted to reducing sexual assault would benefit by integrating a deep resistance to institutional racism. Additionally, focusing on queer male survivors, a majority of whom are Black, helps with challenging rape myths that position survivors as primarily white heterosexual women and assailants as disproportionately Black men. White heterosexual women may benefit from frameworks that privilege gender and white gay men may benefit from those that privilege sexuality, yet intersectional approaches remain necessary for multiply marginalized survivors and for moving away from frameworks that challenge one form of inequality but nevertheless reinforce another.

Beyond the intersectionality of this text, it remains important to focus on sexual assault against queer men because research has shown that this population experiences high rates of this violence.[20] While scholarship varies in estimating the extent to which queer men experience sexual assault, Rothman and coauthors' review of seventy-five studies revealed that for gay and bisexual men, these estimates ranged from 11.8 percent to 54.0 percent, with a median estimate of 30 percent.[21] Comparing these figures with research on the general US population, these authors concluded that gay and bisexual men "may be at increased risk for sexual assault victimization."[22] Fewer studies have explored racial differences among queer men, although some evidence suggests that queer people of color experience sexual assault at higher rates than their white counterparts.[23]

Examining sexual assault against men, queer or otherwise, could certainly be done in unproductive, anti-feminist ways. Specifically, the lack of mainstream attention devoted to men's assaultive experiences could be used to engage in an anti-feminist argument that dismisses gender in-equality and positions social conditions as unfairly "favoring women." To be sure, the common media focus on white women survivors is not ben-efiting many white women who have been sexually assaulted either. Media representations of sexual assault have frequently reproduced traditional gender ideology by positioning white women as needing "protection"— discourse that contributes to gender inequality.[24] Instead, I focus on sex-ual assault against queer men, not to dismiss any emphasis on women survivors across racial lines or their experiences of structural oppression, but to expand feminist understandings of this violence to include a wider range of survivors. Broadening our understandings of who constitutes a sexual assault survivor helps not only with accounting for a wider range of experiences but also with showing how systems of oppression such as heteronormativity and institutional racism play an equally important role as gender inequality in shaping what many survivors experience.[25]

ORNELL'S EXPERIENCES

In this study, many participants' experiences differed from traditional rep-resentations of sexual assault. Take, for example, Ornell, a thirty-seven-year-old Black gay man who grew up in a small, mostly white town.[26] At this time, during his youth, he regularly experienced harassment from the police, including from one officer who used racial slurs against him. He also experienced racist and homophobic harassment at school, from both teachers and classmates, and he did not feel supported by his family due to their homophobia.

At the age of eighteen, he moved to New York City, where he first lived in a homeless shelter for three years. He continued to experience po-lice harassment throughout his time in the city, as he said that he was stopped by the police "on a weekly basis." These experiences typically in-volved some version of a "stop and search," in which he detailed a process whereby "the cops would pat me down for no reason" and sometimes "take me down to the station for disorderly conduct." Ornell described himself as "feminine," as his gender expression included him wearing ear-rings and ripped jeans, and he said that he is often profiled by the police based on discriminatory notions that he is "up to no good and shouldn't be walking the streets."[27]

While living in the homeless shelter, Ornell met and fell in love with a man, Andres. He then moved in with Andres after they had been dating for a few months. Ornell described a process of escalating verbal disputes that eventually resulted in Andres hitting and pushing Ornell several times. A few weeks after this abuse began, Andres raped Ornell, forcibly holding him down by the throat and covering his mouth. Approximately two weeks after the rape, Ornell and Andres got into an argument, which prompted one of their neighbors to call the police. When the officers came to the apartment, Ornell told them that the couple had been fighting about a sexual assault, which he said the officers "turned into a joke" that included one of them asking, "You're sitting here wearing earrings, and you expect us to take you seriously?"

Experiences such as Ornell's have been marginalized by approaches that overlook the role of race, sexuality, and gender expression in relation to sexual assault. By centering such experiences, analyses of sexual assault can help to challenge inequalities based not only on gender but also on race and sexuality. How Ornell spoke about his experiences also contrasted with some dominant understandings of sexual assault against men. For example, research has shown that male survivors frequently feel emasculated—like "less of a man"—after a sexual assault and then strive to reclaim or reassert a masculine sense of self.[28] In contrast, as Ornell reflected on the assault, he said that he did not feel emasculated after the rape because "I never felt masculine to begin with." An understanding that sexual assault leads male survivors to feel emasculated did not reflect how most Black queer men and queer men of color in this study responded to this violence. In fact, these participants sometimes complained about others wanting them to "admit" to feeling emasculated, even though they did not feel this way. Conversely, white queer men, even those who identified as feminine, typically felt emasculated. Thus, in focusing on queer men of color's experiences, some dominant assumptions—such as those that presume emasculation—begin to slip away.

Further, as Ornell's experience with disclosing the sexual assault to the police officers reveals, Black queer male survivors often cannot rely on the police to improve their situation. Ornell's experiences of being profiled by the police before the assault demonstrate the importance of understanding these practices through an intersectional lens, as race, sexuality, and gender expression simultaneously shaped what he experienced. Black gender-expansive or gender-nonconforming participants described many profiling experiences in which they perceived the police as targeting their gender expression as well as their racial identity.[29] These experiences cannot be fully understood by focusing only on race, gender, or sexuality, but instead require deeper consideration of their overlap. A phrase such as "racial profiling" does not fully encapsulate such experiences because these participants thought that the police had targeted them in part due to their gender expression. The benefits of an intersectional approach thus provide a better sense of many individuals' experiences than frameworks that focus on one system of oppression. The complexities of Ornell's experiences would be flattened or obscured through an approach that explored only race, gender, or sexuality.

OUTLINE OF MY MAIN ARGUMENT

With this application of intersectionality, this book has implications more broadly for advocacy and scholarship devoted to sexual assault. Traditional approaches that focus on the assaultive experiences of white women or white gay men are not always explicitly exclusionary of multiply marginalized survivors, as groups such as Black women or Black queer men may appear representationally, but the intersectional critique of these frameworks is that whiteness often remains centralized and that racial inequality continues to be marginalized from much of this work.[30] In contrast, I argue that by adopting an intersectional approach, attempts to reduce sexual assault can become more radical, beneficial, and transformative. Specifically, focusing on the comparatively intense forms of marginalization that Black queer men experience reveals the extent to which many survivors are not supported in a US context, as well as the necessity for change.

Overall, the chapters in this book reveal widespread structural marginalization experienced by queer male survivors—especially by those who are Black—and demonstrate that anti-queer prejudice cannot explain much of this systematic inequality. For instance, my research shows that queer men of color described feeling "lonely" after their assaultive experiences to a much greater extent than their white counterparts, as the former felt more isolated from a variety of domains, including but not limited to LGBTQ communities and institutional resources provided by groups such as the police. Examining the experiences of white queer male survivors undoubtedly reveals a lack of some institutional support as well—the vast majority of white participants had negative experiences when reporting a sexual assault to the police, for example—yet work devoted to reducing sexual assault would miss many of the forms of social isolation experienced by queer men of color if sexuality or anti-LGBTQ prejudice remained the primary focus.

Compare the experiences of Marcel, a twenty-seven-year-old Black gay man, and Allen, a thirty-eight-year-old white gay man. Both of these participants had an assaultive experience that was intra-racial—where the assailant was the same race as them. Marcel's experience occurred during a casual sexual encounter—often colloquially known as a "hookup"—where a man raped him, while a man Allen dated spiked his drink with a date rape drug and then raped him when he was unconscious. Only Marcel, however, repeatedly emphasized how lonely and isolated he felt after his assaultive experience. He thought that he could not rely on the police for support—saying, "My community, we don't trust the police because what are they going to do?"—and he thought that other gay men who are not Black might be dismissive of his assaultive experience, saying, "Other gay guys just look at this as a 'Black thing.'"

Black queer men, and queer men of color more broadly, often spoke about their marginalization from LGBTQ communities, which they sometimes described as infused with racial inequality or set up to benefit white gay men.[31] Moreover, although white participants typically had negative experiences when reporting an assaultive experience to the police, they did not have the extensive history of being profiled and harassed by police officers that most Black queer men described. These experiences then shaped Black queer men's hesitancy or unwillingness to report an assault to the police and intensified their concerns about not having others whom they could rely on for support. In short, white queer men were more institutionally supported than queer men of color and did not face structural marginalization to the same degree.

Accounting for structural marginalization remains particularly important in the context of sexual violence because survivors' social positions—that is, where they are located in relation to power and inequality—affect not only how they will be treated by various institutions and communities but also how others will perceive their claims of sexual assault. In this study, Black queer men experienced and worried about discourses of blame that white queer men did not. Most participants described feeling that they should have been able to prevent a sexual assault through physical force, with others sometimes even asking questions such as, "Why didn't you fight back?" Respondents often spoke about this question in relation to masculinity. However, given a history of racialized discourse that has associated Black men with "strong" or "aggressive" masculinities, Black queer male survivors described being asked this type of question more than non-Black participants. Consequently, rape myths that "men cannot be raped" due to their assumed strength have different racialized effects, systematically disadvantaging Black male survivors who confront masculinizing stereotypes. In this sense, I show that feminism and intersectionality can improve understandings of sexual assault against men, not only women.

Despite contentions that intersectionality has run its course, Patricia Hill Collins has recently argued that intersectional approaches have merely begun exposing and resisting unequal power relations and can expand to many areas of study to improve understandings of how systems of oppression simultaneously structure social life.[32] It is in this spirit of expanding the scope of intersectionality that I have written this text, as a considerable body of masculinities scholarship has argued for greater attention to the ways that men as well as women are intersectionally situated in relation to social hierarchies.[33] Together, all of the following chapters—whether they focus on emasculation, discourses of blame, or experiences with the police—reveal that the structural barriers confronting queer male survivors vary significantly based on their social location. Given this variability, queer male survivors should be understood not as monolithic but as heterogeneous. The "differences" described herein should also then be understood as the outcome of social processes, not as reflecting some natural or essentialized difference between social groups.

Intersectionality has sometimes been critiqued for being too fixed on identity or for being too static—that is, not fluid enough—yet in *Violent*

Differences I show that the tools of intersectionality can expand traditional understandings of sexual assault, providing more comparative knowledge on multiple groups of survivors.[34] This understanding of intersectionality as an expansive approach—not fixed or rigid at all—helps with broadening bodies of scholarship, such as sexual assault research, in new and beneficial directions. In particular, this approach illustrates the continued need to understand systems of oppression as overlapping, rather than assuming that challenges to one system of inequality will benefit survivors who are oppressed in multiple ways.

Although the intersection of race, gender, and sexuality receives the most attention in this book, related aspects of inequality, including biphobia, transphobia, and stigmatizing notions of HIV, are also explored. As such, this analysis reveals the multifaceted ways that queer male survivors are situated in relation to privilege and disadvantage. Most of the men in this study identified as gay, yet I draw attention to the unique experiences of bisexual and pansexual participants, especially in chapter 3, to destabilize a straightforward emphasis on "queer men"; this category is not necessarily as clear-cut as is often assumed. Indeed, it remains important to include the experiences of transgender men in analyses of sexual assault, given that this group faces particular challenges and forms of abuse that their cisgender counterparts do not.[35]

Gay and bisexual men have historically been stereotyped as childhood sexual abusers and most cisgender participants described others they knew who held these stereotypes, yet transgender men detailed these notions even more frequently in relation to their gender identity.[36] Santiago, a forty-nine-year-old Latino transgender man, explained that "people think of trans people as predators, not people who experience [sexual assault]." Certainly, attempts to pass anti-transgender bathroom bills have commonly relied on such prejudicial assumptions.[37] These notions then make it particularly difficult for transgender survivors to have their claims believed, as others may perceive transgender people through a predatory lens. Throughout this book, I have expanded approaches for understanding sexual assault against queer men more with regard to race, yet I hope that future work will continue to build on my analysis of bisexual, pansexual, and transgender men to add further knowledge regarding these groups' experiences.[38]

ANTI-QUEER UNDERSTANDINGS OF SEXUAL ASSAULT

In this text, I argue for a decentering of not only whiteness but also hetero-sexuality. Scholarship focusing on LGBTQ people's assaultive experiences has pointed to the frequency of a heteronormative framework in much of the media landscape devoted to sexual assault.[39] Typically, such hetero-normative approaches simply exclude any mention of LGBTQ people or identities, but more overtly anti-queer frameworks may highlight sexual assault against queer men in ways that pathologize this group, or LGBTQ people more broadly. With regard to childhood sexual abuse, anti-queer perspectives have traditionally positioned such abuse as causing an indi-vidual's queerness.[40] According to this prejudicial understanding, sexual abuse can "make" someone queer. Several participants in this study ex-plained that others had made this type of statement to them. For example, Emerson, a twenty-five-year-old Black and Latino bisexual man, said that his mother linked his experiences of sexual abuse at a young age—in which his father had sexually abused him—to his bisexuality as an adult. When he first told her that he was bisexual, at the age of eighteen, she asked him, "Is this because of what your father did?"

Even more common than those reactions, participants described others' responses that positioned their queerness as contributing to an assaultive experience. Shane, a forty-nine-year-old white gay man, explained that when he was young his brother responded to learning about Shane's expe-riences of sexual abuse by saying, "If you weren't 'out there' being gay, this wouldn't happen." Broadly speaking, this type of perspective associates queerness with negative consequences such as sexual abuse, as some un-derstanding exists that taking on this identity will expose oneself to harm-ful effects. The implied message in such narratives is to avoid queerness, or outward expressions of it, which are associated with male femininity or gender nonconformity.

Relatedly, outsiders may construct queer men's assaultive experiences in punitive terms. For example, Sherman, a fifty-three-year-old Black gay man, worried about others responding in the following way if he disclosed an assaultive experience that occurred during adulthood: "Like maybe [sexual assault] is not so bad because gay people need to find God any-way. . . . Like we deserve it for being gay." This punitiveness may be framed in religious ways—with sexual assault viewed as "God's punishment" for queer people—but such perspectives more generally associate queerness with negative characteristics. From anti-queer perspectives, sexual assault against queer men arises not out of heteronormativity but because of queerness itself.

In contrast, throughout this text, I challenge these stigmatizing ideas that position queerness as a cause of sexual assault or abuse. Sexual assault against queer men must not be understood in these ways, as my research shows that queer male survivors frequently struggle with such associations. Thus, these ways of framing sexual assault against queer men should be understood as reinforcing the struggles that queer male survivors already experience. Further, with regard to gender expression, an important shift of focus needs to occur: it is the stigmatizing of male femininity, rather than this attribute itself, that leads some assailants to commit sexual assault against men.

SURVIVORS' CHALLENGES AND
THE CONTEXT OF THE ASSAULT

Despite the many differences outlined throughout this book, survivors across the lines of race, gender, and sexuality will recognize many of the forms of victim blaming presented here. As a considerable amount of feminist work has shown, much of US culture remains infused with pathologizing notions of survivors—as deceitful or disturbed, for example—and respondents in this study often spoke about how others' perceptions of them changed a considerable amount, usually for the worse, when revealing an assaultive experience.[41] Outsiders may perceive survivors as "biased" with regard to sexual assault, while conversely constructing non-survivors as "objective" or free of bias. These ideas contribute to the marginalization of survivors' voices and experiences. For bisexual, pansexual, and transgender participants, I show that concerns over being perceived as deceitful were particularly pronounced, due to negative stereotypes of these groups that link them with untrustworthiness. Consequently, although pathologizing notions of survivors exist for a wide range of groups, respondents' experiences revealed important differences in this regard.

In spite of these differences, scholarship has shown that groups ranging from service providers to the general US public frequently hold negative views of queer male survivors—in particular, by drawing on stereotypes of queer men as "hypersexual."[42] Conversely, consistent with a long line of feminist scholarship, I argue that a desire for consensual sex should not be understood as a sign that one has relinquished their right to sexual autonomy.[43] Once again, a shift needs to occur in which this violence is understood as originating not through the survivor's attributes or actions prior to the assault, but through the assailant's perpetration of harmful behavior.

Engaging in a hookup by going over to someone else's place remains a rite of passage for many queer men; even this "rite of passage" notion assigns such practices a temporary status, as queer men may engage in casual sexual encounters on a more permanent basis. A pathologizing of queer men as "hypersexual" is also an intersectional concern, as Black participants were particularly likely to have others assign sexualizing notions onto them. Indeed, as scholarship has shown, Black queer men's sexualities often provoke panic, fear, or anger in especially high degrees, with the overlap of heteronormativity and institutional racism constructing Black queer men's sex practices through a pathologizing lens.[44] As a result, although sexualizing stereotypes exist for many queer men, I argue for a more intersectional consideration of this pathologizing.

Before beginning this project, I had incorrectly presumed that I would find little victim blaming among queer male survivors in terms of focusing on "promiscuity." Instead, some respondents—disproportionately those who identified as masculine—positioned other queer male survivors as blameworthy for desiring consensual sex. These forms of victim blaming may be comfortable as a defense mechanism—after all, this line of thinking contends, if one avoids "promiscuity" then one is largely safe from such assaults—yet the most common context in which participants experienced sexual violence as an adult involved a relationship. However, respondents never argued that relationships between men lead to sexual assault and should therefore be avoided. I argue for greater attention to queer men's participation in casual sexual encounters, since my findings indicate that others may blame survivors in particular who have assaultive experiences in this context. Moreover, since many survivors experience sexual assault in relationships, intimate partner violence and male sexual victimization should not be understood as mutually exclusive.

In contrast to my focus on assaults that occur during a hookup or a violent relationship, arguably the most common media framework for representing sexual assault against men, queer or otherwise, has focused on rape in carceral settings. Even the phrase *male rape* may bring to mind images of a jail or prison, as popular films such as *The Shawshank Redemption* have focused on these contexts.[45] Queer men may experience sexual assault in such settings, yet the problem with these stereotypical representations is that this violence becomes segmented off to a particular institutional sphere, rather than being understood as a phenomenon that occurs more pervasively. If scholarship on this topic is correct that approximately 30 percent of queer men experience sexual assault, then these forms of violence clearly cannot be relegated to a specific institutional arena. Emphasizing queer men's assaultive experiences in prison has a history in academic scholarship as well, given that some of the first studies focused on this context.[46] Research diverges on the frequency of sexual assault in jails and prisons—and some evidence suggests that guards rather than other prisoners commit or coordinate a preponderance of this violence—yet most studies indicate that the U.S. public tends to overstate the prevalence of rape against male prisoners, believing that it has reached "epidemic" levels when it has not.[47]

THINKING INTERSECTIONALLY ABOUT MEN, MASCULINITIES, AND QUEERNESS

Beyond sexual assault, men and masculinities scholarship has frequently called for more attention devoted to the intersection of masculinities with power structures based on race and ethnicity, among other forms of inequality.[48] Raewyn Connell's original, influential formulation of hegemonic masculinity—those forms that legitimate gender inequality—drew important attention to how these masculinities have most frequently been linked with whiteness and heterosexuality.[49] Conversely, subordinate masculinities have been associated with homosexuality and marginalized masculinities have been linked with racial and ethnic minority groups.[50]

This formulation brought significant attention to a hierarchy of masculinities, yet subordinate masculinities were implicitly associated with a white femininity or a white queerness and marginalized masculinities were linked in part with heterosexual masculinities of color. Positioning men of color as heterosexual and male femininity or male queerness as white excludes queer men of color. Subsequent work has provided more intersectional analyses, accounting for racial hierarchies in queer male communities and gender and sexuality inequalities in communities of color.[51] Intersectional scholarship has shown that queer men of color experience not only racism and anti-LGBTQ prejudice from mainstream arenas but also oppression in their racial and LGBTQ communities.[52] For instance, in LGBTQ arenas, racial hierarchies associate queer men of color with pathologizing stereotypes, such as a hypermasculinity or a stigmatized femininity, often sexualizing and eroticizing them as well.[53]

In this text, I build on this intersectional work that has drawn attention to negative constructions of queer men of color's gender expressions, yet I demonstrate how these ideas affect queer male survivors. Specifically, Black participants who described themselves as feminine experienced more negative reactions to their disclosure of sexual assault than white queer men who identified in this way. Consistent with work from Black LGBTQ scholars, I argue that scholarship in masculinity studies and beyond has to be careful about reinforcing notions of male femininity as implicitly white.[54] A whitening of male femininity and male queerness contributes to the structural marginalization experienced by Black queer men with feminine gender expressions. These notions become especially problematic for Black queer male survivors who then see their white counterparts—and, more broadly, white women—sometimes positioned as "ideal" victims.[55] Conversely, accounting for the assaultive experiences of Black queer men with feminine gender expressions helps to move away from a whitening of victimhood, as well as of male femininity and male queerness.

THE TRANSFORMATIVE BENEFITS
OF AN INTERSECTIONAL APPROACH

An intersectional approach for studying men, masculinities, and sexual assault takes gender inequality seriously but understands patriarchy as intertwined with heteronormativity and institutional racism. Outside of intersectionality, individuals may assume that privileging one form of inequality is most effective for combatting structural oppression. This line of thinking contends that a mainstream audience will find it easiest to understand the harmful effects of one system of inequality and may sympathize the most with singularly marginalized individuals such as white heterosexual women or white gay men. The problem with this approach, from an intersectional perspective, is that it assumes the benefits granted to the more privileged members of a social group will subsequently be granted to the more marginalized; some scholars have thus referred to this approach as a "trickle-down" form of social justice.[56] The intersectional critique of such frameworks is that the more marginalized benefit very little, if at all, and in some cases may even be harmed further, as their more pressing needs continue to be sidelined.[57]

Instead of a trickle-down approach, intersectional frameworks call for addressing the oppressive experiences of more marginalized individuals. The benefits of this approach, a "trickle-up" or more transformative type of social justice, extend to considerably more people, transforming multiple systems of oppression at the same time. In this sense, intersectionality involves a reorientation of priorities, advancing more radical forms of social change and redirecting attention toward more marginalized groups' experiences.

Intersectionality has sometimes been depoliticized on places such as the internet, and more broadly in media or by multinational corporations, whereby it is reduced to a simple politics of inclusion or representation, as if merely including or drawing attention to a multiply marginalized group is sufficiently intersectional. However, this emphasis on inclusion or representation can limit the transformative potential of intersectionality by simply including a greater number of multiply marginalized people into frameworks that fail to take their interests seriously.[58] Mainstream gay-rights advocacy, for example, has sometimes incorporated LGBTQ people of color in superficial or representational ways, while simultaneously continuing to privilege sexuality and marginalize queer people of color's concerns.[59] This point is in part about the limits of representation, but it is also about making sure that the radical edges of intersectionality are not blunted. The aim of an intersectional perspective is not to include a more diverse group of people into already unequal systems but to reorganize those systems in fundamental, more equal, ways.

For white LGBTQ people such as myself, internalizing the politics of intersectionality requires being more critical of our investments in whiteness—that is, the ways that we have been conditioned to understand whiteness and the attributes associated with it as the most central or valuable to US society. Out of the normalizing of whiteness comes assumptions that it should be privileged; for this reason, individuals may disparage work that centers the perspectives of racially marginalized people, including Black queer men. I became interested in intersectionality because I like how it requires us to grapple with our role in social inequalities, ultimately working toward their decline. As a white and middle-class gay man, I am granted a lot of privileges that many of the men I interviewed for this book are not. Although I listened to them carefully and write this book from the perspective of a survivor myself—which I describe more in the methodological appendix—conducting this research has only made me more aware of the ways that my whiteness has granted me privileges that other survivors do not have. Focusing on survivors with various perspectives and identities has some benefits, but by using an intersectional perspective, I hope to show that the value of this approach is less about inclusion or representation and more about adopting a critical approach toward multiple systems of oppression.

STUDYING SEXUAL ASSAULT AGAINST
QUEER MEN INTERSECTIONALLY

In advancing an intersectional approach, I argue that sexual assault advocacy and scholarship should avoid naturalizing a framework of masculine assailants assaulting feminine individuals.[60] Of course, some forms of sexual assault involve men with masculine gender expressions committing violence against individuals with feminine gender expressions—indeed, many participants in this study experienced an assault that could be characterized in this way—yet other violations remain difficult to comprehend if this model becomes instituted as the predominant one. A framework of masculine assailants assaulting feminine survivors may reinforce heteronormativity and does not encapsulate many forms of sexual assault involving LGBTQ people.[61] For instance, some of the men in this study argued that they were "more masculine" than their assailants, but felt that they would not be believed due to gendered notions that construct "real" or "true" survivors as feminine. Further, strengthening understandings of masculinity as inherently forceful and femininity as naturally susceptible to this force can increase rather than reduce the enactment of many forms of sexual assault.[62] After all, if individuals continue to see men and masculinities as inherently forceful, then many men may also perform masculinity in line with these gender expectations.

Given that Black and Latinx men are especially likely to be stereotyped in masculinizing ways, this concern is also an intersectional one, as the naturalizing of survivors as feminine can be used to marginalize the assaultive experiences of Black and Latinx men. A model of masculine assailants and feminine survivors may appear explicitly gendered and not racialized, yet because ideas about feminine vulnerability and victimhood are disproportionately associated with whiteness, and because racialized stereotypes link Black and Latinx men with not only masculinity but also stigmatized attributes such as crime, I argue that this model is also implicitly racialized. Thus, I contend that analyses of sexual assault would benefit by expanding beyond seemingly race-neutral frameworks that position survivors as feminine and assailants as masculine. This argument is not to deny that dominant constructions of masculinity contribute to many forms of sexual assault, but to advance an analysis that takes seriously how understandings of this violence may reinforce heteronormativity or racial inequality. In short, the tools of intersectionality help with problematizing some current approaches and with shifting toward more productive approaches for the future.

DEFINING SEXUAL ASSAULT AND OTHER TERMINOLOGY

Considerable scholarly debate has occurred regarding how sexual assault should be defined and operationalized.[63] Researchers have sometimes avoided definitions that focus on consent because a significant and expanding body of scholarship has critiqued this emphasis, as well as mainstream advocacy approaches that rely on consent, such as a "yes means yes" framework.[64] A common working definition of sexual assault refers to specific acts; for example, Charlene Muehlenhard and coauthors have defined it as involving "two types of sexual acts—sexual penetration and sexual touching (i.e., nonpenetrative sexual contacts)—obtained by force (including threats of force) or incapacitation."[65] Attempted rape is included in this definition, as are forms of assault in which someone lacks the capacity to consent, such as through drugs or alcohol. The emphasis on "sexual touching" or "nonpenetrative sexual contacts" obtained through force or the threat of force is designed to broaden understandings of sexual assault beyond rape, or penetration of a bodily orifice. Rape is a type of sexual assault, but not all forms of sexual assault are rape.[66]

In this text, I use a broader understanding of sexual assault that includes those forms mentioned by Muehlenhard and coauthors, while also accounting for what other researchers have characterized as "unwanted sexual contact."[67] Conceptualizing sexual assault as including unwanted sexual contact helps draw attention to a broader spectrum of assaultive behavior, as participants in this study sometimes understood experiences as harmful or assaultive that were not part of Muehlenhard and coauthors' definition. In particular, the use of "unwanted sexual contact" is more inclusive of acts that do not necessarily involve "force" or "threats of force."

Including these acts remains important in light of research showing that survivors may "freeze" or become silent during an assault for a range of reasons, such as compliance with sexual scripts or fear that the assault will become more violent.[68] In these cases, the assailant may not necessarily use physical "force," or even the threat of force, but the act may nevertheless feel assaultive given that the survivor did not want it to occur. Survivors may also experience pressure or psychological manipulation to engage in a sex act against their will; in this sense, "force" should be understood broadly, as including verbal or emotional coercion.[69] These acts are included in my definition of sexual assault as well.

Although I conceptualize sexual assault broadly, readers of this book should be aware that most participants came to the interview planning to discuss an adult experience of anal rape, which had usually occurred within the last five years.[70] Fifty-four of the sixty participants had at least one adult experience of anal rape, and these participants usually spent the most time speaking about those experiences, even though they were asked about many sexual violations. As a result, although it remains important to account for other forms of sexual assault, as the anus is not the only "site" where this violence against men occurs, most but certainly not all of the experiences described in this text are incidents of adult anal rape.

Throughout this book, when I refer to "rape," I use this term to refer to an assaultive experience in which a participant was anally penetrated; this choice is designed to account for how understandings of rape against men have usually been conceptualized in these terms.[71] At the same time, I refer to those incidents as sexual assault as well as rape because I am not interested in furthering divisions between rape and other forms of sexual assault. Moving beyond conventional approaches that define sexual violence in narrow and reductive ways—such as "back alley" representations of rape in which the assailant is positioned as a stranger—remains necessary, and part of my aim is to broaden perspectives regarding these issues.

Beyond sexual assault, I use the phrase *criminal-legal system* instead of *criminal justice system* because the latter expression implies that these institutions are designed to provide "justice," when a lot of scholarship has shown that they have not historically done so.[72] The phrase *criminal-legal system* is more descriptive, rather than framing these institutions in positive terms. Other scholars have used the phrase *criminal punishment system* to reframe this apparatus in a less positive, and arguably more accurate, way, pointing to how these institutions are designed primarily to punish, not facilitate justice.[73]

In this text, I also use *assailant* rather than *perpetrator*, given that this latter term has more frequently been racialized and classed in problematic ways, reinforcing notions that sexual assault is committed primarily by marginalized groups, such as low-income Black men. Similarly, a racialized perpetrator/victim dyad, in which the former is constructed as Black or Latinx and the latter is positioned as white, has often informed media representations of sexual assault.[74] For this reason, I use *survivor* more than *victim*, although the latter is used in some cases, especially when referring to victim blaming. Finally, I use *gender expansive* more than *gender nonconforming* because the former phrase positions such gender expressions in a more agentic or positive way. Concurrently, I have used *gender nonconforming* at times because it was the discourse that participants more commonly used.

CHAPTER OUTLINE

The chapters of this book focus on queer men's experiences and perceptions of sexual assault, with data collected from sixty in-depth interviews conducted in Atlanta and New York City from July 2016 through August 2017 (see the appendix for a description of the research methods). In chapter 1, I examine the particular challenges facing Black queer men and emphasize the blame that these participants experienced from others. Respondents' experiences demonstrate that questions such as "why didn't you fight back?" should be understood in relation to not only masculinity but also race. Chapter 2 focuses on participants' negative experiences when reporting a sexual assault to the police. In particular, I emphasize the importance of age, gender expression, and sexuality, in addition to race, in participants' interactions with the police.

Chapter 3 focuses on the ways that participants blamed themselves for their assaultive experiences, particularly in the context of a hookup. Respondents often drew attention to feelings of dirtiness and disgust, which I contextualize in relation to contemporary understandings of sex between men. This chapter also focuses on the particular challenges confronting bisexual and pansexual participants, in addition to those who identified as nonbinary or transgender. In chapter 4, I draw attention to racial and ethnic differences with regard to emasculation. Participants' narratives demonstrate that emasculation is a racialized, as well as a gendered, process for queer men—one that does not arise automatically from being a man who has been sexually assaulted but one that springs disproportionately from whiteness.

In chapter 5, I examine how participants constructed hierarchies of victimhood, or an ordering of who "counts" as a real or legitimate survivor of this violence. This chapter includes an analysis of how queer male survivors may reinforce some social inequalities, especially sexism. Chapter 6 focuses on participants' experiences with regard to outing, or having aspects of their identity disclosed without their consent. This chapter includes multiple forms of nonconsensual disclosure, as participants frequently had negative experiences with coming out as queer in the past—some of which involved them being outed by others—which then usually made them more fearful about revealing their assaultive experiences. Moreover, this chapter includes concerns related to HIV and BDSM—practices involving bondage, discipline, dominance and submission, or sadomasochism—as respondents spent the most time describing fears of being outed as HIV positive or as participating in BDSM. In the conclusion, I end by outlining some productive paths forward. Tensions exist between work hoping to reduce sexual assault and advocacy opposed to mass incarceration. Thinking through these tensions and intersections remains an important goal of my work, as I conclude by advancing an anti-punitive or anti-criminalization approach to combatting sexual assault.

1 "Why Didn't You Fight Back?"

BLACK QUEER MALE SURVIVORS
AND DISCOURSES OF BLAME

Participants' assaultive experiences sometimes clearly reflected gender inequality. Take, for example, the experiences of Latrelle, a forty-nine-year-old Black gay man, who was sexually assaulted on multiple occasions by his former partner, Dominic. Latrelle described a process in which Dominic "wined and dined" him at the beginning of their relationship, before they lived together. Once his partner moved in with him, Latrelle said that Dominic "wanted to be in control" and wanted "to show that he's masculine." The physical violence began when Dominic demanded that Latrelle cook for him, becoming physically abusive if the food was not made to his satisfaction. The first experience of sexual assault, which occurred approximately six months into their relationship, involved Dominic forcibly grabbing Latrelle's genitals. One week later, Dominic raped him.

Sexually assaultive experiences occurred throughout the remainder of their relationship, usually in the middle of the night. Latrelle explained, "If I said 'no,' it didn't matter, he'd just take what he wanted." Immediately after the first incident of rape, Dominic demanded that Latrelle cook a steak for him. Latrelle described Dominic as "manipulative" and said that he "messed with my mind" to the point where "I didn't know which way was up." Dominic would control Latrelle's behavior and then insist that he never did so; this lying and manipulation seemed designed to confuse Latrelle, or make him question his perception of reality.[1] He also explained that he was fearful of leaving, saying he felt that Dominic would "hunt me down if I left him." When discussing why he thought Dominic had committed the abuse, Latrelle said that his former partner "saw masculinity and violence as very linked, like it's almost like being masculine meant being violent."

Latrelle advanced a critique of masculinity here. Indeed, Latrelle probably would not have experienced this abuse if Dominic had not associated violence and control with masculinity. These associations must not be understood as exclusive to heterosexual, cisgender men, given that the privileging of masculinity remains widespread in queer male communities, as well as in broader US society.[2] At the same time, although accounting for masculinity remains important when exploring sexual assault against queer men, analyses of heteronormativity should also be central to these examinations. For instance, how can Latrelle's experience not be understood as yet another reiteration of what happens within some abusive heterosexual relationships but be understood on its own terms, without reinscribing heterosexuality as the standard by which queer relationships are compared? Focusing solely on masculinity can lead to a number of potential problems, reproducing a heteronormative framework and reinforcing the biases of a heteronormative audience. Queer relationships are more frequently compared to heterosexual ones, rather than the opposite, because heteronormativity encourages us to do so. In effect, sexual assault against queer men needs to be analyzed in a way that challenges heteronormative dynamics and assumptions rather than in a way that upholds them.

The problem with focusing solely on masculinity in relation to male sexual victimization is not only that it risks reproducing heteronormative assumptions but also that it may prevent attention to the role of racial inequality. Although Latrelle's assaultive experiences were among the most obvious in terms of how toxic masculinity appeared to affect his assailant's violent behavior, other important aspects of what happened would be obscured by focusing exclusively on masculinity. Latrelle explained that he did not contact the police because "I've always just thought of the police as not being there for guys like me." He also then later said, "What are the police going to do, except maybe blame me for it?" This blame may be related to gender and sexuality as well as race or ethnicity, but centering Black queer men's experiences reveals that they confront many forms of police harassment that their white counterparts do not. By focusing only on masculinity, examinations of sexual assault would miss the important role of race in shaping many survivors' experiences.

One such area in which racial inequality may shape survivors' experiences is in relation to how others respond to their disclosure of a sexual assault. In this chapter, I focus on discourses of blame that Black queer men encountered disproportionately, showing that racialized and gendered notions of "strength" informed their experiences in some unique ways. Specifically, I highlight Black participants' negative experiences with disclosing an assault, which helps to show how stereotypes and patterns of language work to the systematic disadvantage of Black queer male survivors.

THE ROLE OF RACE AND GENDER IN FRIENDS' AND FAMILY MEMBERS' NEGATIVE RESPONSES

About two-thirds of participants had told at least one other person about a sexual violation they had experienced. The remaining respondents had not divulged their assaultive experiences to anyone; I was the first person they had ever told about what had happened to them.[3] Participants who experienced a sexual assault in the context of a hookup were the least likely to have told others about this experience, usually out of a fear that they would be blamed for "putting themselves" in a situation involving consensual sex. Conversely, respondents who had told others were disproportionately those who experienced sexual assault when they were under the age of eighteen or when they were in a relationship as an adult. Participants who had been in an abusive relationship typically revealed their assaultive experiences to others who knew their former partner, believing that this person would then be supportive of their exiting the relationship given that one or more sexual assaults had occurred.

In general, participants who experienced this violence in a relationship described others' responses, usually from a friend or family member, as negative. The most common response involved others saying that they "would have killed" someone who had abused or sexually assaulted them. Respondents generally viewed this reaction as unsupportive because it established their behavior as insufficient or not dramatic enough, implying that they should have done more to end the abuse. Research on intimate partner violence has nevertheless shown that leaving or attempting to leave an abusive relationship is one of the most dangerous times for survivors, given that this is when assailants are especially likely to commit murder and to threaten the survivor's safety.[4]

A lot of the reactions that participants described from others involved a positioning of relationship violence as involving primarily physical or sexual abuse, yet these relationships usually included other abusive dynamics, such as control, psychological manipulation, and threatening behavior. Much of the literature on intimate partner violence and sexual assault has shown that multiple forms of abuse occur simultaneously and do not exist in isolation of one another, as a range of emotionally, physically, and sexually violent acts compound one another and have a cumulative effect on survivors.[5] Consequently, it may be easy for outsiders to believe that they would simply end an abusive relationship, but such intimacies are likely much harder to leave when finding oneself in them, where love and affection may exist, as well as possible emotional manipulation.

Further, research indicates that the general US population and even social service providers assisting survivors of intimate partner violence perceive this abuse as less serious when involving same-gender couples than different-gender ones.[6] Thus, heteronormative assumptions inform perceptions of which survivors deserve care or empathy. However, less is known regarding racial differences in terms of how others may respond to queer male survivors.

In this study, Black queer men experienced two types of negative responses more frequently than non-Black participants. The first of these reactions involved some version of "why didn't you physically prevent the assault?," while the second entailed a discourse that pointed to the "dangerous" nature of the assailant, implying that Black queer men "should have known better" than to become romantically involved with their former partner. Black participants also worried about encountering these forms of blame more than their non-Black counterparts. In this chapter, I show that such reactions arose from a complex interplay between race

and gender expression, as perceptions of Black queer men as either masculine or feminine structured these responses.

Regarding the first of these reactions—"why didn't you physically prevent the assault?"—Black queer men usually described this response in
relation to strength. Black and non-Black participants in this study identified similarly in terms of gender expression; both groups had roughly
equal percentages of respondents who identified as masculine or feminine, as well as gender nonconforming.[7] Despite these similarities in gender expression across racial lines, I found some differences in the extent to
which respondents discussed strength.

While almost two-thirds of Black participants mentioned "strength"
or "being strong," only two of the fourteen white participants did so.[8]
Similarly, only one of the nine non-Black people of color who identified as
Latinx or Asian mentioned strength, which indicates that these dynamics
may not apply to queer men of color more broadly as much as Black queer
men specifically. Black participants were more likely than other respondents to describe outsiders' reactions focusing on the assumed strength of
the survivor. For instance, Jalen, a twenty-four-year-old Black gay man,
was in a violent relationship with an ex-boyfriend, Stephen, for a year and
a half. Stephen had also met many of Jalen's friends and family members.
One year after exiting the relationship, Jalen told his sister that Stephen
had been abusive, which included raping him multiple times throughout
their relationship. Jalen explained that his sister responded skeptically, as
she asked, "Why didn't you stop him?" Jalen believed that her response
was due to differences between himself and his former partner in terms
of gender expression: "I'm a little more masculine, so I think she didn't
believe me that he could physically do it."

When I asked Jalen to explain how this response made him feel, he elaborated: "It caused more trauma. . . . A man is supposed to be stronger than
that. . . . Like it doesn't matter if you're more masculine, someone can still
pick something up, and bam, hit you. . . . 'Why didn't you fight back?' Like
I'm so tough that I can always fend off someone attacking me. . . . [When
he was raping me] my body just went numb, you don't know what to do."
Here, I want to draw attention to how questions such as "why didn't you
stop him?" or "why didn't you fight back?" are raced as well as gendered.
That is, the idea Jalen mocks, "Like I'm so tough that I can always fend

off someone attacking me," is likely to be directed toward some racialized, gendered bodies more than others. White men who are perceived as masculine will confront these notions as well, but given a history of racialized discourse that has associated Black men with "strong" or "aggressive" masculinities, these responses are likely directed disproportionately toward this group of men.

When Black participants described others' reactions focusing on physical strength, they sometimes connected these responses to stereotypes of Black men. For example, Kemal, a thirty-seven-year-old Black gay man, had two assaultive experiences in which his former partner had raped him during their relationship. He described his mother's response as unsupportive when he told her about these assaultive experiences. She asked Kemal, "Why didn't you get him off of you? Aren't you strong enough to do that?" When I asked Kemal where he thought these ideas come from, he mentioned stereotypes of Black men:

> I just think from images you see on TV, not necessarily gay men, just Black men in general, you know, just always getting a lot of girls, with flashy jewelry—and athletics and sports. With the world, what's projected, is rapper, athlete, or thug. And all of those three are hypermasculine images. . . . Someone who sees Black gay men as masculine or whatever, they're going to have a hard time seeing a Black gay man as sexually assaulted, so it makes that barrier harder to get through. . . . Growing up African American just has a label—as a man, you're supposed to be strong, you're supposed to be hypermasculine, and that just lends itself to not wanting to come forward with certain things, such as being assaulted, getting raped. Even if you don't see yourself as so masculine, other people still will.

Kemal later described himself as "feminine" and "not a very masculine guy," but argued that stereotypes of Black men may be applied to individuals such as himself. Undoubtedly, Black men who do not perceive themselves as masculine contend with these racialized stereotypes. As Kemal highlighted here, these ideas can make it difficult for some Black men to tell others about their assaultive experiences and for outsiders to recognize this group as survivors.

When I asked Kemal about how these ideas related to his mother's response, he said, "I'm supposed be a 'strong Black man,' so it's like the second someone puts their hands on me, I should be able to defend myself."

Hegemonic standards of masculinity encourage men to retaliate against challenges or signs of disrespect and to avoid showing emotions associated with weakness. Participants' experiences in this chapter provide further support for a long line of masculinities scholarship showing that when men are harmed, others may respond in ways that encourage toughness or retaliation.[9] Broadly speaking, these responses are part of a hierarchical approach to masculinity, where those forms that are associated with stoicism, strength, and physicality are granted more esteem than those associated with weakness or passivity. Others' responses saying that participants should have resisted or fought back against their attackers—rather than encouraging male survivors to engage in activities associated more with femininity, such as finding care—reveal how dominant masculinities remain linked with strength and a repudiation of femininity.

For Black survivors, research has shown that Black community-based norms may place a high value on being emotionally resilient in the face of ongoing adversity, including sexual assault.[10] Thus, outsiders' responses focusing on Black male survivors' strength may imply that the survivor should be able to handle the traumatic aftermath of the assault on their own. The implication of these statements focusing on physical strength was often not only that Black male survivors should have done more to stop the assault physically but also that they should now convey emotional strength in dealing with its aftereffects. Other research has shown that stereotypes of Black women as inherently strong can lead outsiders to perceive them as less traumatized than other survivors and can create some community-based pressures discouraging them from speaking out about their assaultive experiences from Black men.[11] These notions of a "strong" Black survivor, then, contribute to the silence and invisibility surrounding Black Americans' assaultive experiences.

In relation to LGBTQ people, previous sociological work has shown that Black LGBTQ people are often well integrated into their race-based communities, participating in Black social networks and institutions such as churches, families, and neighborhoods.[12] Scholarship has also shown that homosexuality has historically been linked with whiteness, as well as weakness, and may lead to notions of racial authenticity whereby the most "authentic" Black identities become constructed as heterosexual.[13] For this reason, Black queer men, especially those with feminine gender expressions, may face notions that they have "given in" to whiteness or weakness by identifying as queer.[14] The suggestion, then, that Black queer men should have retaliated against their assailant has different implications for Black queer men than it does for their white counterparts, as statements encouraging Black men to be "strong" may imply a repudiation of not only femininity but also characteristics associated with whiteness.[15]

Although Black queer men across multiple gender expressions detailed others who had perceived them as strong, these participants varied based on this matter as well. Specifically, Black respondents who described themselves as masculine, or at least not feminine, detailed these struggles to a greater extent than Black participants who described themselves as feminine. In one sense, I want to be careful about exaggerating these differences, given that Black queer men who did not view themselves as masculine also sometimes struggled with others' perceptions of themselves as strong. To be sure, Kemal, said, "Even if you don't see yourself as so masculine, other people still will."

Nevertheless, Black men who described themselves as masculine spoke the most about concerns related to others perceiving them as strong. One of these participants, Donald, a twenty-eight-year-old Black gay man, was sexually assaulted once by an abusive ex-boyfriend. Donald described himself as masculine and said that after he disclosed this experience, an acquaintance of his started telling others he knew that Donald's assaultive experience "probably didn't happen" because "he's strong enough to stop it." Donald heard about these comments from friends of his. Similar to Kemal, Donald connected these ideas with stereotypes of Black men, saying, "People see that I'm a masculine Black man, and then just with the stereotype that I'm supposed to be strong, there's this, 'Oh, well he can stop anything that comes his way.'" Another one of these participants, Xavier, a twenty-six-year-old Black bisexual man, characterized this stereotype in relation to aggression: "People think that you're 'more aggressive' and can't be raped."

While critiquing racialized ideas that link Blackness with strength and aggression is important, I want to draw attention to how some well-meaning approaches regarding sexual assault may unwittingly reinforce such ideas. Constructions that position assailants as aggressive and hypermasculine, while simultaneously positioning survivors as feminine and virtuous, can lead to some troubling intersectional consequences by reinforcing racial inequality. In this sense, the gendering of sexual assault as "masculine aggression" committed against "feminine vulnerability" is also an implicitly racialized narrative that positions assailants as men of color and survivors as white. It would be helpful, then, for work focusing on sexual assault to continue to expand understandings of this violence and capture a wider range of experience.

Avoiding this expansion could reproduce some of the silence and shame that queer male survivors already experience. Certainly, expanding sexual assault frameworks is particularly important for LGBTQ people, as gender identities and expressions continue to expand and become more fluid. For LGBTQ people experiencing intimate partner violence, imposing a binary gender model onto queer relationships is not a trivial concern. Such an approach can result in impositions where one individual is constructed as the masculine person in the relationship—or, more bluntly, "the man"—while the other is constructed as the feminine person—or "the woman." These understandings arise out of heteronormative assumptions, yet they can also can lead to the dismissal of violence in which a queer man, perceived as feminine, abuses his male partner who is viewed as "more masculine." Such gendered perceptions of queer male partners also frequently depend on race, as my findings revealed in relation to interracial forms of violence.

INTERRACIAL ABUSE AND RACIALIZED STEREOTYPES IN QUEER MALE COMMUNITIES

While masculinizing stereotypes of Black men exist beyond queer male communities, these ideas are also prevalent in such spaces. That is, in LGBTQ communities, racialized norms link Black and Latinx queer men with masculinizing stereotypes of dominance and aggression and Asian queer men with a pathologized submissiveness.[16] Consequently, queer men of color's gender expressions are then frequently read through the lens of these stereotypes, as either performing them or failing to live up to them. In mainstream LGBTQ communities, white queer men are not essentialized as often. Of course, queer men of color may associate white queer men with essentializing ideas, yet in mainstream LGBTQ communities, gendered stereotypes operate more harshly for queer men of color than for white queer men. A Black or Latinx queer man, for example, performing dominance may be interpreted very differently than a white queer man performing a similar dominance, as only the former may be read as reflecting a "natural" essence associated with their racial group. Conversely, while white queer men may certainly be ridiculed for gender expansiveness, femininity on the part of Black and Latinx queer men is sometimes additionally condemned for failing to enact a masculinity in line with racialized stereotypes.[17] Indeed, Black and Latinx queer men's femininity is less frequently granted the cultural cachet that such gender expressions may generate from white queer men.[18]

In addition, queer men are sexualized across racial lines in some different ways. Sexual acts and positions are often imbued with racialized meaning in LGBTQ communities. Black and Latinx queer men have been stereotyped as preferring masculinized sexual positions such as "topping," the act of penetrating another person during anal intercourse, while Asian men have been stereotyped as preferring feminized positions such as "bottoming," the act of being penetrated during this sex act. White queer men confront less rigid expectations of behavior. The problem with such notions, beyond the naturalizing of sexual positions onto particular bodies, is that they reproduce a racialized "mind/body" binary, in which queer men of color become defined by their sexual prowess. Institutional racism has historically relied on a "mind/body" duality that associates white people with the former and people of color with the latter, yet my argument here is that this binary informs racial inequality in queer male communities as well.[19]

The prevalence of these racial inequalities has not necessarily become easier to address over time, as the mainstream part of the LGBTQ-rights movement has increasingly advanced a representation of sexual minorities as "evolved" regarding a wide range of social issues, including racial equality.[20] These representations have often relied on a positioning of LGBTQ people as white, not to mention male and middle-class, despite the fact that most LGBTQ people are not white and middle-class gay men. Further, queer people of color have continually challenged representations of LGBTQ communities as "free" of racism, and I hope my work here contributes to this ongoing effort of highlighting inequality in these arenas.[21]

Given my white racial identity, Black participants sometimes appeared hesitant to discuss racism in LGBTQ communities, since they did not know how their narratives would be represented by a white gay man. However, race was often explicitly addressed when Black participants described interracial relationships. Most respondents experienced sexual assault from an assailant who was the same race as them, in relationships and in other contexts. Indeed, most violence is intra-racial, given that individuals disproportionately experience sexual assault, and violence more broadly, from someone they know.[22] In light of widespread racial segregation, residential neighborhoods remain divided largely based on race, leading to primarily intra-racial violence in communities.[23] Further, given that individuals largely continue to couple intra-racially, intimate partner violence also tends to follow this pattern.[24]

Conversely, two of the six Black queer men who experienced sexual assault from a white man were assaulted in the context of a relationship. One of these participants, Gene, a fifty-year-old Black gay man, described two friends who responded negatively when he told them about being sexually assaulted by his former partner, a white man. Gene described his friends—both queer men of color—responding unsympathetically: "They were laughing. . . . They thought it was funny—like, 'Oh, you can't handle a white guy?'" Expectations that Black queer men should be strong, or stronger than their partner, and therefore blamed for not physically preventing the abuse, may be particularly pronounced in such interracial relationships, in which physical strength may be mapped onto the Black male partner. To be sure, Gene said, "I think they thought he was weaker because he's white."

With interracial queer relationships, others may disproportionately assign masculinity to the Black or Latinx partner, while linking femininity with the white or Asian person. Of course, gender expression shapes these perceptions as well, yet here I am drawing attention to the role of racial inequality in such evaluations. The question from Gene's friends—"Oh you can't handle a white guy?"—is perhaps a crude articulation of how whiteness may be associated with weakness among some queer men of color, but these perspectives in relation to white queer men also exist in broader US society. Namely, white queer men are frequently associated with weakness in comparison with white heterosexual men.[25]

Given that Gene's friends were both queer men of color—one was Black and the other was Latinx—some individuals may attempt to challenge the privileging of whiteness in queer communities and beyond by ascribing seemingly negative characteristics to white gay men. This response may seem critical of white male homosexuality, linking it with weakness, but when viewed in a larger context, is quite consistent with racialized stereotypes that associate Black men with strength and white gay men with comparably weaker dispositions. The response of Gene's friends also reinforces negative constructions of femininity and reproduces gender hierarchies privileging masculinity over femininity.

The other Black participant who experienced sexual assault from a former white partner similarly struggled with notions that others could blame him for not physically preventing his assaultive experience. Vondell, a twenty-nine-year-old Black gay man, had not told anyone about his former partner, a white man, raping and physically abusing him during their relationship. Vondell mentioned strength more than any other participant, as he said, "I just don't want someone telling me that I should have been strong enough to stop it" and "[I] don't need to hear that I was stronger than him—'how could he rape you?'" Vondell's description of himself as stronger than his former partner was atypical among participants in this study, including among Black respondents. In fact, participants across racial lines more frequently said that they were physically weaker than their former partner, perhaps to preempt any accusations that they could have physically prevented the assault.

Black respondents sometimes argued that others perceived them as physically stronger than they viewed themselves, which indicates that Black queer men may confront notions that they are stronger than their partner even in cases in which they are not. Nevertheless, I am not interested here in determining differences in physical strength among queer men in relationships. Instead, I am interested in how ideas around physicality remain implicated in racial inequality and how these understandings may shape responses to Black, queer male survivors.

COMPLICATING PHYSICALITY

Historically, including during the 1990s and early 2000s, anti-feminist "men's rights" discourse gained a considerable amount of traction by emphasizing gender symmetry, or equal rates of abuse across gender lines, in terms of women's and men's violence in heterosexual relationships.[26] For this reason, in part, discussions of physicality have a contentious history in feminist scholarship. To combat these notions of gender symmetry, feminist research at the time pointed out that forms of violence may differ in terms of whether they are abusive, retaliatory, or preemptive, highlighting that women's violence in heterosexual relationships may occur before they are about to be abused or after they have already been hit.[27] This scholarship also highlighted how similar forms of violence can differ substantially in their effects.[28] In more everyday language, all hits and punches are not equally severe in their consequences. Still, although differences in physical strength may lead to significant discrepancies in the amount of harm a partner can cause, it is not always the physically stronger person who is abusive.

Focusing too heavily on physicality risks imposing a heterosexual model onto queer relationships. Moreover, given that Black men are especially likely to be associated with physicality in this way, such emphasis can lead to troubling racial implications, in which Black men become instituted as the strongest and most likely individuals to commit sexual assault. A decoupling of Blackness from physicality remains necessary, yet it is also more useful to understand intimate partner violence as occurring because of an investment in characteristics such as control or mistreatment rather than because of differences in physical strength. It may not be comforting to internalize the notion that most individuals can cause great harm to a romantic partner, but in hoping to move beyond reductive analyses that attribute men's enactment of sexual assault to physical strength, discussions of physicality should remain complex rather than straightforward.

ZACHARY'S EXPERIENCES

Although I continue to center Black queer men in the rest of this chapter, some comparative data that includes a white participant may help in elucidating these racialized notions of Black men as strong. When respondents told others about their assaultive experiences in a relationship, their friends or family members typically knew the assailant's race or ethnicity, since they had met. In other contexts, outsiders may not know this information, unless the survivor includes it in their description. One of the two cases in which a white man was sexually assaulted by a Black man involved Zachary, a forty-four-year-old gay man, who went home with a man he had met at a gay bar. Zachary told one of his friends, a white woman, about the assault, and described her as responding "sympathetically," but said that she became "less sympathetic" when she found out the man was Black. When I asked Zachary why he thought her response changed after learning this information, he said, "I think she thought I should know better than to go home with a Black guy."

On the one hand, I want to suggest that the stereotypical linking of Black men with strength may lead others to dismiss Black queer men's assaultive experiences as acts they should have been able to prevent through physical force, including and maybe even especially when the assailant is a white gay man. On the other hand, with Zachary here, his friend did not use racialized associations of Black men with violence, danger, or aggression to underscore the severity of the assault. In fact, she used such notions to problematize Zachary's actions.

With examinations of sexual assault against queer men, it remains important not to reinforce notions of white gay male vulnerability, as such understandings often involve an implicit contrast with a "dangerous perpetrator," which has historically and continually been linked with Black men. Nevertheless, in this case, Zachary's friend used these stereotypes to harm a white queer male survivor, as she blamed him more for the violence after learning that the assailant was Black. This response indicates that others may position Black men as "dangerous" or as potential assailants due to racialized stereotypes. As I show in the following section, Black queer men, particularly those who described themselves as feminine, encountered these reactions even more frequently, in which others blamed them for coupling with a "more masculine" Black man.

ACCOUNTING FOR GENDER EXPRESSION AND MALE FEMININITY

As my results reveal, even Black queer men who did not view themselves as particularly masculine had others assign stereotypical understandings of Black masculinity onto them. At the same time, it remains important to avoid reinforcing notions of Black men as primarily or disproportionately masculine. In focusing too much attention on "strength" in relation to Black masculinity, research can inadvertently marginalize the experiences of Black queer men who do not view strength as especially relevant to their lives. Black participants who described themselves as feminine were more likely than other Black queer men to argue that others do not usually perceive them as strong. For instance, Ornell, a thirty-seven-year-old Black gay man, had an assaultive experience in which an ex-boyfriend raped him once. After the assault, Ornell said that the two of them fought a lot and that he left the relationship three months later. He mockingly referred to his former partner as someone who "had to be seen as masculine at all times."

Ornell also had not told any of his friends or family members about this assaultive experience. He imagined others "not being supportive" because he worried that they would turn it into "something I brought upon myself." However, when asked if he was worried that others would blame him for not physically preventing the violence, he said: "People wouldn't say 'why didn't you stop him?' They'd say, 'Oh, you must have wanted it, you've always been craving dick'. . . . [or] 'Why did you get with that guy, anyway? We always told you he was up to no good.' . . . There is sort of that 'strong Black man' stereotype. I've never really felt like that applies to me. I'm feminine, so people don't see me that way." Analyses of Black masculinities, including mine up until this point, have often focused on the effects of this "strong Black man" stereotype that Ornell referred to here.[29] Even so, some Black men, disproportionately those with feminine gender expressions, may feel as if such stereotypes do not usually shape how others perceive them.

Overall, for Black participants who described their gender expression as feminine, they generally worried about encountering a response constructing the assailant as potentially "dangerous" or attributing the assault to the survivor's sexual desire—"craving dick," as Ornell bluntly phrased it here. Ornell argued that these notions exist in his racial communities as well: "A lot of Black [heterosexual] people think that Black gay men are just sex, sex, sex all the time. . . . Then they see one of us 'crying rape'—'no way, it was just sex.'" Of course, this type of response may also be directed toward white queer men who are perceived as feminine. Nevertheless, due to stereotypes sexualizing Black queer men, others may perceive this group's assaultive experiences particularly through the lens of sexual desire. The sexualization of queer men needs to be understood intersectionally because Black participants who described themselves as feminine struggled the most with pathologizing notions that position them as extraordinarily sexual.

Another one of these participants, Herman, a thirty-six-year-old Black gay man, also had a former partner sexually assault him. Herman described his ex-boyfriend as increasing his controlling behavior incrementally, at first limiting the amount of time he could spend with his friends and then forcing him to engage in sex acts he did not want. He characterized his former partner as "a little masculine, but not too much." Herman had only told one other person—his brother—about his assaultive experiences, which happened in the context of him becoming angry at his brother for remaining friends with his ex-boyfriend, even after they had separated.

Herman described his brother's response as "not good," because "he thought that I wanted it . . . like it couldn't have been rape because it was two gay guys, so we must have just been having sex." Given cultural notions that stigmatize queer men, particularly queer men of color, as "hypersexual," others may dismiss these survivors' assaultive experiences as consensual. Further, Herman responded in the following way when asked about whether others might blame him for not physically preventing the assaults:

> People don't view me as strong, because I'm feminine and gay. I have skinny arms and legs. I don't look like someone who could ever beat someone else up, so I don't think it's about that. . . . I worry more that they'll say, "Why didn't you get out the second he raped you? Was it really rape then? Are you sure some part of you didn't like it?" . . . I just think that's what people think of a feminine guy. Like something is wrong with you anyway that made you "that way," so maybe you brought it on yourself.

Men's femininity has often been pathologized as inevitably leading to negative consequences.[30] Such notions are not only cautionary—avoid male femininity, this line of thinking contends, because it is bound to lead to unhappiness or undesirable outcomes—but also punitive, as they naturalize, justify, or dismiss harmful events directed toward men with these gender expressions. Moreover, Black queer men's femininity may be especially chastised on these grounds, as failing to measure up to culturally approved standards of Black masculinity.

In the literature on male survivors, as well as in mainstream discussions of sexual assault, Black queer men who identify as feminine have received troublingly little attention.[31] Possible silences may occur if work on sexual assault focuses primarily on stereotypes of Black men as strong, masculine, or aggressive. Black participants who described themselves as feminine remained aware of these stereotypes, and occasionally even said that others assigned such notions to themselves, but different stereotypes associated with Black male femininity and Black queer sexuality usually appeared as, or even more, relevant to them.

With my previous research, I have highlighted how gender hierarchies in LGBTQ communities are constructed along racial lines; that is, in these communities, Black queer men are disproportionately associated with pathologized gender expressions such as "hypermasculinity" or "hyperfemininity."[32] In this sense, white queer men's feminine gender expressions may be interpreted through the lens of "male femininity," while similar gender expressions of Black queer men, or queer men of color more broadly, may be stigmatized to a greater extent as suddenly "hyper" in their expression of femininity. In short, it remains important to pay attention to how stigmatized gender expressions in LGBTQ communities and beyond are associated with marginalized racial groups.

Although participants across racial lines experienced negative responses based on prejudicial understandings of male femininity, Black queer men most frequently worried about others blaming them in relation to their assailant's gender expression. This response occurred primarily when a Black queer man who described himself as feminine had coupled with a Black man who was typically perceived as masculine. For instance, Reymond, a fifty-three-year-old Black bisexual man, explained that his former partner sexually assaulted him twice when they were having consensual sex, choking him and grabbing various parts of his body. Reymond described this man, Marshall, as "the kind of guy no one would think is gay," given his gender expression. At the same time, it was common knowledge in Marshall's neighborhood that he had sex with men because he did not keep this information hidden. Reymond described Marshall as someone who dealt drugs and who was perceived as belonging to a gang, even though Reymond said that he did not.

When I asked Reymond about his concerns regarding possible negative responses from others, he said, "Well, like, 'Why would you get with that guy? Everyone knows he's dangerous.'" This discourse of "danger" was something I heard from Black queer men who described themselves as feminine more than any other participants. Reymond, similar to most of these respondents, did not struggle with notions that he should have physically prevented the assault. Instead, he repeatedly described his fears that others would blame him for "not knowing better" than to become involved with a man such as Marshall. "Danger" is a very racialized word in the United States, as it remains associated with Black men with masculine gender expressions.[33] In these cases, Black queer men who described themselves as feminine worried that such notions of a "dangerous" Black masculinity would be used against them, to suggest that they should have avoided the relationship from the beginning and thus deserved some blame for coupling with a man who was perceived as violent or dangerous.

Reymond thought that these perceptions of Marshall were largely unearned, as he said that Marshall "never hurt anyone." When I asked, "Well, what about you?," Reymond responded, "Oh, I just meant in terms of his public persona. . . . He was very much a 'people's person.' . . . I never saw him threaten anyone else, be violent." Perhaps this focus on "danger" remains consistent with larger understandings of "the rapist," in which some assumption exists that it is fairly easy to distinguish between men who would rape and men who would not.[34] Reymond's emphasis on Marshall as a "people's person" is perhaps an attempt to challenge such notions, as individuals who commit sexual assault frequently exhibit more "regular," or even positive, characteristics, as rapists may be kind, generous, or charming in many situations, and cannot typically be easily identified.

At the same time, a Black male drug dealer, while not commonly positioned as queer in the dominant US cultural imagination, remains a heavily pathologized figure, associated with danger. While white men who deal drugs are stigmatized as well, the notion of a "white drug dealer" does not hold the same cultural weight as that of a "Black drug dealer." Further, the same stereotypes do not exist around masculine white men, as this group is more commonly normalized and not as frequently associated with danger. As my results show here, these differences have significant effects on Black queer men who enter into relationships with Black men who are perceived as masculine, as the former struggle with concerns that others will blame them for entering into such relationships.

While Reymond said that "everyone knew [Marshall] was gay," another participant, Clayton, a thirty-two-year-old Black gay man, described encountering a similar reaction in relation to a man he dated, who was considered on the "down low," or "DL," for short. A considerable amount of scholarship has problematized this notion of Black men on the DL, given that white men who are not out have more frequently been viewed sympathetically, as "suffering" in "the closet" where they are not yet able to "be themselves."[35] Here, Clayton's ex-boyfriend, Theo, and two of Theo's friends raped him as a form of punishment for outing Theo without his consent; Clayton told others that the two of them had been having sex. Clayton expressed regret during the interview, saying, "I should not have done that," but felt that others had blamed him more for becoming involved with Theo than for outing him, as Clayton described a cousin who said, "I told you not to get involved with him" because "that's just asking for trouble." White participants who had coupled with a "closeted" white man did not describe these responses, as such men are not associated with violence or danger to the same extent as their Black counterparts.

As Clayton's experience reveals, Black men on the DL may commit sexual assault, yet the prevalence of this stereotype in the United States likely leads to an overestimation of the frequency of this sexual violence. Moreover, this stereotype may serve as an easy explanation for why Black queer men appear to experience high rates of sexual assault, preventing deeper discussions of heteronormativity and racial inequality. Quite simply, any narrative that relies on understandings of Black men who identify as DL as inherently dangerous needs to be challenged, as these notions do not help survivors who have experienced violence from such men, but cause them to worry about being blamed by others. This trope of a man of color who cannot openly declare his sexuality because of cultural constraints has long been associated with "danger," as repressed and prone to violence.[36] Some more recent reporting on cisgender men who have murdered Black transgender women has arguably reproduced this trope as well. This reporting often excludes any mention of the assailant; the worry here is that such absences will result in some audiences imagining a Black man on the DL as committing the violence, given that broader structures of racial inequality already encourage this process.

Another one of these participants, Damon, a twenty-six-year-old Black bisexual man, was in what he described as a "friends with benefits situation" with a Black man, Nathaniel, who identified as on the DL. Nathaniel raped Damon once. After the rape, Damon described his continuing to see Nathaniel, as "like a powerful drug, I didn't know how to get out of." Indeed, some survivors remain connected with, and continue to see, an assailant after an assault, for a wide range of reasons.[37] Continued contact with an assailant, in other words, is not an uncommon occurrence, even though outsiders may view this contact as a sign that an assault did not occur. Many of the participants quoted in this chapter spoke about how breaking away from their former partner was not an easy process, as they found it hard to leave, and sometimes left and then returned, or maintained contact because they had not yet come to terms with defining the assailant's actions as abusive. Additionally, assailants often prompted this continued contact by reaching out to survivors after an assault. At times, respondents described these actions as part of the psychological manipulation they experienced.

Damon blamed himself considerably for continuing to see Nathaniel after the rape and for becoming involved with him to begin with, as Damon said, "I beat myself up for getting in with a guy who everyone would say, 'Well, he's DL, you know about those DL guys.' . . . I wouldn't want anyone to say, 'Didn't you know what you were getting into?' Blame me for that. Because that's like something I already feel." Damon's self-blame reveals the negative effects that masculinizing stereotypes of Black men can have on Black, queer male survivors. When I asked Damon who he thought specifically would blame him for coupling with Nathaniel, he responded, "Pretty much everyone. . . . White people too, because I'm supposed to know better than to get with 'such a person.'"

Damon said this phrase, "such a person," sarcastically, which suggests that he viewed this idea as predictable or ridiculous. However, even with this critical distance, Damon still worried that these ideas would inform others' responses. His statement that "pretty much everyone" would blame him for coupling with Nathaniel is likely an exaggeration, since it remains important not to position negative responses as inevitable or omnipresent, yet participants in this chapter typically worried about a wide range of people responding in negative ways. Most of the unsupportive reactions outlined here involved friends or family members who were the same race as the participant, but Damon's perception indicates that Black queer men may fear these responses from white people as well, given that racialized stereotypes broadly associate Black men with "hard" or "dangerous" masculinities. As Gail Garfield has stated in her research exploring how Black men interpret harmful stereotypes of them as perpetrators of violence, "In the cultural and social imagining of white America, black men and violence are inexplicably linked."[38]

Overall, I have shown that some Black queer men may be blamed for not preventing sexual violence through physical strength, while others may be blamed in ways that pathologize Black, queer male femininity or in ways that draw attention to the assailant's "dangerous" masculinity. These results depended in part on gender expression, as binary understandings of gender, in which participants thought that others would perceive members of the relationship as either masculine or feminine, were predominant. As such, it would be helpful for sexual assault scholarship to continue to destabilize binary understandings of gender.

Bodies of scholarship have focused on male femininity, but this line of work has not always incorporated the experiences of Black men, including in research on sexual assault.[39] Simply put, it remains important not to advance an understanding of "male femininity" that is implicitly white. At the same time, masculinizing discourse was relevant for multiple groups of Black participants. An assumption of strength prompted the "why didn't you fight back?" response, while a presumption of danger motivated the "you should have known better" reaction. The latter of these responses was experienced disproportionately by Black queer men with feminine gender expressions, which indicates that masculinizing stereotypes of Black men can harm Black queer male survivors who do not view themselves as masculine.

Discourses of blame will undoubtedly vary based on the context of an assault; for example, depending on whether the violence occurred in a relationship, casual sexual encounter, or some other situation. Paying attention to these differences remains important, yet a broader context of overlapping inequalities based on race, gender, and sexuality also needs deeper consideration. As I have shown, discourses of blame are rooted in this overlap.

In developing a more dynamic understanding of survivors' experiences of blame—one shaped not only by the context in which the violence occurred but also by structures of inequality—sexual assault scholarship can enhance knowledge of survivors' challenges. Certainly, in centering the experiences of survivors such as Black queer men, analyses of sexual assault can demonstrate how stereotypes rooted in overlapping inequalities disadvantage many survivors. More broadly, with scholarship on men and masculinities, centering Black queer male femininities helps to destabilize stereotypes of Black masculinity and to challenge constructions of male femininity as implicitly white. This approach also addresses the structural barriers confronting Black queer men with feminine gender expressions, as this group experiences marginalization due not only to stereotypes of Black masculinity but also to constructions that separate Blackness from male femininity and male queerness.

2 Queer Male Survivors and Police Interactions

Previous research focusing on queer male survivors' experiences of reporting to the police has typically emphasized homophobia or anti-queer prejudice, revealing how some police officers respond unsympathetically to this group of men.[1] In one of the earlier studies on this topic, Noreen Abdullah-Khan found that "many officers are unsympathetic and do not take male rape seriously," whereas Philip Rumney's review of this literature indicated that "some police officers and other criminal justice professionals appear to attach to gay men or those they perceive as gay highly questionable assumptions regarding credibility, trauma, and truthfulness."[2] More recent work has similarly shown that some police officers blame queer men for their assaultive experiences, drawing on stereotypical understandings of gay and bisexual men as sexually "promiscuous."[3] For example, Aliraza Javaid's research focusing on the police has pointed to how "gay male rape victims are often seen as having 'asked for it' and are, therefore, blamed for their rape."[4] Overall, this line of scholarship indicates that queer men share some similar experiences with other survivors, as groups such as women and heterosexual men also face victim-blaming responses from the police; at the same time, queer men experience some negative reactions unique to their own social position, informed by overlapping gender and sexuality norms.[5]

Although previous research has provided important insights into how anti-queer prejudice informs police responses to queer male survivors, little remains known in terms of racial differences among this group of men.[6] Queer men may differ based on race in some important ways regarding their experiences with the police, and yet research on queer male survivors has not typically focused on race and sexuality simultaneously. In contrast, I advance an analysis of queer male survivors' experiences with the police that considers intersections of race with gender and sexuality, accounting for intra-racial and interracial differences.

More broadly, beyond queer male survivors, most attention devoted to police brutality in the United States has focused on the effects of institutional racism, as a substantial amount of scholarship has shown that Black men fear and experience less supportive responses than white men.[7] Although race undoubtedly remains important for understanding many forms of police brutality, gender and sexuality have generally received less attention.[8] In this regard, prevailing criminological approaches, despite some noteworthy examples to the contrary, have typically explored issues such as police brutality and racial profiling without considering gender and sexuality.[9] Scholars in the field of critical, queer criminology have pointed to how these exclusions have led to the marginalization of LGBTQ issues from dominant criminal justice frameworks.[10] Consequently, this more critical area of research has argued for a "queering" of traditional criminological scholarship, in which gender and sexuality, as well as race, become understood as central to theorizing on the criminal-legal system.[11]

With regard to mainstream media representations, queer and feminist analyses have pointed out that Black heterosexual and cisgender men's experiences of police brutality have generally received the most attention.[12] This group certainly encounters disproportionately high rates of police violence, yet other research indicates that queer men of color also experience these forms of violence at an elevated frequency.[13] Research shows that LGBTQ people are disproportionately incarcerated as well, particularly queer people of color and those who are transgender or gender expansive.[14] One study, based on a national survey of inmates in US prisons and jails, found that the incarceration rate of self-identified lesbian, gay, and bisexual people was more than three times that of the general adult population; in comparison to heterosexual inmates, this study also showed that sexual minorities were more likely to have been sexually assaulted while incarcerated.[15]

Building on scholarship that has explored LGBTQ people's experiences with the police and the criminal-legal system more broadly, I argue that an intersectional approach improves understandings of queer male survivors' interactions with, and perceptions of, the police. Focusing specifically on whether participants were surprised by a negative police response, I reveal intra-racial differences within the categories of "white queer men" and "queer men of color."[16] For instance, this analysis reveals that queer men of color remain far from monolithic in how they perceive negative police experiences, as some of these participants were surprised that officers disparaged their sexuality, whereas others were not surprised. Overall, my results reveal complex differences among queer men of color based on gender expression and among white queer men based on age.

In total, twenty-three of the sixty respondents reported an experience of sexual assault to the police; all twenty-three participants reported only one experience and the vast majority, twenty-one, characterized the police response as negative.[17] Here, I focus specifically on queer male survivors' negative experiences in the context of reporting a sexual assault, although part of my analysis extends more broadly to profiling practices directed against queer men. The twenty-one respondents included in this analysis are disproportionately those who had been sexually assaulted in a relationship. Many of these participants spoke about how they would not have contacted the police in a different situation but felt compelled to do so, given the intimate partner violence they were facing.

Most of these participants, sixteen of the twenty-one, contacted the police to report an assaultive experience. The other five respondents had a neighbor contact the police on their behalf or had reached out to the police to report another matter, such as being locked out of their apartment, and then revealed the assault once the officers were present. A majority of these respondents were reporting generally abusive behavior from their partner, as physical and sexual violence were part of the same relationship, yet a sexual assault is usually what prompted them to contact the police. Twelve of these twenty-one participants were queer men of color, while nine were white queer men.

Among these twelve participants of color, police distrust was consistently expressed. All twelve of these respondents explained that they did not trust the police prior to their reporting of sexual assault and that they had been racially profiled by officers in the past. Thus, none of these participants were surprised that the police responded unsupportively. Moreover, these twelve participants all thought that anti-queer prejudice played at least some role in the negative response. Most frequently, they described officers as relying on stereotypes of queer men as consistently desiring sex, which reframed their assaultive experiences as consensual. Despite these similarities, the perceptions of queer men of color differed in important ways based on gender expression, with six participants expressing surprise that the police had disparaged their sexuality and the other six not expressing surprise regarding this matter.

"I DIDN'T THINK THEY WOULD BRING UP MY SEXUALITY"

Among the six participants of color who expressed surprise, all identified as Black and did not describe themselves as feminine or gender non-conforming. All of these respondents were not surprised that the police responded unsupportively to their assaultive experience, but they were surprised that their sexuality played a role in the negative response. For example, Vondell, a twenty-nine-year-old Black gay man, contacted the police after an abusive former partner had raped him. He thought that the officers blamed him for the assault, in part because of his sexuality, as he said, "They were acting like just because I'm gay that I want this to happen and like I'm craving sex 24/7." Vondell could not recall everything the officers had said to him, but he characterized their attitude as "condescending" and said that they were asking him a lot of questions that involved "our sex life and what I like in bed—like I wanted it."

All of these participants had previous experiences in which they had been racially profiled, yet they did not have any prior police interactions in which officers had disparaged their sexuality. Indeed, Vondell described a history of racial profiling in which he was approached by police officers in the New York City neighborhood where he grew up; at these times, he was searched, sometimes for drugs and other times for an unstated reason. These experiences have often been referred to as a "stop and search" or "stop and frisk."[18] In regions of the country in which walking is less common than New York City, these stops may occur more in the context of driving, at least for those who can afford a car, as the phrase "driving while Black" has been used to characterize this phenomenon in which Black Americans are disproportionately surveilled due to racialized assumptions of guilt and suspicion.[19]

Vondell said that the most recent time this had happened to him was a few weeks before the interview, when he was walking on the street and a police car pulled up next to him. Then, one of the officers asked him to spread his legs and let them search him. When this happened, Vondell was walking in a wealthy, predominantly white, neighborhood of New York City. He referred to this experience as "embarrassing" and "humiliating." Beyond the search, he was not reprimanded or punished in any way, but when Vondell had these experiences during his youth, he recalled several times in which he was ticketed or arrested, including for behavior he did not do. He had two experiences as a teenager in which police officers planted drugs on him when he was stopped and searched. Both times involved officers putting drugs in his belongings, such as a backpack or a wallet. He reframed these incidents by characterizing them as an example of a "stop and plant" rather than a "stop and search."

Given this history, it may be surprising that Vondell reported his assaultive experience to the police. All sixty participants in this study had one or more experience of sexual assault, and a majority of these respondents, thirty-seven, did not report any of their experiences. The most common reason given for not reporting was a concern that the police would not take the violence seriously. Almost half of the participants who did not report also spoke about their fear that the police would mock or belittle what had happened to them. This concern was primarily borne out when participants such as Vondell reported a sexual assault. Vondell said that he had these concerns as well, but went to the police station with an understanding that "nothing would probably happen" and that he was "fine with that . . . [but] hoped that they would at least talk to [his ex-boyfriend]." He reported the assault, in other words, with the hope that his doing so would lead to the reduction or elimination of his former partner's abusive behavior.

Regarding the officers' negative response to the assault, Vondell said, "I know the police don't support people like me. . . . I wasn't surprised that they talked to me in that aggressive way. All of my previous incidents didn't have anything to do with me being gay, so I guess that part of it was surprising. . . . I didn't think they would bring up my sexuality." Vondell expressed surprise that the police mentioned his sexuality, given that an officer had never previously remarked on this aspect of his identity. All six Black respondents who expressed this surprise described a history in which officers had not perceived them as gay or bisexual, at least not to their knowledge. These participants felt that race was central to their previous police interactions or thought that officers in the past had perceived them as Black, implicitly straight, men.

The surprise that these respondents expressed arose from a complex interplay of race, sexuality, and gender expression. For instance, Antonne, a fifty-eight-year-old Black gay man, was sexually assaulted by a man he had met on a gay hookup app and had invited over to his apartment. After Antonne reported this experience to the police, an officer asked him, "Well, why would you invite him over to your place?" This officer's response could certainly be directed toward a heterosexual survivor, given that it is consistent with the sort of victim blaming that many women encounter after they have been sexually assaulted.[20] Still, Antonne thought that homophobia was informing the officer's reaction, as he said, "His whole demeanor was, 'This is disgusting.' . . . He hated gay people."

In comparison with his previous experiences with the police, however, Antonne explained that this situation differed: "[Police officers] don't really think I'm gay when they meet me, they just see me as a Black man, so this was the first time I've really had a police officer respond in that way. . . . I haven't had good experiences with the police, but this was the first time that me being gay had anything to do with it, so that part of it was surprising. . . . Because I'm masculine, they usually just see me as a Black straight guy." The cultural association of gender conformity with heterosexuality played an important role here, as others may perceive Black queer men who largely conform to dominant constructions of masculinity as heterosexual in many contexts. Conversely, these participants thought that their reporting of a sexual assault was the first time that an officer had known or assumed they were queer. At times, these respondents did not explicitly disclose their sexuality to the officers, but they thought the police had presumed they were homosexual or bisexual, given that the assault had usually occurred in the context of a relationship or a sexual encounter with another man.

One of these participants, Dannell, a forty-one-year-old Black bisexual man, thought that the police response would not have been quite as negative as it was in the context of a sexual assault due to him revealing his sexuality. He explained that sometimes he thinks "people are more comfortable [with me] when they find out that I'm bi . . . because then I'm less threatening." Perceptions of Black men as "threatening" may be softened when they are perceived as queer or feminine. In this sense, the overlap of Blackness and queerness does not always increase the amount of discrimination one may face, as the latter identity may lessen outsiders' stigmatizing perceptions of Black men. Of course, Black queer men face forms of discrimination that their heterosexual and cisgender counterparts do not, and, as I show in the next section, Black queer men who described themselves as feminine or gender nonconforming experienced many forms of police profiling that targeted their gender expression.[21] Indeed, although Dannell expected the police officers to be more empathetic in the context of him reporting a sexual assault, this expectation was not supported by what happened.

Similar to Vondell, introduced earlier, Dannell also contacted the police with the goal of ending his ex-boyfriend's abusive behavior. However, unlike other participants in this chapter, the police officers who came to Dannell's apartment committed physical violence against his ex-boyfriend, Benjamin. The officers also arrested Benjamin on domestic violence charges. This experience of one partner being arrested may be relatively uncommon for queer couples more broadly, as research indicates that the police are more likely to arrest both partners in cases of same-gender intimate partner violence than in different-gender ones and are more likely to arrest no one when both partners are the same gender.[22] Thus, both dual arrest and nonarrest are more likely in same-gender intimate partner violence situations than in different-gender ones, the latter of which more frequently involve the arrest of one person.

Dannell said that the intimate partner violence became worse after Benjamin was released from jail. He also described Benjamin being arrested as something he was "OK" with, or neutral about, since he wanted the violence to stop, but Dannell said that he "did not want it to happen like that," with the officers beating up his former partner. In particular, Dannell viewed the police violence against his ex-boyfriend as making matters worse or more dangerous for him, as he felt that Benjamin became angrier as a result of what happened. Although the police violence was directed primarily toward Benjamin, Dannell explained that he was not immune from this force either. When the police officers were hitting Benjamin, Dannell said that he was primarily yelling for them to stop, but that he also tried to intervene at one point, which resulted in one of the officers elbowing Dannell in the face and giving him a bloody lip. When the officers were beating Benjamin, Dannell said that they were using homophobic language about himself by asking Benjamin questions such as, "You like to rape faggots?"

Among the men who did not report any of their assaultive experiences to the police, I often heard concerns about possible repercussions from their reporting. Men of color were considerably more likely to make these arguments than white participants. Most commonly, queer men of color explained that they thought nothing would be done after their reporting; these respondents characterized contacting the police as pointless or as a waste of time. However, about one-third of the participants of color who did not contact the police described a fear that officers would be physically violent toward them or a romantic partner. Dannell did not describe having these fears before contacting the police, but said that once the officers were in his apartment, he began to feel this way. He explained that both he and Benjamin had to listen to "a lecture" from one of the officers about how they needed to be more considerate of their neighbors. Dannell said that the difficulty in this type of situation is that "you must be respectful," but that it is easy for something to be viewed as "disrespectful" when one is describing a painful experience, in a tense situation.

He also communicated that "if I'm 'too respectful,' then I'm being disrespectful," as forms of respect from Black men may be viewed as arrogant or patronizing by some officers. This discourse around "respect" was also something that I heard from participants of color more than white respondents, as police interactions may be especially tense for Black and Latinx individuals, given that the slightest sign of "disrespect" may be viewed as a norm violation and may, consequently, result in a violent or aggressive response. In this sense, white Americans tend to be granted more leeway in their interactions with the police, while a respectful/disrespectful framework structures how some officers evaluate people of color. As Dannell explained, Black men frequently have to balance this fine line, where they do not want to be perceived as "disrespectful," but also have to work at avoiding perceptions of themselves as "too respectful." Other participants of color contextualized this balance around notions of "deference" or "politeness," yet the larger point was similar, in that these respondents worried that their actions, or those of their partner, would not be read as appropriately deferential and, therefore, could be subjected to an unsupportive or even violent response.

When I asked Dannell about his prior experiences with the police when he was young, he described that time period as one in which he was subjected to the most intense policing, as he said that he was stopped and searched for drugs "all the time" in his low-income neighborhood. Class and age undoubtedly remain important for understanding police profiling practices, as younger, low-income men tend to experience more profiling than their older and wealthier counterparts.[23] Class prestige can and does shield individuals across racial lines from some experiences of police harassment or brutality. At the same time, it remains important not to reduce these experiences to a matter of social class, as race is also significant, given that low-income men of color experience a greater share of police violence than their white counterparts.[24] Thus, both race and class need to be accounted for, rather than privileging one over the other.

Participants spoke about the effects of class less than those of race, perhaps reflecting larger dynamics in the United States in which class often remains unacknowledged due to meritocratic notions that arise from the ethos of the American Dream. Respondents were college educated at a higher rate than the general US population and a significant number had grown up in middle-class homes—particularly those who were white—yet most participants experienced some economic precarity and did not appear to have much disposable income; this trend points to some downward mobility. Several respondents had also experienced homelessness for an extended period of time. Most typically, this homelessness coincided with the time when an assailant had sexually assaulted the participant, or the assault led to some economic precarity, and ultimately, homelessness.

For instance, one of these participants, Xavier, a twenty-six-year-old Black bisexual man, was working as a janitor when his former partner sexually assaulted him. The first assault involved physical force, as his ex-boyfriend held him down by the throat. After this assault, Xavier began to show up late to work and was eventually fired, which made him economically dependent on his ex-boyfriend for shelter and other necessities. Subsequent assaults involved coercion or pressure, in which his former partner would insist on their having sex, sometimes when Xavier was drunk, until he relented. Some of these coercive assaults involved his ex-boyfriend financially threatening Xavier if he refused to have sex, saying things such as, "I can always kick you out if you don't want to." His partner worked in a traditionally feminine occupation, while Xavier described himself as "kinda masculine," which again indicates that forms of sexual assault against queer men do not always involve masculine assailants or feminine survivors.

Xavier's negative police experience in the context of reporting a sexual assault occurred when his former partner assaulted him a second time using physical force. When this happened, Xavier called the police. The officer who arrived at their apartment did not seem to take the violence seriously and began to joke around with Xavier's former partner. Xavier thought that the officer was biphobic or homophobic because "he refused to give me the time of day" or "look me in the eye." Xavier was surprised by this response because he had not had any previous experiences in which he felt that anti-queer prejudice had informed a police officer's response toward him, although he had been racially profiled in the past.

A few weeks after this second assault involving physical force, Xavier moved out of his ex-boyfriend's apartment into a homeless shelter. This occurred approximately six months after the first assault, after Xavier had lost his job. He described the first several shelters he was placed in as "very bad" in terms of seeing and occasionally even experiencing physical violence, yet two years later, he found one in which he felt safer and more comfortable. When I asked him about other experiences with the police, he referred to this time period when he was homeless, saying, "That's the other big time I experienced [police harassment]." Since he was homeless, he often did not have money for new clothes or even food. He thought that police officers perceived him as homeless or low income during this time and subjected him to more intense policing than he had experienced prior to then.

He described multiple occasions in which police harassment occurred during this time of his life. One such example involved him being ticketed for fare evasion when he jumped over a New York City subway turnstile; the police officer who ticketed him spoke down to him and called him a racial slur. Other experiences did not involve name calling, but consisted of him being profiled or ticketed for loitering, usually when Xavier was in a relatively wealthy area or one in which a lot of tourists congregated. Loitering, a criminalized term for hanging around a public place for a protracted period of time, is a charge that officers apply disproportionately to individuals perceived as low income.[25] Since race affects judgments of class—a middle-class Black person, for example, may be perceived as lower income than a middle-class white person, even if their income and wealth are the same—this overlap again points to the importance of examining race and class simultaneously. Xavier's experience also reflects larger trends in which homeless people are subjected to high degrees of policing, as "quality of life" laws criminalize many acts such as panhandling or sleeping in a public place that are associated with homelessness and, more broadly, poverty.[26]

In sum, while social class is undoubtedly important, all of the respondents in this section identifying as Black remains significant, as these participants believed that officers in the past had typically devoted attention to their racial identity. This approach toward Black men reflects a larger cultural context in the United States in which Blackness is "marked" as hypervisible and policed disproportionately based on prejudicial assumptions of danger and criminality.[27] Still, while officers may profile some Black queer men primarily based on their racial identity, the results presented here, especially when compared with findings in the next section, indicate that this experience exists disproportionately for Black queer men who do not identify as feminine or gender nonconforming.

"THE POLICE ARE DISRESPECTFUL BECAUSE I WALK A CERTAIN WAY AND DRESS A CERTAIN WAY"

In contrast to participants in the previous section, six other respondents of color—all of whom identified as either Black or Latino—were not surprised that police officers negatively addressed their sexuality when they reported a sexual assault. For instance, Justin, a sixty-two-year-old Black gay man said, "I expect the cops to be homophobic, so it wasn't surprising," and Mendez, a twenty-seven-year-old Black and Latino bisexual man, said, "I wasn't surprised, the cops can be very insulting of my sexuality." Another participant, Ornell, a thirty-seven-year-old Black gay man, explained his reasons for not being surprised by the negative police response: "No, I wasn't surprised, I've had a lifetime of the police targeting me because I'm a feminine gay man. . . . So, them addressing my femininity was just like, 'Yeah, I've heard this one before, what else you got that's new?'. . . They're very disrespectful of my race and my sexuality, so that's why I don't trust them to help me no matter what I'm going through." These participants usually had expectations, informed by their past experiences, that they would not encounter a positive police response and then found their expectations confirmed when disclosing the assault. The key difference, however, between these respondents and the Black participants in the previous section was that respondents here described a history in which officers had chastised their sexuality or gender expression.

As research has shown, outsiders may perceive gender-expansive people as "making trouble" or "being disruptive," and groups such as the police sometimes profile individuals based on these assumptions.[28] Gender nonconformity also intersects with social class in important ways, as others may assign a low-income status to gender-expansive people, given cultural associations that link subversive gender expressions with disorder.[29] For this reason, others may surveil gender-expansive individuals, especially those who are Black or Latinx, based on understandings that they "do not belong" in locations reserved for individuals with class prestige.

The participants in this section varied in describing their gender expression, with some referring to themselves as feminine and others as gender nonconforming. Despite this variation, all of these respondents detailed past experiences in which they felt that they had been profiled based on their gender expression, as well as their racial identity. These experiences also typically involved some version of a "stop and search." Ornell, for example, described a police officer in the past who referred to him as an "AIDS monkey," among other disparaging names, in the small town where he was born and raised. This officer also arrested Ornell on a variety of nonviolent charges. As a result, although profiling on the street may be particularly common in pedestrian-friendly cities such as New York City, this practice is also not exclusive to them, as Ornell had been profiled in this way when he lived in a small town.

Ornell had similarly encountered such profiling since moving to New York City, as he underscored that officers have targeted him in part due to his gender expansiveness: "They see that I'm wearing something queer. . . . My ripped jeans, my earrings, and they think that's a sign that I'm up to no good and shouldn't be walking the streets. So that's where the searching and the taking me down to the station comes in." The assumption that Ornell may be "up to no good" can arise from a host of prejudicial attitudes toward Black queer men, including not only stereotypes around crime and drug use that officers may ascribe to Black heterosexual and cisgender men but also negative ideas around sex work that the police may assign to Black LGBTQ people.[30] To be sure, Ornell described several occasions when officers found a condom on him and then brought him to the police station for questioning about sex work.

Given his past experiences of being profiled and arrested, Ornell said that he "would never call the police for help." Instead, when he was arguing with his abusive ex-boyfriend, a neighbor called the police on them. This behavior from outsiders can potentially expose survivors to more distress or harassment, stripping them of control regarding how they would like to proceed. Similar to Ornell, four of the six participants in this section did not contact the police to report a sexual assault, but then revealed this experience once the officers were present. The friend, who was also a neighbor of another participant, called the police, and two respondents only contacted law enforcement because a former partner had locked them out of their apartment. In comparison with participants in the previous section, respondents here did not view the police as potentially hospitable to queer men and, thus, sometimes did not report a sexual assault for that reason.

The experiences of Black queer men in the previous section were relatively similar to some dominant understandings of racial profiling, as police officers in the past had profiled this group based on their Blackness but had not disparaged their sexuality. Conversely, when considering the challenges of queer men of color who described themselves as feminine or gender nonconforming, a more intersectional understanding of how they are profiled remains necessary, as the phrase "racial profiling" does not account for how race, sexuality, and gender expression simultaneously shaped many of their police interactions. These participants' experiences did not involve the officers first racially profiling them and then subsequently disparaging their sexuality or gender presentation, but involved the officers targeting their gender expression from the very beginning. Consequently, prejudicial understandings of gender expansiveness lead to forms of profiling against some people of color. Scholarship remains necessary that centers, rather than marginalizes, these experiences, which would help with underscoring the role of gender and sexuality in profiling practices and the criminal-legal system more broadly.[31]

While respondents who were not surprised that the police had disparaged their sexuality typically emphasized the importance of race, sexuality, and gender expression, they also sometimes emphasized contextual variation, as the relevance of these aspects may vary depending on the situation at hand. Another participant, Jeremiah, a twenty-two-year-old Black gay man, explained that "there are some situations [with the police] where my sexuality plays more of a role and some situations where my race does." When asked how he makes this determination as to the role of racism and homophobia, he said, "I can't pinpoint it as 'Oh, in this case it's all about this, or in this case it's all about that,' but it's just something that I know in my bones—like I can tell when it's more about one of those things than the other, but it's usually about both."

Jeremiah also explained that he was not surprised by the unsupportive police response given his past experiences: "No, I wasn't surprised. I've seen the police be very rude about my sexuality in the past—that's why I didn't want them there in the first place." Most Black participants, regardless of gender expression, described their past experiences as leading to some hesitancy to reach out to the police; these respondents, after all, were less likely to contact law enforcement than white participants. Nevertheless, although the framework of "racial profiling" may account for the experiences of Black queer men who conform to dominant standards of masculinity, participants such as Jeremiah viewed the police as hostile to their queer identity as well as their racial identity.

Several of these participants, including Ornell and Jeremiah, said that they are stopped and searched about once a week in New York City.

White or middle-class Americans may find this frequency hard to believe, but other gender-expansive queer men of color who lived in low-income neighborhoods made similar statements. This constant surveillance can result in a variety of negative consequences, as individuals subjected to it may not only end up spending unnecessary time in jail but also experience adverse psychological effects, as the harm and frustration that accompanies such profiling or harassment is likely to wear individuals down. Cumulatively, these practices may function as a form of "slow death," defined as the physical wearing down or deterioration of a population.[32]

Public attention to police brutality in the United States has tended to focus on cases of death or murder, yet those incidents also need to be contextualized in relation to more routine forms of profiling. In this sense, while cases of murder may be useful for gaining more widespread attention on problematic policing practices, these cases represent only a fraction of the problem. Instead, more pervasive forms of profiling remain important to highlight because much of the activism against policing has occurred in light of this broader context, in which many people of color are protesting due to a fear that they could be murdered and a concern that they will continue to be profiled or harassed. In short, these policing practices—and the activism against them—exist in a larger environment of white supremacy that assigns stigmatizing characteristics such as danger, mistrust, and criminality onto people of color more frequently than their white counterparts.

Although race remains important, many participants' experiences revealed the centrality of gender and sexuality as well. Respondents in this section typically argued that the more gender expansive they appeared, the more likely they were to be harassed by the police. Juan, a forty-seven-year-old Latino gay man, repeatedly drew attention to his gender expansiveness throughout the interview, explaining that "the police are disrespectful because I walk a certain way and dress a certain way. . . . If I get really decked out, that's when they'll be the most disrespectful." Police officers and others may perceive gender nonconformity as "drawing negative attention" toward oneself and then profile or harass people with such gender expressions based on these prejudicial notions. For gender-expansive participants, their negative police experiences often involved a ridiculing of their gender expression. Police officers also sometimes made biphobic, homophobic, or transphobic comments to these respondents.

Juan, who experienced sexual assault in the context of a relationship, did not want to report his abusive ex-boyfriend to the police, but did so after his former partner had locked Juan out of his own apartment. When two officers came to his building, Juan told them that his partner had also raped him twice, which one of the officers responded to by asking, "Don't you guys like rough sex anyway?" Juan interpreted "you guys" to mean gay men, as this question reframed his assaultive experiences as consensual and drew on sexualizing stereotypes of gay men. When asked whether he was surprised by this response, Juan reflected on his past experiences: "No, it wasn't surprising, I've never really had a positive experience with the police, except for maybe if I just have to ask for directions or something. . . . They can tell that I'm feminine from the way I talk and then they get this attitude of, 'Oh, he's one of these smart ass queens.' . . . I wasn't surprised so much as angry at myself for not trusting my gut, and not calling them. But what are you supposed to do when someone is hitting on you, wailing on you?" Juan regretted calling the police and wished that he had followed his instincts not to do so, as he described experiencing some fear before reaching out to them and then felt as if these concerns had been substantiated when the officers responded unsupportively.

Policing remains important to explore in relation to Latinx people, not only those who are Black, as Latinx individuals make up one of the largest growing segments of the US prison population.[33] Statistics are sobering with regard to the increased criminalization of immigration, as over two hundred jails and prisons for immigrants currently operate within the United States, a sharp increase over time.[34] Juan was the only participant in this study who identified as undocumented, and he spoke about how his lack of citizenship made him more fearful when the police arrived at his apartment. He feared that the officers would learn about his undocumented status and that he would then be arrested and deported. Juan felt especially fearful that his partner would reveal this information to the officers. Further, he described how he had avoided going to the hospital before this time due to a fear that his undocumented status would be reported to the police.[35] Thus, immigration status remains an important dimension of inequality for understanding survivors' unwillingness to reach out to the police or, more broadly, to social service agencies.

Juan's question "But what are you supposed to do when someone is hit-ting on you, wailing on you?" points to the powerlessness that queer men of color may experience in light of abuse. Survivors more broadly may have this emotional response, yet my findings indicate that queer men of color experience a lack of support more than their white counterparts, as the former felt less aided and more marginalized by social institu-tions, including but not limited to the criminal-legal system. These per-ceptions may lead to understandings that social institutions have largely failed queer male survivors of color and that they must rely primarily on themselves in light of this structural marginalization. Survivors' sense of powerlessness may also be particularly intense after experiencing an unsupportive police response, as individuals often have relatively little recourse when confronting such reactions. That is, police brutality and other negative responses are difficult to pursue charges against, or even to report to other authority figures, given the powerful position of law en-forcement in implementing punishment. Violence from the police, then, may feel qualitatively different than violence from civilians, given that the former cannot be as easily contested.

"SO MUCH FOR PROTECT AND SERVE"

Similar to participants of color in the previous sections, all nine white respondents with negative reporting experiences thought that anti-queer prejudice played at least some role in the unsupportive response. In con-trast to queer men of color, however, some white participants expected the police to respond supportively. White queer men differed based on age in this regard. Specifically, white participants under the age of forty were surprised by a negative police response, while those over forty were not. To reflect age differences among white participants, I have referred to those above the age of forty as "older" and those below the age of forty as "younger." The "younger" category roughly correlates with the commonly used generational label of "millennials," whereas the "older" category com-prises "Generation X" and "baby boomer" generations.

Of course, these categorizations are imperfect, given that age operates as a continuum more than a dichotomy and differences obviously exist between the generational categories of Generation X and baby boomers. Moreover, although I have used forty as the separation point for the sake of clarity, the category of "over forty" officially comprises white participants aged from forty-four through seventy-seven and "under forty" encompasses those from twenty-six through thirty-eight. While the findings based on this analysis should be viewed as suggestive rather than definitive given the relatively small number of white respondents in this study, age was nevertheless the most salient factor in shaping the amount of surprise that white participants expressed.

Younger white queer men were the only participants who expressed surprise at the negative police response to their reporting of a sexual assault. For instance, Charlie, a twenty-six-year-old white queer man, said, "I didn't expect them to be that rude," and Allen, a thirty-eight-year-old white gay man, said, "I didn't think they would be blaming me like that." Allen's assaultive experience involved a man spiking his drink with a date rape drug and then raping him when he was unconscious. When Allen reported this assault, he said that the police officers asked him, "Are you sure you didn't want it?" This line of questioning from the officers focused on Allen's sexual desire and included other questions, centering most on their belief that Allen had taken the date rape drug voluntarily. One of the officers asked, "Are you sure you didn't take it? Sometimes people forget." While date rape drugs may be taken recreationally, it is illegal to assault an unconscious person, given that they do not have the capacity to consent.[36] Allen regretted contacting the police, and when I asked him at the end of the interview what he would like to see done to help other survivors, he said, "Make sure to tell them not to contact the police," as he felt that this experience had traumatized him further.

Another one of these participants, Danny, a thirty-one-year-old white gay man, experienced intimate partner violence from an ex-boyfriend who had raped him four times during their seven-year relationship. Once, when his partner was abusive, Danny called the police, which prompted two officers to come to his apartment. Describing their response, he said, "They were just very condescending, like I was wasting their time or something. When I told them that he raped me in the past—'Well, you can't rape the willing,' one of them said that to me. . . . I thought they would be like, 'What can we do to help you?' but that was the furthest thing from their minds. It was very un-policeman-like—like, so much for 'protect and serve.'"

Participants across racial lines experienced sexualizing comments from the police, yet Danny's reaction differed from that of queer men of color and white gay men older than forty. His construction of the negative police response as "un-policeman-like" relies on an understanding of the police as typically supportive; none of the participants of color or older white respondents made such statements. This racial difference among participants is consistent with previous research revealing that men differ across racial lines in their understandings of the police as providing "safety" or support—a perception expressed disproportionately by white Americans.[37] At the same time, white participants typically had negative police experiences in the context of sexual assault, which suggests that their whiteness did not shield them from an unsympathetic response.

Another white respondent under the age of forty, Francis, a twenty-seven-year-old queer man, called the police after a man had spiked his alcoholic drink with a date rape drug and then raped him. During the interview, he described the police as blaming him for the violence, as one of the officers told him, "You should be more careful who you drink with." Francis explained his surprise at this response: "I was surprised by that, because I don't know anyone who has had something like that happen. So, it was just surprising that here I am in the middle of this thing I only see on TV. . . . I thought they would be nicer." Francis expected a more positive response because he did not know anyone who had a negative police experience; he also did not have any undesirable experiences of his own, prior to this incident. His positioning of this response as something "I only see on TV" indicates the degree to which Francis, as well as individuals in his social networks, had not encountered such a reaction. Undoubtedly, this anticipation of a positive, or at least not entirely negative, response cannot be separated from his whiteness.

Still, given that white respondents older than forty did not respond in this way, Francis's perception should also be understood in relation to his age. Understanding younger white queer men's evaluations necessitates not only accounting for race but also considering the context in which these participants were raised. Historically, during the 1950s and 1960s, sexual minorities, including those who were white, were broadly associated with criminality, which resulted in a wide range of policing practices, including, perhaps most famously, bar raids.[38] Although such raids have not disappeared, as they have been reported against undocumented LGBTQ people and other queer people of color, their widespread use has undoubtedly decreased since their zenith in the 1950s and 1960s, when it was frequently illegal for homosexuals to congregate with one another.[39]

These participants younger than forty were born no earlier than the late 1970s; two were not born until the 1990s. Thus, they grew up in a context in which they either were very young during Ronald Reagan's administration and the AIDS crisis or were not alive at all during that time. Irrespective of their relationship to the 1980s, these participants came of age at a time in which they were not experiencing the anti-gay discrimination prevalent in the 1950s and 1960s, some of which was enacted by the police, such as at Stonewall. They were also not present for much of the activism in the 1970s that developed in response to police violence.[40] Forms of police brutality against white queer men and others certainly persisted into the 1980s and beyond, with particularly aggressive policing directed toward queer men during the AIDS crisis and toward gay and bisexual cruising zones, as well as LGBTQ sex workers, continuing through the present day.[41] However, younger white queer men's responses need to be contextualized relative to the social changes that have transpired since the 1970s, in which mainstream gay-rights groups have increasingly forged alliances with the police.[42] LGBTQ advocacy historically constructed the police as an agent of queer oppression, yet a divide began in the 1970s, which has continued until the present, in which some LGBTQ groups still challenged the criminal-legal system while others began to call for greater policing.[43]

White queer men, similar to other social groups, should be understood as intersectionally situated in relation to systems of oppression and as differing based on a wide range of characteristics such as age, social class, HIV status, and geographic location. While it remains important to emphasize the negative effects of policing on LGBTQ people of color, less work has explored how white queer men may now be helped, or harmed, by law enforcement.[44] On the one hand, my work here indicates that younger white queer men may increasingly view the police as a source of protection, with little of the skepticism that previous generations expressed more frequently. That is, younger white queer men may no longer be growing up in a context in which they are encouraged to view the police as working against their interests. If the findings here reflect larger trends, then serious challenges exist for LGBTQ work that hopes to resist punitive strategies, as many younger white queer men may now view criminalization as offering them greater safety.

On the other hand, the police may not provide as much "protection" or support for younger white queer men as they expect, at least in the context of sexual assault. As a result, great potential for revealing some of the ways that the police do not support queer men, including those who are white, resides in this disjuncture between the assistance that younger white participants expected to encounter and the unsupportive reaction they actually experienced. It remains important to avoid positioning white queer men's negative experiences with the police as worthy of greater attention than those of LGBTQ people of color. Nevertheless, it is also important to highlight the many contexts in which queer men across racial lines may encounter unsupportive police responses. Queer men's experiences will undoubtedly differ across racial lines in these contexts as well, yet some younger white queer men may be unaware of the degree to which the police have historically not served their interests and the extent to which officers may continue to respond unsupportively in some situations.

The interviews for this research project occurred before the 2020 protests in response to the murder of George Floyd and others. Many younger white LGBTQ people engaged in these protests, which suggests that more critical perspectives among this group may exist more broadly. Regardless, scholarship on white LGBTQ people's perceptions of the police remains necessary, including research that accounts for generational differences. For the younger white participants, I can only speculate as to the reasons they did not generally have any prior negative police experiences. The neighborhoods in which they lived did not appear to leave them exposed to routine policing, given that they described only rarely interacting with the police. For white queer men, social class and gender expression will undoubtedly play an important role in shaping police interactions, yet younger white participants, even those who grew up in poor neighborhoods or who described themselves as gender nonconforming, did not have the extensive history of profiling experiences that queer men of color described.

"I SHOULD HAVE BEEN SURPRISED, BUT I WASN'T"

White respondents older than forty differed from their younger counter-parts, in that the former did not express surprise at a negative police re-sponse. For instance, Zachary, a forty-four-year-old white bisexual man said, "It wasn't surprising to me in the least," and Chad, a forty-eight-year-old white gay man stated, "I wasn't surprised at all." While Zach-ary's assaultive experience occurred several years prior to the interview, Chad's happened when he was eighteen, during the 1980s. Both of them occurred in the context of a relationship. Chad contextualized the negative response—which involved the officers snickering—in relation to dominant understandings of homosexuality at the time, as he said, "You have to re-member, this was at a time when being gay was seen as the plague." Zach-ary also contextualized the negative police reaction, which involved the officers casting doubt on his claims, in relation to the social context—in this case, modern stereotypes regarding bisexuality—as he said, "They think I'm confused about my sexuality. Then that translates into 'Oh, you must be confused about whether [a sexual assault] happened.'"

Three of these participants had reported to the police during previous decades, yet the other two respondents encountered negative police re-sponses in the past five years. Thus, especially when coupled with results from the previous section, these negative experiences should not be un-derstood as a relic of the past or as a phenomenon that has disappeared, even for white queer men. Indeed, as Zachary emphasized here, biphobia persists and may inform how the police interact with bisexual men.

Another older white participant, Melvin, a fifty-nine-year-old gay man, described an experience in which he was stabbed by a man in a public park. Melvin was performing oral sex on the man when this occurred. When the police showed up at the hospital, Melvin explained that they laughed when he described what happened. He contextualized this negative response in relation to his experiences with the police during the 1980s, when extensive homophobic hysteria existed with regard to the AIDS crisis: "In the '80s, the police used to go to these places where gay men would have sex and rough us up. I saw this guy I had sex with get his face pounded in by two cops. . . . So, I know what police brutality looks like. I didn't really expect them to be any better these days, but this was just proof of that."

While younger white queer men usually explained that they did not know anyone with negative police experiences, their older counterparts had more frequently been targeted by the police when they were young or, if not, they knew others who had. These older participants had also grown up in a context in which white queer men were more often subjected to routine policing. Of course, the time period that these respondents referred to varied depending on their age. Another one of these participants, Paul, a seventy-seven-year-old white gay man, mentioned bar raids that he had experienced during the 1950s and 1960s and said that these experiences "taught me not to trust the police." Similar to Melvin, Paul's experience involved officers laughing when he described the sexual assault, only this time in the context of a relationship. Paul was also not surprised by this response, as he said, "I should have been surprised, but I wasn't. . . . [Being] a young gay man in the sixties taught me that I should never be surprised by them."

These age differences among white participants, taken with the differences among queer men of color based on gender expression, indicate that scholarship on LGBTQ people's perceptions of the police would benefit by examining aspects beyond race and sexuality, including age and gender expression. Still, in comparing the experiences of these older white participants with those of queer men of color, race becomes an obvious and important factor for understanding queer men's interactions with the police. Outside of some of their recent experiences of reporting sexual assault and confronting a negative response, most white queer men older than forty did not have another negative police encounter in over a decade. In contrast, queer men of color had continual experiences of racial profiling and, at times, had more interactions in which the police had disparaged their sexuality or gender expression. As a result, although this chapter has focused primarily on intra-racial differences, variation across racial lines also remains important to examine.

Although the white queer men in this study generally had negative police experiences, it is also possible that this group of men would have received a more positive response if the form of violence they experienced had been different.[45] Previous research has shown that the police, as well as media, tend to take seriously forms of public street violence enacted against white gay men, given that this violence is consistent with the "stranger danger" framework that the criminal-legal system routinely prosecutes.[46] Even in my previous research, white gay men who experienced stranger-based forms of violence on the street typically encountered supportive police responses.[47] Consequently, it is important to remain attuned to different forms of violence and how such contextual variation may shape queer men's experiences with the police. Further, it would be useful for future advocacy and scholarship to question who benefits and who is harmed by a continued reliance on the criminal-legal system to solve social problems such as sexual assault.

HISTORICAL CHANGE AND FUTURE POTENTIAL

The findings throughout this chapter may be considered sobering or disheartening because they reveal a lack of support for many queer male survivors, yet I also find a lot of hope or encouragement in some of the social changes that have occurred over the past ten years. When I conducted the research for my first book, *Violence against Queer People*, starting in 2006, Black Lives Matter did not yet even exist, and barely any attention, at least in mainstream media, focused on LGBTQ people's experiences of police brutality. That book in part became a text about police violence against LGBTQ people of color because many of the participants I interviewed had those experiences. However, at that time, anti-LGBTQ violence was typically understood through the lens of attacks from strangers on the street, not state-sanctioned forms of violence such as those that occur through the criminal-legal system.

While understanding violence as constituting primarily stranger-based attacks has not disappeared, more attention since that time has been devoted to Black LGBTQ people's experiences of police brutality, due in large part to the work of individuals associated with the Movement for Black Lives.[48] This change in public discourse has likely altered how LGBTQ people understand forms of violence, including some of their own experiences. I view these changes as largely positive, as I have noticed with my research that queer people of color I interviewed prior to the advent of Black Lives Matter were less likely to underscore the severity of their experiences of police brutality than those I interviewed for this project. Based on my research, these social changes that have taken place have helped individuals with such experiences to understand them as harmful and to feel more open or comfortable speaking about them.

The work of Black Lives Matter and other social justice groups focusing on police brutality can be understood as queer activist labor, as LGBTQ people have increasingly figured into representations of police brutality.[49] This emphasis can be pushed even further in the future, yet part of my goal in this book is to emphasize some possible connections, as well as tensions, between advocacy devoted to combatting mass incarceration and to reducing sexual assault. While I return to this argument more in the conclusion, my point here is that advocacy focusing on sexual assault could learn from the work of Black Lives Matter by pushing understandings of sexual violence in more intersectional directions.

Analyses of sexual assault would also benefit by further connecting this violence with police brutality. After all, violence from the police includes sexual assault. For instance, one participant, Anthony, a fifty-nine-year-old Black gay man, was sexually assaulted by a police officer when he spent time in prison. Research also indicates that Black and Latinx women, as well as transgender people of color, experience high rates of sexual assault from prison guards and police officers.[50] An intersectional approach can help to connect these two concepts—sexual assault and police brutality—and to show how anti-criminalization work can reduce some forms of sexual assault. In effect, the challenge for future work is to expand further the intersectional imagination of our approach to these issues, revealing some possible connections between seemingly discrete social problems.

Although I cannot speak to the demographic breakdown of all of the officers participants described in this chapter, among those respondents who divulged this information, a substantial minority were women or people of color. A majority of the officers participants identified in this chapter were white men. However, given that a significant percentage involved female officers or male officers of color, this dynamic reveals a more structural problem beyond white men's racism and anti-queer prejudice. In particular, an array of officers across race and gender lines appear to engage in practices demeaning queer male survivors.

Academic work can help in this regard by contextualizing individuals' police experiences in relation to systems of oppression. Certainly, my work here is consistent with previous scholarship that has demonstrated the effects of structural inequalities on individuals' experiences of police brutality.[51] Part of how systems of oppression operate and become reproduced is by establishing some bodies—disproportionately, those that are Black, Latinx, low-income, transgender, or gender-expansive—as more "suspect," disruptive, or dangerous, and therefore more "deserving" of policing, than others.[52]

While in this sense my analysis here has been consistent with most research focusing on police profiling practices, I have argued for a more truly intersectional approach that considers gender and sexuality as well as race and ethnicity. This approach accounts for the experiences of multiply marginalized individuals, whose challenges cannot be fully understood through prevailing frameworks that focus on only one form of inequality. An intersectional approach helps to capture what is going on with many individuals' police interactions, revealing complexities that cannot be explained by race-only or sexuality-only frameworks.

3 Survivors' Self-Blame and Differences within the Queer Umbrella

Survivors' self-blame has usually been examined by psychologists.[1] However, as a sociologist, I was less interested in trauma or participants' psychological experiences and more interested in the ways that self-blame may be implicated in power relations. In this chapter, I show that this blame can be understood in sociological ways, in relation to structures of inequality. Specifically, respondents' self-blame was often implicated in US-based understandings of male queerness, as a majority of participants—forty-one—described feeling "dirty" or "disgusting" after the assault.[2] Indeed, this was one of the most common emotional reactions that respondents described.

Overall, participants differed considerably in the amount of self-blame they expressed. Some blamed themselves throughout the interview, while others blamed themselves very little or not at all. Of course, some of the respondents who blamed themselves very little may have felt uncomfortable with expressing any self-blame in the context of an interview, but nevertheless felt this way at other times. Still, I do not want to naturalize the blame that survivors may feel as inevitable, given that a few participants spoke about self-blame as something they had felt in the past but did not feel anymore, or as something they never really felt. Most

respondents, however, went back-and-forth, sometimes blaming themselves and at other times resisting this blame. In this sense, participants
usually struggled with this matter in a nonlinear way; as such, their self-
blame fluctuated a fair amount.

This blame also took on many different forms. Some participants, for
example, appeared to internalize notions that their queerness may have
contributed to the sexual assault, while others did not struggle with this
matter. Similarly, some respondents grappled with their behavior before
the assault, while others did not. Consequently, queer male survivors' self-
blame should be understood as varied, and any attempt to point to trends
or similarities must be viewed in this context.

Despite this variability, when participants described feeling "dirty" or
"disgusting," they often referred to prejudicial understandings of sex between men. For instance, Brian, a nineteen-year-old Latino gay man, was
approached by a man on the street who asked Brian if he wanted to have
sex at the guy's apartment; the man raped Brian after they started to have
consensual sex. Most of the sexual assaults that participants experienced
in the context of a casual sexual encounter involved an initial meeting on
the internet. Brian also described several assaults in that context, as he
told me that three men he had first met on the internet did not stop penetrating him after he told them to "stop."

His assaultive experience with the man he met on the street first involved Brian performing oral sex on the man and then they began to have
anal sex, where Brian bottomed. Before describing this experience, Brian
said, "I'm not sure if this counts as a sexual assault," and then explained
what happened: "Like it was hurting, I didn't want it anymore, but he just
kept going. . . . I said 'no,' he just kept going. . . . [When it was over], I felt
dirty, just sitting there with my thoughts. I definitely didn't ask for that,
but at the same time, I brought that on myself to an extent. . . . It feels like,
'Oh my god, is what people always said the way it is?' Like, 'This is what
happens when you're gay.'"

Growing up in a heteronormative society, participants likely became aware
of notions that sex between queer men may be deemed "dirty," "disgusting,"
or "immoral." While sex between two heterosexual people is comparatively
normalized, sex between individuals of the same gender is more commonly
linked with perversion. Even how the phrase "gay sex" circulates in some

media and social circles often has a bit of dirtiness implied in this expression. In particular, anal sex between men may be stigmatized as "disgusting."

These perceptions have deep historical roots in the United States, as sodomy laws, which were not declared unconstitutional until 2003 with *Lawrence v. Texas*, provide one example of how these understandings have been codified into law. For queer male survivors, then, a sexual assault may bring forth these negative ideas. Brian addressed this pathologizing, drawing particular attention to homophobic narratives that link homosexuality with negative outcomes such as sexual assault. To be sure, an anti-LGBTQ understanding of what I have focused on in this book would use queer men's assaultive experiences as evidence of the many problems and harmful events that purportedly arise from queerness.

Such a framing of sexual assault against queer men deserves problematizing. Surely, assailants' actions need to be understood as producing these violations, not survivors' sexualities. These associations link two aspects— queerness and sexual violence—that have no "natural" connection with one another. On the one hand, participants sometimes seemed to internalize these ideas, questioning whether their queerness had contributed to harms directed against themselves. On the other hand, respondents often expressed a deep ambiguity when responding to questions about blame, as they acknowledged that they sometimes felt it, but also spoke about these ideas as if they were wrong or prejudicial. That is, even as participants struggled with some anti-queer narratives, they also usually resisted the notion that their sexual identity had led to the assault.

Another respondent, David, an eighteen-year-old Black gay man, struggled relatively little with self-blame in relation to an assault that had occurred during a hookup, after he went over to the apartment of a gay male couple to have consensual sex. He explained his reasons for not telling anyone about the assault in the following way: "People will think, 'Well, why'd you go over there? Isn't it partially your fault then?'" In some ways, David was atypical in comparison with most participants who had these experiences because he did not seem to blame himself, at least when he was speaking with me. I remarked on this matter at one point during the interview, telling him that most of the other men I had spoken to appeared to blame themselves more than he did. He responded, "That's a struggle. I do blame myself sometimes, too. . . . I just don't think it's helpful for me to get through my day by asking myself, 'Why did you go over there?'"

Participants with assaultive experiences that occurred during a hookup were the least likely to have told anyone about the assault. This trend arose from their concern that outsiders could blame them for an assault in this context. Several participants also questioned whether their experiences were "really" assaultive, given that they had first pursued consensual sex. Similar to Brian, another participant, Mendez, a twenty-seven-year-old Black and Latino bisexual man, stated, "I'm not sure if this counts," before describing an experience of rape. Mendez first went over to a man's apartment with the intention of having consensual sex; they had been speaking with one another on Grindr, a gay hookup or dating app, for several weeks.

The assault involved the man refusing to stop penetrating Mendez when he became uncomfortable and tried to stop having sex. Mendez said, "I started to freak out. . . . I was very uncomfortable, like squirming, and then he just started grabbing me tighter and forcing himself in me." I was surprised to hear participants undermine the severity of their experiences by saying "I'm not sure if this counts" before recounting a sexual assault such as this one. This type of statement should be understood in relation to broader ideas concerning what "counts" as rape and sexual assault. Indeed, I heard such statements most frequently from participants who had been assaulted in the context of a hookup.

Respondents who were sexually assaulted in this context often thought that some audiences would dismiss their assaultive experiences, given that outsiders could criticize their actions before the violation as purportedly setting the stage for an assault. These constructions arise out of a sex-negative approach, in which individuals may position consensual sex as leading to negative consequences. It remains important to challenge such notions, as a wide range of feminist work has characterized this emphasis on survivors' sexual activity as a form of victim blaming.[3] Combatting this violence necessitates focusing on the social conditions that lead assailants to violate someone else's sexual autonomy, not survivors' attributes or behaviors.

At the same time, mainstream media narratives generally focus on violations that occur in non-sexualized contexts and that involve no consensual sex before the assault, perhaps out of a concern that many audiences will blame a survivor who experiences this violence during a hookup.[4] The danger of such portrayals, especially when they repeatedly occur, is that they reproduce an implicit contrast, in which some survivors are cast as "blameless," given that they did not "put themselves" in a sexual situation, while others are cast as "blameworthy," or as playing some role in what occurred. These divisions reproduce a framework of "personal responsibility" for addressing sexual assault; such a framework has been central to many mainstream media representations of social problems in the United States, including sexual violence.[5]

The problem with understanding sexual assault through the lens of personal responsibility is that it reinforces these discourses of blame and demands that individuals "behave more responsibly" without insisting on deeper, more profound changes that give rise to the violence in the first place. Instead of emphasizing individualistic solutions, I advance a more social approach by examining queer male survivors' self-blame through a sociological lens. This analysis reveals how such blame varies depending on a survivor's social location and how the challenges queer male survivors face differ based on their sexuality and gender identity. Specifically, I detail some unique experiences of bisexual and pansexual participants, as well as those who are nonbinary or transgender, highlighting significant differences among queer men.

BISEXUAL AND PANSEXUAL PARTICIPANTS' EXPERIENCES

For bisexual men, their assaultive experiences often differed in some important ways from what gay men experienced. In particular, although others may dismiss gay men's sexual identities at times, bisexual participants had these experiences more frequently. Kamar, for example, a forty-year-old Black and Latino bisexual man, had an assaultive experience in which a gay man he met on Grindr raped him. After going over to the man's house, Kamar talked with him for a short amount of time before they started to have sex. During this discussion, Kamar said that the man became agitated when Kamar affirmed his bisexuality rather than identifying as gay. Kamar's Grindr profile said that he was bisexual, but during their conversation this man said, "You can't be bi and 'a bottom.'"

Kamar now blamed himself for not leaving at that moment, as he told me, "I think it was my fault, I wish I would have been smarter about it and left right then and there." When initially describing the assault, Kamar also said that this man "decided to have a little fun with me" rather than explaining what had taken place. Participants sometimes characterized an assault in this undermining sort of way—"a little fun"—to avoid describing specific details about what had happened to them. After some time in which these respondents became more at ease with the interview, they typically explained the assault in more detail, although doing so was sometimes difficult for them. Certainly, Kamar later said, "I'm starting to feel really emotional talking about this."

While Kamar described blaming himself, he also did not back away from defending his desire to have sex, as he stated, "I came there for sex, so that's what I was gonna do." Kamar explained that they were having consensual anal intercourse, but then the man began to grab Kamar's nipples to the point that it was causing him pain. Kamar then attempted to stop having sex, when the man put his hand around Kamar's chest, forcing him against the bed and raping him. Besides grunting loudly, the man did not say anything during the assault and Kamar's bisexuality was never mentioned again. Still, Kamar drew attention to several ways that biphobia may have informed his assailant's actions, as he said, "There's something where gay men will play with you differently when they find out you're bi. . . . I don't know, like it's a tussle in bed." When I asked him about whether this dynamic had to do with a masculinizing of the position of topping and how some men may interpret this sexual practice as a "role" that involves power and dominance, Kamar responded, "Yeah . . . also, it's like fine if you're 'a top,' but then it's a problem if you're 'a bottom'—'you're not really bi then, and I'm going to show you that you're not.'"

The assailant's statement, "you can't be bi and 'a bottom,'" draws on notions of bisexual men as confused. Historically, bisexuality has been dismissed as not a "real" or legitimate sexual identity, with individuals being rigidly categorized as heterosexual or homosexual based on a partner's gender.[6] More broadly, the dismissal of bisexuality as not "real" or authentic comes from a privileging of the heterosexual/homosexual binary, in which sexualities outside of this construction are frequently forced into it. A male-centeredness is often built into this dismissal as well, given that outsiders are more likely to characterize bisexual men as "really" homo-sexual, while bisexual women are more frequently labeled as "truly" het-erosexual. The end point in both cases is desire for men. The statement of Kamar's assailant also indicates an association of bottoming with homo-sexuality, as this act may be naturalized as an essentially homosexual or feminized position. As his experience indicates, individuals may become angry at bisexual men for troubling this assumed association.

Additionally, Kamar described how perceptions of bisexual people as "selfish" or "greedy" may structure aggressive or violent approaches toward himself: "People think you just want everything, and so then they can take it. . . . Like it's open season." These notions can lead assailants to assume that bisexual people want a sex act to which they did not consent. Among the twelve bisexual men, ten spoke about understandings of bisexual people as "selfish" and expressed concern that these ideas would inform others' responses to their disclosure of a sexual assault. Lee, a thirty-eight-year-old Asian bisexual man, described this dynamic as "people will look at it like maybe if you weren't so selfish and greedy, this wouldn't have happened to you." Notions of "you want to have your cake and eat it too" imply a greedi-ness to bisexuality, as if one is selfishly asking for too much. In contrast, a lot of bisexual activism has emphasized the value of fluid sexualities, draw-ing attention to the benefits of fluidity in expressions of sexuality.[7]

While most bisexual participants mentioned this selfishness stigma, bisexual men who experienced a sexual assault in a relationship also addressed stereotypes around cheating. Another bisexual respondent, Xavier, a twenty-six-year-old Black and Latino man who was sexually as-saulted by a gay male partner in a relationship, mentioned how biphobia can lead to intimate partner violence: "I worry that I will be questioned [by partners]. . . . Like, 'What about you, what were you doing?'. . . People think that bi people will cheat. That's where the attacks can come from." Intimate partner violence against bisexual people may occur due to stereo-types around cheating, as homosexual or heterosexual assailants may at-tempt to control their bisexual partner through physical or sexual abuse. To be sure, research indicates that bisexual people experience intimate partner violence at considerably high rates, due in part to sexualizing stereotypes that essentialize bisexual people as cheaters and, more broadly, as "promiscuous" or untrustworthy.[8]

In addition to the twelve bisexual participants, two respondents identified as pansexual. Pansexuality, which may be collapsed with bisexuality in
mainstream media, is often interpreted as a sexuality in which individuals
announce their attraction to all genders or to people regardless of gender
identity. The origin and increasing use of pansexuality is designed to be
inclusive of transgender people, given that traditional understandings of
sexuality may imply an attraction toward cisgender individuals. An additional purpose of pansexuality is to help move away from binary understandings of gender that assume only two genders exist—an assumption
that excludes nonbinary individuals and others who may identify beyond
the categories of woman or man.

Of course, a hierarchical positioning of pansexual people as "more
evolved" than bisexual people remains problematic, given that the latter
played an instrumental role in the development of pansexuality.[9] Pansexual people may also identify as bisexual depending on their audience.
Thus, these identities are not always mutually exclusive.[10] Here, I am less
interested in distinguishing between bisexual and pansexual participants
and more interested in drawing attention to the challenges that pansexual survivors may experience. I make my claims cautiously here, given
that only two of these respondents participated in this study, yet I hope
future scholarship will center such survivors' experiences to expand on
my analysis.

One of these pansexual participants, Samuel, a thirty-seven-year-old
Black man, described being sexually assaulted by a gay man at a house
party. Unlike most participants in this chapter, Samuel and this man did
not have any consensual sex, although Samuel initially thought about
doing so, since he was attracted to the man. Samuel also told me that
he prefers to top if he has sex with men. At the party, the two men, after
speaking with one another for a few minutes, went into a bedroom to talk
some more. He said that he then started getting "creepy vibes" from this
guy, which included the man continually pushing for the two of them to
"mess around."

Samuel described this conversation as lasting "maybe five minutes,"
and then the next thing he knew, he woke up or regained consciousness
with most of his clothes off, feeling pain in his genitals. Samuel concluded
that the man had drugged his drink, likely with a date rape drug, causing

him to pass out. The man gave Samuel money after this happened, which Samuel viewed as designed to "keep [him] quiet." He took the money, but blamed himself afterward for doing so: "I beat myself up [for that]. . . . Like did I take that because I 'asked for it' in some way? Because I wanted it to happen?"

Samuel had not told anyone about this experience, and when he explained his reasons for not telling anyone, he said that he worried, similar to a lot of other participants, that "no one is going to believe me." Although queer male survivors experience some overlapping struggles, bisexual and pansexual men also confront some unique challenges, as Samuel mentioned that others could interpret his experiences through the lens of "confusion." He said, "People don't understand [pansexuality]. They're confused by it. . . . They think I'm making up my identity." Bisexual participants also worried that others may think of them as "confused" about their sexuality. Samuel here stated that others may not understand pansexuality, which indicates not necessarily that others may think of pansexual people as "confused" but that they may be unclear as to what it involves. Regardless of the precise meaning of "confusion" in this case, the part of Samuel's statement that I did not hear from gay male participants was this assertion, "They think I'm making up my identity." Transgender respondents, as I detail later in this chapter, mentioned these notions as well, and bisexual participants often implied them, suggesting that others may perceive them as not "truly" bisexual.

Outsiders may view gay men as "making up" their identities or being "confused" about them, but these notions are also likely becoming increasingly passé, at least in comparison to what bisexual and pansexual people experience. For example, the relative newness of pansexuality in comparison to homosexuality is likely to lead to some important differences. Samuel's hesitancy to tell others about his assaultive experience must be understood in relation to a broader context in which pansexuality may be positioned as an "invented" identity. These ideas likely led to his concern that others may "think I'm making up my identity."

In queer theory and elsewhere, sexualities scholars have frequently underscored that all sexual identities are socially constructed—or "invented," if one wants to use stronger and arguably more negative language.[11] Indeed, in the United States, heterosexual and homosexual identities did not arise until the nineteenth century and did not come to be understood as mutually exclusive "opposites" until even more recently, in the mid-1900s after World War II.[12] Consequently, queer theorists and others in sexuality studies view heterosexual and homosexual identities as socially constructed. With regard to pansexuality, individuals who do not identify in this way may view it as an "invented" identity because they did not become aware of this discourse until relatively recently. Rather than these individuals then engaging with how their sexual identities are also implicated in social processes, such reactions assign a special status to "new" sexualities, which become positioned as socially constructed. In short, these understandings serve to naturalize sexualities such as heterosexuality and marginalize those such as pansexuality.

"PEOPLE THINK YOU'RE TRYING TO FOOL THEM": NONBINARY AND TRANSGENDER EXPERIENCES

Centering the perspectives of nonbinary and transgender participants helps to show these groups' unique experiences. Certainly, gender identities are often essentialized as well as sexualities, as some assumption exists that gender entails "who one is" rather than an attribute that is also historically and contextually dependent.[13] In this study, two participants identified as "nonbinary men." Both explained that their pronouns are "he or they." One of these participants, Sergio, who was twenty-two-years-old and Latinx, said that he identifies as "a nonbinary man . . . meaning that I don't have a problem with people seeing me as a man, but I see myself as a 'messy man'—like partially a man, but partially something else."

Obviously, given that I recruited participants through the language of "queer men" and not "nonbinary individuals," this study attracted men primarily with binary understandings of gender.[14] Nevertheless, including these two nonbinary participants in my analysis points to the need for more research focusing on this group of survivors. When listening to these participants, I felt that their experiences were important to include in this book and that their identities fit under the umbrella of "queer men," regardless of how imperfect that designation may be. It remains important for academics not to impose our understandings of gender and sexuality onto others, as both of these respondents explained that they did not view the categories of "men" and "nonbinary" as mutually exclusive.

Sergio did not identify as transgender, while the other nonbinary participant, Clyde, did. Clyde, a thirty-three-year-old Black and Native American transgender man said that he is "open" and "fine with 'man' or 'nonbinary.'" Clyde was the only respondent in the entire sample to be sexually assaulted by a woman past the age of eighteen. The assault happened when Clyde went over to the apartment of a female friend of his girlfriend; this friend lived across the hall from him. Clyde described the friend as liking him romantically, but he was not interested in dating her. The two of them also commonly asked one another for favors, given that Clyde was dating her friend.

The assault occurred when he was helping her in the bathroom, as she pushed him to the point that he slipped and fell, hitting his head on something hard, likely the sink or bathtub. He lost consciousness and then woke to her on top of him trying to orgasm, with him feeling pain in his groin area. When explaining his reasons for not telling his girlfriend, Clyde said, "I didn't want to come in between two friends, for something little." This downplaying may reflect cultural discourse in which sexual violence committed by women has disproportionately been positioned as causing relatively little harm to male survivors.[15] Four other respondents had assaultive experiences with women assailants, although they all occurred under the age of eighteen, and these participants similarly undermined the seriousness of the sexual abuse more frequently than respondents with male assailants.

While undermining the severity of the assault at times, Clyde also underscored the possible role of transphobia, as he thought that a fascination with transgender men's genitalia contributed to the assault. He said, "Like there's this 'Oh, what's under there' thing that people have with trans people." Indeed, when mainstream media representations have presented transgender issues to cisgender audiences, the narrative has sometimes focused on genitalia, with crude divisions between transgender people who have undergone genital surgeries and those who have not.[16] Such divisions can result in the invasive questioning of transgender people, which their cisgender counterparts do not typically experience. These distinctions also support the normalizing of cisgender bodies, as a voyeuristic approach toward transgender people may be predominant throughout such representations.

Even well-meaning media attention that focuses on the lack of access for some transgender people to genital surgeries is arguably part of this cultural emphasis on genitalia. Here, I hope to resist or critique this focus on genitalia, while simultaneously highlighting a larger transphobic context that positions transgender people's bodies in a variety of negative ways. Comparing participants based on gender identity, transgender men described assailants who had characterized their bodies as "nasty" or "disgusting" more frequently than their cisgender counterparts.[17] For instance, two transgender participants, Santiago, a forty-nine-year-old Latino queer man, and Grey, a thirty-five-year-old white queer man, experienced sexual assault from cisgender male partners. Both Santiago and Grey described themselves as primarily attracted to men, although both of them had dated women in the past as well. Their assailants also both used demeaning language about their bodies during the abuse. Additionally, both assailants started using physical violence when these participants were transitioning. One difference, however, was that Santiago began transitioning before meeting his former partner, while Grey did not begin this process until he was in a relationship with his ex-boyfriend.

Santiago began transitioning in his early forties; after starting this process, he also met and fell in love with his former partner, Lorenzo. Santiago described this relationship as "loving" at first, but said that it "turned dark" when he moved into Lorenzo's apartment after they had been dating for a few months. Lorenzo began to control Santiago, demanding that he stop working and seeing his own friends. Santiago now thought that these actions were designed to make him financially and emotionally dependent on Lorenzo. The first sexual assault occurred after they had lived together for approximately four months. Lorenzo sexually assaulted Santiago about ten times throughout their relationship; half of these assaultive experiences involved rape, and all of them involved Lorenzo hurting Santiago's genitalia.

Perhaps surprisingly, in light of this abuse, Santiago described Lorenzo as supportive, at least superficially, of his transitioning process, which included paying for most of his medical treatments. Yet, Santiago viewed this support as part of Lorenzo's manipulation, since he would justify his abuse by apologizing and saying, "I let you be a man." Santiago's decision to transition, in other words, was positioned as something that Lorenzo had "allowed" him to do, implying that he should be grateful to Lorenzo and should not complain about the abuse he was experiencing.

In this sense, cisgender men may use the social pathologizing of transgender identities to position their transgender partners as "lucky" for any amount of support they receive. Since cisgender identities are not pathologized, but normalized, they are considerably less likely to be used in this way. Further, Lorenzo sometimes demeaned Santiago's transgender identity, once referring to him as "really a woman" and another time as someone who would never be able to "change that disgusting body." Santiago described these comments as designed to "break my spirit" and as intended to make him question whether Lorenzo "really cared for me or not." Santiago explained that these comments damaged his sense of self-worth and led him to blame himself for the abuse, as he frequently felt as if "maybe I deserved it." He found it hard to leave the relationship since he had little money and nowhere to stay, but he told a friend, a transgender woman, about the abuse a year and a half after it had begun, and then moved in with her.

While similar in some ways, Grey's assaultive experiences differed in that he had met his former partner, Jason, before Grey began transitioning. Grey and Jason dated for several months and then Grey moved in with Jason. The abuse began much later than in Santiago's relationship because Jason was not physically abusive for the first year that he and Grey were together. Grey spoke with Jason about wanting to transition from the beginning of their relationship, but said that Jason would usually change the subject, likely due to his discomfort with the topic at hand. Once Grey began the transitioning process, he felt that the relationship "changed a lot," as Jason became angry and verbally abusive.

Jason was first physically abusive when the two of them got into an argument, which culminated in him making a veiled threat, "If you wanna be a man, then you better step up to the plate." When Grey responded, "Or what are you gonna do?" Jason hit him. Jason's construction, "If you wanna be a man," relies on notions that transgender men are not men from the beginning, assigning primacy to genitalia or sex assigned at birth. The notion that being a man involves "stepping up to the plate" also relies on traditional understandings of masculinity, as cisgender men may be violent toward transgender men due to notions of manhood as something that one must achieve or accomplish, including possibly through physical violence. Cisgender men may be violent toward transgender women as well, yet the opposite type of statement, "If you wanna be a woman, then you better step up to the plate," does not appear as culturally tenable in the United States, in light of different ideals regarding femininity and masculinity.

As Grey continued his transitioning process, Jason became abusive on a more regular basis and escalated his violence, using objects to intensify the brutality of his abuse. At times, Jason would demean Grey's body and appearance, telling him that "no one will love you now that you look like that." Jason's abuse was primarily physical, not sexual, although one time after being physically abusive, when he was drunk, Jason also raped Grey. For several months, Grey said that he "stopped transitioning," hoping that the abuse would end, which he now regretted because he did not feel as if it was healthy for him "to try and be someone else" for another person. When the abuse did not stop, Grey felt he had to leave the relationship. Similar to Santiago, Grey moved in with a friend who was a transgender woman, continuing his transitioning process during this time.[18]

Overall, Grey's and Santiago's experiences reveal that transgender men face some qualitatively different forms of abuse than cisgender queer men, including when possibly transitioning and with insulting comments being made about their bodies.[19] Still, similarities between transgender and cisgender participants also merit some attention. Transgender men experienced sexual assault in relationships and hookups—similar contexts as their cisgender counterparts. It remains necessary to account for this overlap and not present transgender people in an objectifying or voyeuristic way. For example, although two of the transgender men experienced sexual assault in the context of sex work, not all transgender people engage in this line of work. A frequent positioning of transgender people as sex workers can lead to a voyeuristic approach, in which transgender people are set apart from more everyday arenas and are constructed as marginal or unimportant to US society.

At the same time, two transgender participants experienced sexual assault in this context, and it is important not to overlook these experiences or the structural conditions that lead transgender people to engage in sex work.[20] One participant, Jude, a thirty-nine-year-old white transgender queer man, was the only transgender man in the sample who explained that he did not have any interest in medically transitioning. Not all transgender people want to have gender confirmation surgeries, yet structural barriers to obtaining them also remain widespread.[21] Jude did not, then, experience violence while transitioning, but instead had two assaultive experiences that occurred in sexual situations. The first happened in the context of sex work, while the second occurred during a hookup. With this second experience, Jude went over to the apartment of a man he met online and they began having consensual sex, but then Jude became uncomfortable, and eventually fearful, when the man started pressuring Jude to do things he did not want to do.

When Jude tried to get up from the bed, the man pinned him down and raped him, referring to Jude as "nasty," among other homophobic and transphobic insults, while covering his mouth to keep him from yelling. In focusing on queer men hooking up or seeking consensual sex, traditional representations may position this figure as cisgender, yet Jude's experience demonstrates that transgender men encounter this violence as well. Consequently, despite some important differences from their cisgender counterparts, transgender men should not be excluded from representations of sexual assault that occur in the context of a hookup.

Conversely, transgender men were more likely than gay cisgender men to fear that others would perceive their experiences through the lens of "deceit," as Jude worried that others might think that he had "lied" about his gender identity to the assailant. Another one of these participants, Leonard, a fifty-five-year-old Black transgender man, described an experience in which two cisgender men raped him. The assault occurred when Leonard was a sex worker and a man approached him on the street. Leonard said that cisgender men often approach transgender people in this context, propositioning them for sex, regardless of whether they are sex workers or not. The night of the rape, Leonard went back to the apartment of the man who had approached him, under the assumption that Leonard would be paid to have sex with him.

When Leonard arrived at the apartment, one of the man's male friends was also there. Leonard performed oral sex on the man whose apartment it was, and then after he got up to leave, the man hit him on the back of the head. The two men beat up Leonard, punching him repeatedly, and then both of the men raped him. He said that the men were calling him a "faggot" during the assault, and saying things such as "this faggot doesn't know what she is" and "this faggot is nasty" when referring to his body. The use of nonhuman language here—"what"—as well as a misgendering indicates that the assailants likely held dehumanizing attitudes toward Leonard and transgender people more broadly. When I asked Leonard if he had told anyone about this experience, he said that he had only told other transgender sex workers because "I don't think anyone else would believe me," and then he added, "Because when you're trans, people think you're trying to fool them."

Transphobic narratives often position transgender people as deceitful, based on prejudicial assumptions that transgender identities involve concealing who they "really are." These views rely on an understanding of sex assigned at birth as primarily a fixed attribute that cannot or should not be changed. Due to a naturalizing of the gender binary, cisgender identities may be constructed as reflecting a "natural" alignment between gender and sex assigned at birth, while transgender identities become conversely pathologized and positioned as reflecting "someone you're not." For transgender people, it remains important to challenge understandings of sex assigned at birth as a fixed and lifelong attribute, as such notions lead to the naturalizing of cisgender identities and the pathologizing of transgender ones.

All of the transgender men who were assaulted by a male stranger said that the assailant "knew" they were transgender before the assault, even though I never asked for this information. For example, Leonard said, "He knew I was trans, it was an area where only trans people work." A trope exists in the United States where anti-transgender violence has often been presented through the lens of "deception" such as with "transgender panic" cases in which a cisgender man murders a transgender person.[22] These media narratives have positioned such attacks as occurring not because of a cisgender male assailant's transphobia but because of the victim's refusal to reveal their transgender identity from the beginning, thereby framing the violence as understandable. Thus, outsiders may position anti-transgender violence as justified if they view a cisgender male assailant in a sexual encounter as becoming enraged when finding out an individual's transness. These interpretations occur because transphobic stereotypes already pathologize transgender people as deceptive, enabling others to view these forms of violence as involving a dishonest transgender victim. Contending with such notions, transgender participants likely attempted to foreclose this possible interpretation by stating that their assailant was aware of their transgender identity from the beginning.

Many transgender people may not, or do not hope to, "pass" as a particular gender, experiencing violence for this very reason, yet here I am questioning why it remains important for cisgender people to know if and when a transgender survivor revealed their transness. This violence should be contextualized in relation to transphobia. It is also significant to note that the dismissal of anti-transgender violence in this way occurs primarily when the assailant is a cisgender man. One should question whether a cisgender woman committing similar violence would be dismissed in this way.[23] Some assumption exists that cisgender men will respond aggressively to being "tricked." Moreover, while most scholarly attention on anti-transgender violence has focused on cisgender male assailants and transgender women, Leonard's experience reveals that transgender men also encounter violence from this group of men.

Similar to many other participants, Leonard blamed himself, saying, "I could have been more aware, I wish I was less trusting of people. . . . I shouldn't have gone over there." However, unlike most of the cisgender men in this study, Leonard experienced this violence in the context of sex work. On the one hand, further criminalizing sex work will exacerbate the challenges facing many transgender people, given that the police frequently profile and arrest them based on assumptions that they are sex workers.[24] In transgender advocacy, this criminalizing of everyday behavior such as walking on the street has been referred to as "walking while trans."[25] For this reason, a lot of transgender advocacy has attempted to reduce funding for the criminal-legal system.[26] Transgender people experience widespread discrimination in the formal employment sector, preventing them access to many middle-class jobs, to say nothing of the structural barriers they face in housing and educational settings.[27] To improve the material conditions of transgender people's lives, it would be helpful to rectify such barriers rather than further criminalizing sex work.

On the other hand, glossing over the sexual violence that transgender people experience in sex work is also unhelpful. Several transgender participants noted that sexual assault against sex workers often goes unrecognized; Leonard, for example, argued, "People think a prostitute can't be raped." Assumptions remain widespread that sex workers have already consented to whatever their client may want.[28] Additionally, perceptions of sex workers as unworthy of respect may inform how others treat such survivors. Indeed, research indicates that the US public tends to perceive sex workers as less deserving of empathy than many other survivors.[29]

SELF-BLAME: ACCOUNTING FOR SIMILARITIES AND DIFFERENCES AMONG QUEER MALE SURVIVORS

Overall, participants typically oscillated between self-blame and resistance to these notions. For instance, Jayden, a forty-five-year-old Black gay man, had an assaultive experience in which two male heterosexual friends of his cousin raped him, while his cousin looked on and laughed. Jayden, as well as all three of the men, were drunk and high on marijuana and crack cocaine when the men committed the rape. He described his oscillation between self-blame and trying not to blame himself in the following way:

> I felt embarrassed because that was forced on me. It wasn't like I wanted it, but I kept asking myself, "Did I really enjoy it?" It was questions that I kept asking myself: "Did I enjoy it? Did I want it to happen?" . . . People will think, "If you weren't gay, it wouldn't have happened. You shouldn't be that way, anyway. God doesn't like gay people. He doesn't like homos and faggots." . . . I've consistently blamed myself for it. Deep down, I know it's not my fault, but I still blame myself because of the drug use.

Jayden's narrative here is consistent with a lot of the themes introduced in this chapter, as he blamed himself and struggled immensely with homophobic discourses, perhaps internalizing some of them in the process, and yet he could also resist these ideas on some level, saying, "Deep down, I know it's not my fault." As reflected by Jayden's reference to religious discourse, queer male survivors' self-blame was informed by various social institutions, including religion, media, and the family.

In examining participants' self-blame, I found that they often reflected on the assault and then blamed themselves for things they had, or had not, done. In this sense, individuals who have not experienced sexual assault have to be careful about questioning survivors' behaviors before the assault; such responses may reinforce the blame survivors already feel. By listening to respondents' self-blame, I discovered that these concerns were fairly extensive, as most participants worried about having their assaultive experiences dismissed in a variety of ways. Some of these concerns overlapped considerably with what research has shown for other survivors, while other challenges appeared specific to queer men.[30] Further, these concerns differed among queer male survivors themselves, as bisexual and pansexual men had some unique experiences, as did transgender men in comparison to their cisgender counterparts. Queer male survivors—and perhaps more broadly, LGBTQ survivors—should be understood not as homogenous but as varied. That is, as differing in important ways based on aspects such as sexuality and gender identity. What remains necessary is work that accounts for these complex similarities and differences among survivors, while also reframing attention away from approaches that focus on a survivor's behavior before the assault and toward broader solutions that address social inequalities.

4   Racial Differences Regarding Emasculation

Research has shown that male survivors frequently feel emasculated, which has been defined as "feeling a diminished sense of strength or as feeling like 'less of a man,'" after these survivors experience a sexual violation.[1] Indeed, emasculation has remained central to much of the theorizing on male sexual victimization.[2] These studies have found that male survivors often feel "broken" as a result of this violence and then attempt to reclaim a masculine sense of self.[3] In a review of this scholarship on emasculation, Aliraza Javaid has stated that "rape humiliates, degrades, undermines, and weakens the victim's masculinity" and that "this process, consequently, feminizes the weaker victim's body, taking away his manhood and emasculating him."[4] Conversely, by examining the narratives of queer male survivors, I argue that this emphasis on emasculation, while an important part of how some white queer men respond to sexual assault, nevertheless provides an incomplete picture of many queer men of color's responses. Instead, participants of color interpreted their experiences through alternative frameworks, such as "loneliness" and "troublemaker" discourses, that were implicated in challenges they faced due to their social position.

Focusing on assailants, Gabrielle Ferrales and coauthors have found that sexual violence against men and boys often "communicates an emasculating message to individual victims."[5] The aim of my work here is not to dispute these results, as participants also frequently perceived their assailants as attempting to emasculate them. At the same time, although assailants may use sexual violence to emasculate men, results from this study indicate that such attempts do not automatically lead male survivors to feel this way. In focusing on complex intersections of race and gender expression, I argue that emasculation should not be naturalized as an inevitable response from queer male survivors.

Overall, only six of the forty-six participants of color said that they felt emasculated from one or more of their experiences of sexual assault, while twelve of the fourteen white respondents said that they felt this way.[6] In this chapter, I compare the perceptions of participants of color with those of white respondents. While other parts of this book emphasize the variation within each of these groups, this chapter focuses primarily on the differences between them. These differences should be understood as the product of social hierarchies, rather than the result of queer men of color's strength. Black Americans' traumatic experiences in particular have sometimes been presented in this way, as racialized notions of strength have led to the minimization of their pain.[7] However, the narratives of Black participants, and more broadly of queer men of color, revealed not a lack of pain—as they highlighted many harmful experiences—but the rejection of emasculation as a framework for understanding their experiences.

Throughout this chapter, to reflect participants' views, I refer to "ideal" and "dominant" forms of masculinity rather than those that are "hegemonic," as respondents evaluated their experiences in relation to what they perceived as ideal and dominant masculinities. James Messerschmidt has distinguished "hegemonic masculinities," which legitimate gender inequality, from "dominant" and "idealized" forms, which may or may not reinforce such inequities; thus, they are not equivalent to hegemonic masculinity.[8] Nevertheless, the results presented here have important implications for masculinity studies, revealing that participants evaluated their experiences and understandings of emasculation in different ways depending on where they were structurally located. These results are consistent with previous work showing that white queer men and queer men of color, even with similar gender expressions, have some different connections with masculinity as well as queerness, yet I show that it is not only expressions of masculinity that must be understood in expansive and intersectional ways but also understandings of its loss.[9]

PARTICIPANTS OF COLOR'S NARRATIVES RESISTING THE FRAMEWORK OF EMASCULATION FOR INTRA-RACIAL FORMS OF ASSAULT

Instead of describing feelings of emasculation, queer men of color emphasized other emotional responses such as loneliness that arose out of a sense of social isolation they felt from broader communities and institutions. Take, for example, the response of Kemal, a thirty-seven-year-old Black gay man who described a violent experience in which an older Black man he had been dating raped him one night, two months into their relationship. After Kemal explained that he did not feel emasculated, he described his reasoning in the following way:

> I felt like a lonely man—a sad man—not a broken man. It was hard for me to get out of bed, I would just stay there all day and cry. He was seen as a good, upstanding citizen—the kind of Black man that everyone looks up to. Even though he was gay, he was very masculine. Me? I'm very feminine. So, he would be believed. The police wouldn't have supported me, me being a feminine Black gay man. That's why I felt lonely. . . . I've just never thought of myself as the perfect role model sort of guy. That all-American sort of guy. Being a Black gay man, feeling emasculated is not something I ever struggled with, because I was feminine to begin with. There was nothing to be broken.

When the violence was intra-racial, most queer men of color highlighted challenges related to their social position and compared themselves with their assailant to argue that they did not feel emasculated. Here, Kemal compared himself with his ex-boyfriend, whom he thought would be believed over him, given their different gender expressions. Kemal described hierarchies among men of color, as his assailant may be "the kind of Black man that everyone looks up to." In this sense, hierarchies exist among Black men based on gender expression, even if idealized masculinities more broadly remain disproportionately linked with whiteness.

During the interview, when Kemal mentioned "the perfect role model sort of guy" and "that all-American sort of guy," I interpreted these statements as referring to Black masculinities that conform to what Evelyn Brooks Higginbotham has characterized as a "politics of respectability"—that is, cultural norms in Black communities that encourage practices or characteristics, such as gender conformity, that may appeal to more mainstream groups.[10] Kemal also expressed concern that he would be ostracized by some others in his racial communities if he disclosed his assaultive experiences, which is consistent with research showing that Black women who call attention to intra-racial forms of sexual assault may be thought of as traitorous for disclosing Black men's assaultive behavior.[11]

Kemal's statements here, however, regarding "the perfect role model sort of guy" are more ambiguous on the page than they appeared to me during the interview, as he may have been referring to idealized white masculinities. Indeed, later during the interview, Kemal said that feminine Black gay men are "at the lowest part" of US society, in terms of their structural location. Regardless of the precise group he was referring to, Kemal's "looking up" to esteemed masculinities did not produce feelings of emasculation, as it did for white participants, including those who identified as feminine. Kemal repeatedly emphasized the distance he felt from masculinity, as he later during the interview once again stated, "I don't feel connected to masculinity, so it didn't feel like something I could lose."

As shown in the table in the appendix, participants of color were not any more likely to identify as feminine than white respondents; a similar percentage of participants across racial lines also described the distance they felt from masculinity. Still, queer men of color typically underscored this distance to highlight how they could not "lose" something they never possessed. Alternatively, male femininity for white queer men did not produce the same response. This racial difference also held for participants who described themselves as masculine. Respondents of color with masculine gender expressions generally resisted meanings of emasculation, albeit not as emphatically as participants of color who described themselves as feminine.

Among the thirty-eight respondents of color who said that they did not feel emasculated from an intra-racial experience of assault, thirty of them emphasized the distance they felt from dominant constructions of masculinity.[12] Further, thirteen described themselves as feminine. These participants responded to questions concerning whether they felt emasculated with statements such as "no, I was a very feminine child" or "no, I was always feminine." The framework of emasculation remains limited for understanding their experiences, given that this approach may be interpreted as assuming some initial investment in masculinity, which becomes lost, damaged, or broken afterward. In contrast, as Kemal said, "There was nothing to be broken." Another one of these participants, Mateo, a fifty-six-year-old Latino gay man, similarly said, "I'm not a masculine guy, so I don't think anything could be broken."

Rather than emphasizing emasculation, queer men of color reframed my questions on this topic to highlight other concerns that they viewed as more important. As Kemal expressed, an emphasis on feeling "lonely" was mentioned by considerably more queer men of color than white queer men; twenty-three respondents of color described feelings of loneliness, while only two white participants conveyed this emotion. This response arose from a variety of factors, but generally involved ideals, communities, or institutions that participants of color felt excluded from, such as policing agencies or dominant standards of masculinity, as Kemal described.

Although most white queer men also emphasized to some degree the disconnect they felt from dominant masculinities, only participants of color privileged feelings of loneliness over those of emasculation. For instance, Marcel, a twenty-seven-year-old Black gay man, described a violent experience in which a man he had initially met online cut him with a knife while they were having sex. Marcel explained that he did not feel emasculated after this experience:

> No, I didn't feel that way. I felt lonely, more than anything. My community, we don't trust the police because what are they going to do? . . . My family wasn't supportive [of my sexuality]. Other gay guys just look at this as a 'Black thing' or like if I wasn't so horny, this wouldn't have happened—so who did I really have to go to? I felt all alone, it was very scary. . . . People know that I'm gay from the start because I talk like how a gay Black man talks, so I've never thought of myself as the "ideal man." I've always been very flamboyant, just very gay-acting, and I've always felt more of an affinity toward femininity, so as far as being emasculated and having to be tough, I never felt that way. I don't know if I had any masculinity to begin with.

Once again, gender expression remained relevant here, as Marcel underscored his "affinity toward femininity" to reject notions that he felt emasculated. Marcel also highlighted the lack of assistance he likely would have received from the police, as well as his experiences of familial homophobia and his concern that some gay men would minimize the assault. The cumulative result of these challenges led to feelings of loneliness, not emasculation, as Marcel felt marginalized from multiple arenas and struggled to find avenues of support. Queer men of color more routinely expressed this marginalization than their white counterparts, as the former experienced racial inequalities within LGBTQ communities that the latter did not face, in addition to feeling marginalized from some heterosexual communities of color and more normative white, heterosexual arenas.

While participants of color characterized their feelings in terms of "loneliness," they most frequently spoke about this response as arising from a sense of social isolation they felt from broader communities and institutions. This social isolation included feeling locked out of several domains, such as: (1) race- or sexuality-based communities; (2) idealized constructions of masculinity; (3) institutional resources provided by groups such as the police; and (4) credibility regarding their claims of sexual assault. Most participants of color mentioned at least three of these aspects of social isolation, while white queer men usually addressed only one or two of them. Consequently, this loneliness discourse needs to be understood in relation to the various ways that queer men of color may be prevented access to resources and institutions in ways that white queer men are not.

In addition to feelings of loneliness, participants of color repeatedly emphasized the disconnect they felt between themselves and other groups of men. These contrasts involved a wide range of groups; most frequently, they compared themselves with masculine queer men of color, given the context of the violence. Across racial lines, respondents typically compared themselves with multiple groups of men within the same interview and some of their comparisons were ambiguous as to the precise group with which they contrasted themselves. Nevertheless, for participants of color, the second most common comparison involved heterosexual men of color. These participants compared themselves with white gay men more than white heterosexual men, perhaps in part because the interviews took place with a white gay male researcher. Regardless of the precise group with which queer men of color compared themselves, the important consistency across most of their narratives was that emasculation was segmented off, away from themselves.

Participants of color sometimes linked emasculation with other, implicitly more privileged, groups of men. For instance, Juan, a forty-seven-year-old Latino gay man, described an abusive relationship that involved sexual assault, in which his former partner had physically abused him on a regular basis and forced him to have anal sex on two occasions. Juan initially described his feelings after being sexually assaulted by using a variety of adjectives—he felt "demeaned," "dirty," and "vulnerable"—but when asked if he also felt emasculated, he distinguished those feelings from emasculation in the following way:

> Emasculated is more like a thing that the biggest guy on campus might feel. I didn't feel it. After it was over, I just cried, and sat there for a long time because I felt so dirty. It is a feeling, like he was getting to some place that is mine. It was just like a sense of fear, a sense of being vulnerable, a sense of not being able to move about freely. That was there in my head. . . . I felt [those things], but emasculated? No, I never felt that way.

Juan distanced himself from emasculation through a comparison with an esteemed masculinity—"the biggest guy on campus"—as he thought that other men, with a different social position, might feel emasculated, yet he did not. While this "biggest guy on campus" may have a lot to lose or may feel as if his masculinity has been severely damaged after being sexually assaulted, most participants of color perceived such responses as outside of themselves.

At the same time, Juan emphasized his feelings of fear and vulnerability. To impose a framework of emasculation onto these emotions, however, is to distort what these participants had to say. Instead, they continually explained that they did not feel as if they had "failed" with regard to their masculinity. Juan's response later during the interview was instructive of this trend: "I knew I wasn't that sort of man that everyone looks up to a long time ago, so I didn't feel like I failed at being a man. . . . [My therapist] wants me to say that I feel that way [emasculated], but I don't."

During these discussions of emasculation, ten participants of color complained about others—usually a friend, family member, or therapist—who had assumed that they must have felt emasculated or who had wanted them to "admit" to such feelings. Such impositions may be understandable given that service providers generally want their clients to become aware of, and speak about, painful feelings, yet my findings here indicate that queer men of color may resist meanings of emasculation not necessarily because they are in denial about their "true" feelings but because they understand such a framework as applicable to more socially esteemed groups of men. Similarly, another one of these participants, Kenneth, a forty-two-year-old Black gay man, said, "Emasculated? Nah, like that's something that a guy on a high perch would feel."

This research did not include groups such as Black heterosexual men, as some scholarship has pointed to this group's feelings of emasculation in other contexts.[13] C. Shawn McGuffey's research, for example, quotes a Black heterosexual male survivor who says, "But if you're a Black man, your manhood is all you really got in a racist society. If that's taken away, you really ain't got nothin.'"[14] Black heterosexual men may perceive sexual assault as threatening one of the few privileges they see themselves as possessing—being viewed as a masculine, heterosexual man. Thus, queer men of color in this study may have resisted meanings of emasculation not necessarily solely due to race but because of the intersection of race and sexuality.

Despite this possibility, what remained striking about some participants' evaluations was how similar they seemed to the narratives of women survivors, as shown in other research.[15] Juan, quoted previously, described "a sense of fear, a sense of being vulnerable, a sense of not being able to move about freely." Emphasizing that men experience fear, constraint, and vulnerability can help to destabilize the gendering of these emotions. However, it remains difficult to draw attention to these responses if sexual violence against men becomes positioned as fundamentally different than sexual violence against women. Focusing solely on men's feelings of emasculation can reinforce this framework of gender difference, as only men, but not women, may be viewed as experiencing such responses. That is, a focus on emasculation can reinforce notions that men perceive their experiences in qualitatively different ways than women, who are implicitly understood as not experiencing emasculation. In contrast, similarities across gender categories, and differences within them, also remain important to explore.[16]

Among the participants who explained that they did not feel emasculated, this resistance cannot be divorced from a larger cultural context that positions men's emasculation in negative terms. Interview research is best at uncovering individuals' perceptions of their experiences, not necessarily how they "really" felt, given that they may be unaware of their emotions or may want to avoid revealing stigmatized feelings.[17] Consequently, some participants may have hesitated to name feelings of emasculation due to shame over believing that they had failed to measure up to dominant constructions of masculinity. Some queer men of color may have also been suspicious of how any claims of emasculation would be represented by a white gay male researcher.

At the same time, participants of color frequently shared painful feelings with me and drew attention to concerns that they viewed as more important than emasculation. Indeed, in sharing their experiences, these respondents may have viewed my comparative racial privilege as an opportunity for them to have their concerns broadcast to a larger audience, given that outsiders may be more likely to listen to a white male academic. Thus, even in this interactional context in which queer men of color spent a considerable amount of time outlining their challenges, they did not typically describe feelings of emasculation. In addition, although it is entirely possible that some respondents may have felt emasculated even when asserting otherwise, it is also essential not to position these men as undoubtedly mistaken or dishonest, as the ten participants of color who complained about others wanting them to "admit" to such feelings did not want such a framework imposed on their response.

While participants differed across racial lines in their evaluations of emasculation, gender expression shaped the degree to which respondents of color rejected this framework. It remains important not to impose a binary model of gender onto queer men, in which they are characterized as either masculine or feminine, given that this imposition would reinforce heteronormative standards. Yet, queer men of color who emphasized their connection with masculinity resisted the framework of emasculation the least intensely. Eight respondents of color described themselves as masculine, or emphasized how connected they felt to masculinity, and rejected meanings of emasculation in relation to intra-racial sexual assault. For example, Marcus, a thirty-seven-year-old Black gay man who described himself as masculine, said, "I didn't feel emasculated. . . . Like maybe if I was straight, then I would have, but I would say 'no.' . . . I see myself as masculine, but not that masculine where I would feel emasculated." Similarly, another respondent, Yamen, a fifty-five-year-old Black gay man, said that he has "always seen himself as a masculine guy" and that "if I was straight, I probably would have [felt emasculated]."

These results indicate important variability regarding gender expression among queer men of color, as only those who felt connected with masculinity described possibly feeling emasculated if they had been heterosexual. In contrast, participants of color who described themselves as feminine typically perceived emasculation as wholly foreign to themselves, as they did not say that they might have felt emasculated "if" their sexuality were different. Of course, queer men of color regardless of gender expression generally resisted meanings of emasculation, as even those identifying as masculine typically denied feeling this way. Still, to homogenize the responses of queer men of color would be counterproductive, given these differences based on gender expression.

PARTICIPANTS OF COLOR WHO FELT EMASCULATED
AND THE IMPORTANCE OF AGE

While queer men of color who felt emasculated as a result of an intra-racial sexual assault are not the main focus of this chapter, five of these participants emphasized this feeling. One of these respondents, Justin, a sixty-two-year-old Black gay man, described an experience in which he was gang raped by four men. When I asked him if he felt emasculated after this experience, he became very quiet and nodded affirmatively, explaining, "That is not supposed to happen to a man." He also said that his assailants were trying to "strip me of my manhood," as they used derogatory words such as *faggot* and *queer* when they raped him. When participants described feeling emasculated, they often focused on the language that their assailants had used. White participants who felt emasculated emphasized their assailants' language even more frequently. As some previous research indicates, words such as *faggot* may be racialized white in a dominant US context as well as in racial minority communities, which suggests that these insults do not necessarily have the same resonance across racial lines.[18] Only two other participants of color had an experience of gang rape—both of whom did not feel emasculated—which indicates that I do not have conclusive data either way as to the effects of a gang rape on respondents' evaluations.

Other than Justin, four of these five participants of color felt emasculated in the context of an experience of childhood or adolescent sexual assault, in which a male family member or stranger perpetrated anal rape against them. Xavier, for example, a twenty-six-year-old Black bisexual man, described feeling emasculated when his stepfather sexually abused him when he was a teenager: "Yes, I did feel that way then." Conversely, he later had an assaultive experience as an adult, but said that he did not feel emasculated: "Not so much then, because I was grown. . . . I wasn't thinking of myself as a little boy who had been hurt." All four of these participants of color explained that they did not feel emasculated after any of their assaultive experiences as an adult.

These results indicate that age may play an important role in structuring perceptions of emasculation. Youth can lead to particular feelings of vulnerability, and perhaps "loss" after an assaultive experience, that older men are less likely to feel. As individuals' gender expressions and identities are more likely to be in the process of development rather than fully formed during childhood and adolescence, these aspects may feel especially precarious and susceptible to change. Young men, in this sense, may experience a particularly strong sense of "loss" regarding their masculine sense of self and then look for ways to regain or reassert this lost masculine sensibility.

Nevertheless, these age differences among queer men of color can also be exaggerated, as most of these participants had experienced childhood or adolescent sexual abuse, and yet most of them said that they did not feel emasculated at that point in time. For instance, Mendez, a twenty-seven-year-old Black and Latino bisexual man, said that he did not feel emasculated as a result of an adult experience because he "never felt like a masculine guy," and then when I asked him about an experience of childhood sexual abuse, he said that it was "the same thing . . . because you're just feeling very hurt at that age." Participants of color were more likely than white queer men to reject the framework of emasculation for their childhood, adolescent, and adult experiences of sexual assault. However, the data were more mixed for childhood and adolescent experiences, given that a slightly higher percentage of participants of color viewed these experiences as emasculating. How participants spoke about their adult and nonadult experiences in relation to emasculation also differed some, as they usually spent considerably more time describing dominant masculinities for victimization experiences that occurred during adulthood.

I note these differences because age remains an important dimension of inequality to account for, and individuals may perceive sexual assault against minors differently than these forms of violence against adults. Despite these age differences, one limitation of this study is that participants often began the interview discussing a relatively recent adult experience, which may have led them to apply their perceptions of emasculation for that experience to earlier forms of abuse. This application of more recent feelings to past experiences may have happened because childhood sexual abuse had frequently occurred long before the interview and was usually more difficult for participants to recall. The results, then, presented throughout this chapter apply primarily to adult experiences, as future research on race and emasculation remains necessary regarding childhood and adolescent victimization.[19]

WHITE QUEER MEN'S EMPHASIS ON EMASCULATION WITH INTRA-RACIAL FORMS OF ASSAULT

White participants' narratives, in contrast to those of queer men of color, were closer to findings from previous research, as these respondents generally described their masculinity as becoming lost or damaged after a sexual violation.[20] For instance, Allen, a thirty-eight-year-old white gay man, described this feeling succinctly: "Yeah, I did feel that way a little bit—it feels like a piece of you, of your manhood, is missing afterwards." These narratives did not usually focus on emasculation in an emphatic way, which happened when white queer men had experiences of interracial violence. With intra-racial forms of assault, white participants sometimes tempered their emphasis on emasculation with modulating phrases such as Allen's "a little bit." Still, in comparison with queer men of color, white respondents typically spent considerably more time discussing, rather than refuting, the framework of emasculation.

William, a thirty-six-year-old white bisexual man, first described an ex-boyfriend who had sexually assaulted him and then explained his feelings of emasculation in the following way: "Yeah, I felt broken for the longest time. It was hard to tell others, but that got easier over time. . . . I never felt like the "ideal man" because I was bi, but [my ex-boyfriend] sort of was because he was masculine. So I felt like I couldn't measure up to him. Like he was just trying to show me that I wasn't as good as him. Emasculation is that sort of thing, where you feel like you haven't 'measured up.'" Here, William emphasized how "it was hard to tell others," but did not describe feelings of loneliness in the same way as many participants of color; instead, he explained that telling others "got easier over time." Throughout the interview, he also did not emphasize any disconnect or marginalization he felt from LGBTQ communities. White participants were less critical of these communities than queer men of color, given that the latter had experiences of racism in these arenas. White queer men also generally expressed less fear than their racially marginalized counterparts of potential police hostility for reporting an assault. Thus, as white respondents felt more institutionally supported and connected than queer men of color, the former spent less time describing feelings of loneliness than the latter.

In addition to differences regarding institutional support, white queer men more frequently emphasized than queer men of color their relatively close proximity to idealized masculinities. William, similar to many participants of color, stated that he "never felt like the 'ideal man,'" yet his narrative differed in that he positioned his white assailant as closer to such ideals and then felt as if he "couldn't measure up" in comparison. The difference between this narrative and those of participants of color is that William thought that his assailant "sort of was" similar to an "ideal man," while queer men of color were not typically comparing themselves with idealized white masculinities and, if they were, they did not make such an intimate comparison. Kemal's earlier statement that Black feminine men are "at the lowest part" of US society was not expressed by white queer men about their own social group, even those who identified as feminine. In this sense, white respondents' sense of "loss" appeared to arise in part from feeling comparatively disadvantaged in relation to a privileged white masculinity.

Another one of these participants, Sean, a fifty-three-year-old white gay man, said, "I felt broken because without [the rape] I would have been thinking about myself more like [the man who assaulted me]. . . . Like a man people look up to." This comparison relies on an understanding of what Sean saw himself as potentially possessing—that is, a status that involves being "a man people look up to." Queer of color participants compared themselves with other queer men of color they thought would be looked up to as well, but those comparisons did not produce feelings of emasculation as they did for white respondents because the latter perceived white masculinities as more broadly valued and felt a sense of loss when making this hierarchical contrast.

At times, white participants evaluated their experiences in relation to an idealized, implicitly white and heterosexual, masculinity, yet most frequently this comparison involved a valued masculine queerness they viewed their assailant as possessing. Francis, a twenty-seven-year-old queer man, compared himself with the man who had sexually assaulted him in this way: "I don't see myself as so different from him, except that he was more masculine. So, for him to do that was like him telling me that I'm not as good as him because I'm not as masculine. Like I won't be this "perfect man" that he thinks he is. So I think that's where the emasculation comes from." Although white participants never mentioned their whiteness as contributing to feelings of emasculation, their racial similarity with masculinities they perceived as idealized likely played an important role here. Indeed, Francis compared himself with his assailant, a man he mockingly referred to as "this perfect man," yet Francis also did not "see [himself] as so different from . . . except that [his assailant] was more masculine."

White participants' narratives should be understood in relation to larger social changes that have taken place in the United States in which some white queer men, disproportionately those with masculine gender expressions, have increasingly been represented in socially esteemed ways.[21] This understanding that masculine white queer men have "made it" may be leading to particular concern for those who do not feel this way, including those with feminine gender expressions, as they continually observe their "more masculine" counterparts figure into culturally valued representations of masculinity and queerness. One of these participants, Chad, a forty-eight-year-old white gay man, initially described his assailant in this way: "He was that sort of 'hot guy' who everyone wants to be." Then, later, when describing the reasons he felt emasculated, Chad said, "You feel like you lost something because you know what you could have had. . . . [My assailant] would be very looked up to. . . . [Because] he's masculine."

Chad identified as feminine and throughout the interview expressed anger at not being granted the same privileges as masculine white men. Emasculation, then, was one of the ways that he could underscore this sense of loss that he felt. White queer men may assume that they should be granted the privileges that come with whiteness, but then feel anger that they are not accorded such privileges due to their femininity or queerness. Conversely, queer men of color also sometimes compared themselves with more privileged white queer masculinities, but did not view such masculinities as something they could attain, likely due in part to racial difference. Overall, the responses of queer men of color and white queer men arose from these groups being differently situated in social hierarchies, as the structural positioning of white participants led to a more intimate comparison with idealized, white queer masculinities, and then an underscoring of their feelings of deprivation.

While differences regarding gender expression were difficult to examine for white queer men, given that only fourteen of these respondents were involved in this study, the few white participants who described feeling connected with masculinity spoke about emasculation in a more matter-of-fact way. For instance, Danny, a thirty-one-year-old white gay man who described himself as being perceived as heterosexual due to his relatively masculine gender expression, said, "Yeah, I did feel that way some, just because when you're a man and someone rapes you, you know you're going to lose something—you go down a peg." While most other white participants "looked up" toward a masculine queerness they perceived as more culturally valued, Danny simply described his masculinity as declining. He did not compare himself with a more masculine, implicitly white, queerness, given that he already occupied a similar position.

Another one of these participants, Norman, a thirty-eight-year-old white gay man who also described himself as being perceived as heterosexual, said, "Yeah, you feel like your manhood has been hurt—that's what it's like for a guy." Even though the number of white queer men with masculine gender expressions is too small to make a conclusive determination, these preliminary results suggest that the intersection of whiteness and queer masculinity may result in a relatively straightforward emphasis on emasculation, due to the comparatively high social status of this group of men. Of course, this group did not emphatically emphasize emasculation, as some previous research suggests for white heterosexual men.[22] In this sense, queerness may temper feelings of emasculation for white men, at least in the context of an intra-racial sexual assault.

SIMILARITIES ACROSS RACIAL LINES AND ASSAULTS FROM WOMEN ASSAILANTS

Although my results in this chapter point to racial differences, some similarities across racial groups existed when participants described experiences in which the assailant was a woman. Only five respondents had this experience—and four of the five occurred in the context of childhood sexual abuse—which means that these findings should be viewed as suggestive rather than definitive. Still, participants across racial lines rejected the framework of emasculation when their assailant was a woman. Two of these respondents were of color, as they were sexually assaulted by a woman during their youth and said that they did not feel emasculated after that experience or after any of their assaultive experiences with male assailants. However, three white participants who were sexually abused by a woman when they were young said that they did not feel emasculated from those experiences, but that they did feel this way from adult experiences with a male assailant.

Regardless of racial identity, then, participants who had assaultive experiences with women assailants perceived these forms of assault similarly in terms of emasculation. That is, they did not view these assaultive experiences as emasculating, irrespective of racial identity. These perceptions may reflect cultural discourse in the United States positioning women's enactment of sexual violence against boys and men as less harmful than other sexual violations.[23] Nevertheless, given that most participants had experiences with male assailants, further research is necessary regarding this matter.

In this chapter, I have generally tried to resist assumptions that make the relationship between forms of sexual assault and perceptions of emasculation appear straightforward. At the same time, participants who spoke about being "overpowered" were more likely to categorize that experience as emasculating than those who did not use this word. Feeling "overpowered" likely remains racialized as well, which means that this dynamic does not necessarily change the overall finding presented here, but it does point to some possible differences regarding the relationship between forms of sexual assault and perceptions of emasculation. Male survivors who had multiple experiences of assault sometimes characterized one form as emasculating, but not others. In these cases, the participant typically drew attention to how an assaultive experience involving an extreme amount of force felt the most emasculating. Other forms of assault involved respondents saying that they "froze." In the sexual assault literature, this experience has been termed "tonic immobility," as individuals in a traumatic situation may experience a form of paralysis when it occurs.[24]

For participants, these sexual violations were less frequently characterized as emasculating than those they perceived as forceful or overpowering. Thus, the form of an assault remains relevant to evaluations of emasculation, yet it is also the case that power relations may supersede these effects and that perceptions of emasculation are not a straightforward process that can simply be determined by examining the type of assault. As I have highlighted, queer men's access, or lack of access, to idealized forms of masculinity shapes understandings of emasculation, as this response cannot be assumed to operate for all men or to be felt in equal measure, but instead will vary depending on where men are situated in relation to structures of inequality.

INTERRACIAL VIOLENCE: A STARK CONTRAST IN PARTICIPANTS' PERCEPTIONS

While the vast majority of respondents' experiences were intra-racial, six Black queer men experienced an assault from one or more white male assailant. These participants rejected emasculation as a framework for characterizing their response and also frequently underscored feelings of loneliness. In addition, they usually highlighted the possibility of them being constructed as a "troublemaker" for telling others about the assault. For example, Brandon, a twenty-one-year-old Black gay man, had an assaultive experience during college after riding home with a white gay man in his theater group. Brandon invited the man to his dorm room, where consensual kissing happened, yet Brandon said that the man "wouldn't take no for an answer" when forcing Brandon's clothes off and raping him. Brandon responded in the following way to a question about whether he felt emasculated: "No, I felt like there was no one I could tell. He was liked by everyone. If I tell people, then I'm the 'troublemaker' who is trying to ruin him. It's 'Oh, this Black guy is trying to ruin him.' Everyone would have taken his side."

Only Black participants emphasized this racialized baggage of being viewed as a "troublemaker" who could be perceived as looking to ruin, or take down, a white man. When asked a follow-up question, Brandon elaborated on his feelings: "I was very sad, I was very scared, I was very lonely. But it wasn't about my masculinity or feeling like I was a 'broken man.' I wanted to talk to others, but I couldn't. People would have attacked me. Like I just wanted to start trouble." This finding that Black queer men did not usually feel emasculated could be used to reinforce mistaken notions that they were not harmed as a result of the violence, reproducing stereotypes of Black men as possessing "superhuman" strength, where their pain is not recognized as real or legitimate.[25] Brandon's response, however, suggests not the absence of pain, as he described feeling "very sad" and "very scared," but a concern with how he would be viewed if he told others about his assaultive experience.

In addition to Brandon's concern about being perceived as someone who "just wanted to start trouble," he described how a Black gay man telling others about being raped by a white gay man could be interpreted not only as an accusation of sexual assault but also as a claim of potential racial bias on the part of the assailant. Brandon thought that he would have felt more comfortable telling others about the assault if he was white because then it would not be read as "me accusing him of being racist." Given larger cultural discourse in the United States surrounding charges of racism as regularly "invented," Brandon's telling others about the sexual assault could have led to debates about whether the man who raped him was "really racist" or not. If others positioned or defended this man as "not racist," then this line of thinking could construct him as someone who would not perpetrate the assault, thereby positioning Brandon as a liar. Black queer men who have been sexually assaulted by white men may fear these racialized responses being used against them, as evidence that they are inventing charges of racism as well as rape, which then furthers their silence.

Significant social class differences between Black queer men and white assailants only seemed to accentuate this emphasis on not wanting to be seen as a "troublemaker." David, an eighteen-year-old Black gay man, was homeless at the time of the interview, as he lived in a homeless shelter after his parents had kicked him out of their house. One of his assaultive experiences occurred after he was looking for sex on the internet and went over to the apartment of a white gay male couple who lived in a wealthy New York City neighborhood. He performed oral sex on one of the men, and then afterward, both of the men raped him. While he was in their apartment, David also saw several photographs of a Black girl, whom David perceived as their adopted Black daughter.

When asked, "did you feel emasculated?" he responded: "It wasn't about that so much as I felt very alone. Like I couldn't tell anyone, like there was no one I could go to. The police wouldn't believe me, my family would have asked why I went there. I tell the police, they're gonna look at it as I'm making trouble. Who is going to believe me, a homeless kid, instead of these two rich guys? 'They have adopted a Black girl and you expect us to believe they raped you? You probably just wanted money.'" These last two sentences involved David mimicking or imagining what he would have been told if he had reported the assault to the police. Here, because of his social position—because he was homeless and Black and young—and because of the race and class standing of the men who committed the rape, he felt especially fearful that others would not believe him. He connected this unlikelihood of him being believed very directly to his social class position when he said, "Who is going to believe me, a homeless kid, instead of these two rich guys?"

David also noted that the police could say that he "probably just wanted money," an accusation that can be used against survivors, particularly those with few financial resources, to protect assailants with social class privilege. Moreover, once again, the perception that others would examine his reporting of the violence through the lens of him "making trouble" superseded feelings of emasculation, as interracial violence against Black queer men elicited these fears, as well as feelings of loneliness. Another one of these participants, Jeremiah, a twenty-two-year-old Black gay man, who was also homeless at the time of the interview, similarly said, "People would see it as me starting trouble if I told on a white guy."

Contrary to these results, other research has indicated that Black survivors have a particularly difficult time disclosing experiences of intra-racial rape, due to community-based pressures in Black communities that may protect Black men or due to broader concerns over how this emphasis could reinforce the denigration of Black individuals or communities.[26] Participants did not speak to these concerns as much as I expected throughout the course of this study, or even as much as when I conducted research for my previous book.[27] This trend may have been because Black participants were worried about how their narratives regarding Black male assailants or Black community-based norms would be used by a white male researcher. It is also possible that the Black men who participated in this project wanted to draw more attention to other concerns, such as their structural marginalization or experiences with the police, that they viewed as more important than these community-based pressures.

Despite these complexities, community-based pressures encouraging silence should be understood as operating not only when the assault is an intra-racial one within Black communities but also when the assailant is white and the survivor is Black, as participants with these experiences spoke about the difficulty of disclosing interracial forms of assault. The context in which the assault occurred shaped participants' concerns as well. For instance, Brandon was at a predominantly white university and was worried in that context about how many white people would respond. These community-based pressures will thus vary depending on the social groups that survivors find themselves surrounded by when the assault occurs.

In stark contrast to Black queer men, two white respondents and one Latino participant described feeling emasculated when experiencing sexual assault from a Black man. Zachary, for example, a forty-four-year-old white bisexual man, referred to his masculinity as "shattered" in response to a question about emasculation: "It felt like my masculinity had been destroyed. . . . He took complete control over me and shattered my manhood into a million pieces." Similarly, Charlie, a twenty-six-year-old white queer man who had experienced this interracial violence, used a vivid metaphor, describing his masculinity as "flying away, like a bird took it." Along with these two white participants, masculinizing stereotypes of Black men also shaped the response of Tario, a forty-seven-year-old Latino gay man, who said the following about whether he felt emasculated: "Yeah, it feels like something is taken from you. He was very aggressive—a big, aggressive Black guy. . . . It is like somebody is getting in some part of you, like a very vulnerable part."

Tario also explained that after this violent experience, which began as consensual but turned into an assault, that he did not have sex with any Black men for ten years afterward, for fear of it happening again. None of the participants made similar comments about avoiding sex with white men after being sexually assaulted by a white man. These narratives, then, arose in part from the cultural "marking" of Blackness, as Tario's under-scoring of his assailant as "a big, aggressive Black guy" appeared to draw on racialized discourse that associates rape and aggressiveness with the bodies of Black men. His language also generalizes from one experience to Black men more broadly, which has been a historical and continual mani-festation of racism. The experience of David, in which he was assaulted by two wealthy white gay men, makes these differences apparent, as describ-ing either of them as "a big, aggressive white guy," does not appear as cul-turally tenable, given that white men are not associated with aggression or masculinizing stereotypes to the same degree. In short, the availability of a racialized discourse to describe Black assailants, but not white ones, structured these narratives.

UNDERSTANDING EMASCULATION
AS AN INTERSECTIONAL PROCESS

These results focusing on interracial violence revealed a stark contrast, in which Black participants who had experienced this violence from a white man did not describe feelings of emasculation, while white and Latino respondents who experienced sexual assault from a Black man forcefully underscored such feelings. Although research has brought important attention to the role of emasculation, feminist scholarship must also begin to think through the silences and obfuscations that occur through analyses that focus primarily on gender or masculinity, as such approaches may prevent attention to racial inequalities.[28] From an intersectional perspective, focusing solely on emasculation as a framework for understanding how men respond to sexual violence may legitimize the narratives of those such as white and Latino participants who had assaultive experiences with a Black assailant, given that these respondents placed the most emphasis on emasculation.

In hoping to resist long-standing racialized myths that associate sexual violence with Black male assailants and white victims, it remains particularly important to avoid naturalizing emasculation as an inevitable male response, as these narratives may work to reinforce already-existing racial hierarchies and obscure the experiences of more marginalized groups of men. Certainly, Black queer men with interracial experiences of assault described racialized pressures to remain silent. These pressures most typically involved concerns over being perceived as a "troublemaker" for reporting a white assailant, yet some Black participants also struggled with cultural discourse that establishes charges of racism as regularly "invented." This discourse could then be used to construct them as lying about their interracial experience of assault.

More broadly, by also considering intra-racial forms of sexual violence, these findings have implications for scholarship on men and masculinities, as I have shown that emasculation is a racialized as well as a gendered process that appears, at least for queer male survivors, most closely linked with whiteness. Rather than understanding masculinity in the context of sexual violence as something that men are consistently concerned about losing or having lost, I have shown that queer men of color did not typically respond in this way. If this finding reflects larger trends, then the perceptions of queer men of color may be particularly useful for thinking about ways to remake dominant forms of masculinity. A considerable amount of feminist work has pointed to problems resulting from toxic masculinity, but noticeably less work has focused on men who do not look for ways to reassert a "lost" masculine sense of self.[29]

Although the findings presented here may only apply to the context of sexual assault, the understanding of masculinity as something that men are constantly striving to reclaim after a traumatic event certainly needs to be rethought, as queer men of color articulated alternative ways of understanding their experiences. These perspectives can be amplified through future research, which can help to draw attention to how multiply marginalized groups of men are moving masculinities away from aspects such as loss or competition.[30] What remains necessary is not only further critiques of dominant constructions of masculinity but also greater attention to groups of men who are remaking masculinities in productive ways. In understanding queer men of color's narratives concerning loneliness and "troublemaker" discourses, their statements reveal widespread structural marginalization from multiple avenues of support and from some ideals in US society, such as those based on masculinity and credibility. Institutional marginalization leads to feelings of loneliness and isolation for many queer male survivors of color, revealing the need to improve structural conditions facing a wider range of survivors.

5 Constructing Hierarchies of Victimhood

Studies examining sexual assault have frequently explored hierarchies of victimhood, or an ordering of who "counts" as a real or legitimate survivor of this violence.[1] Susan Estrich notably referred to notions of "real rape," in which acts of sexual assault have been constructed as serious primarily when they are forceful stranger attacks and involve certain attributes, such as the assailant using a weapon or hitting the victim.[2] More recently, C. J. Pascoe and Jocelyn Hollander have echoed Estrich's framework, problematizing "the stereotype of the frightening stranger jumping out of a dark alley or from behind a car."[3] These representations have been critiqued for a wide range of reasons, as such portrayals often implicitly diminish the severity of other forms of violence—as not "really" rape or sexual assault—and frequently reinforce racial inequality by positioning the assailant as a man of color.[4]

Regarding hierarchies among male survivors, Heather Hlavka has drawn attention to an ordering that "privileges the violation of certain bodies over others," explaining that "those victims who are not suspect and thus represent the 'ideal victim' are on the top tier."[5] On this "top tier," she uses the examples of very young male victims and those who are drugged, while also noting that "the bottom tier includes gay victims presumed suspect and questioned about consent because of their deviant sexuality. Like common rape myths about women, they are 'asking for it.'"[6] Although my research here supports Hlavka's framework in many ways, given that participants sometimes drew on understandings of other queer men as "asking for it," the relegation of "gay victims" to the "bottom tier" leaves unexplored how hierarchical understandings may exist among queer men as well. Some participants constructed hierarchies of queer male survivors, invoking a stereotype of a feminized gay man seeking consensual sex, while other respondents made hierarchical comparisons across gender lines, with women survivors.

This chapter focuses in particular on the two most common ways that participants constructed hierarchies of victimhood, examining the narratives of the forty-one respondents who employed these most common discourses. Specifically, I reveal that queer male survivors' perceptions—not simply those of their assailants—should be understood in relation to a larger social context that includes victim blaming and involves the minimizing of some forms of sexual assault. In sexual assault scholarship, assumptions sometimes exist that centering survivors' perspectives will inevitably improve current approaches toward this violence.[7] Conversely, I show that survivors may reinforce social inequalities, including negative ideas about others who have been sexually assaulted. Thus, I argue that survivor-centered approaches, while important, remain limited, given that broader inequalities shape survivors' experiences and perceptions.

"WOMEN GET MORE SUPPORT": COMPARISONS WITH WOMEN SURVIVORS

The most common response to questions concerning hierarchies of victimhood involved participants arguing that sexual assault is taken more seriously when it happens to women than to men, as thirty-one respondents made this type of argument. Although participants came to this conclusion for a variety of reasons, they usually focused on the challenges confronting queer male survivors, or men more broadly, when making these arguments. In particular, twenty-five of the thirty-one participants emphasized homophobia, biphobia, or anti-queer prejudice potentially confronting queer male survivors, and twelve respondents argued that men will receive less support than women because men may be perceived as stronger and blamed for not physically fighting back. These two responses were not mutually exclusive, as participants sometimes went back and forth between them. Further, due to the intersectional subjectivity of respondents, as queer and as men, it was not always feasible to separate their challenges related to gender and sexuality.

However, among these thirty-one participants, their arguments were typically constructed around gender difference initially, as they spoke about women receiving more support than men, yet they then usually described struggling with stereotypes of queer male survivors as feminine or sexual. Indeed, twenty-two of these participants criticized the stigmatizing of male femininity or queer sexual desire. For instance, Juan, a forty-seven-year-old Latino gay man whose former partner had raped him on two occasions, said the following:

> I guess what really bothers me is that a lot of people see us all as silly little faggots who go around looking for dick anywhere we can find it. They see us as feminine, therefore we can't defend ourselves, and looking for sex— therefore, we can't be raped. And I am [feminine], but that doesn't mean I'm just sitting around waiting to be raped. . . . I want people to know that just because I'm not a woman who was grabbed in an alley that doesn't mean I should be blamed for what happened to me. Women get more sympathy, so people are going to grant them respect, but feminine guys are hurt just as bad, if not worse. Women have it easier.

These participants often highlighted their gendered challenges, such as an association of femininity with weakness or vulnerability, and their anti-queer struggles, such as pathologizing notions of "promiscuity." They also generally struggled with a perception, sometimes substantiated by their experiences, that others would not view them as legitimate survivors. Instead, they feared, or had experiences with, being blamed for the violence; as outlined in chapter 2, when Juan reported an experience of rape to the police, one of the officers responded by asking, "Don't you guys like rough sex anyway?"

While these participants attempted to establish themselves as unworthy of this blame in a variety of ways, one of the more frequent ways they did so was through this comparison with traditional understandings of sexual assault against women. Indeed, Juan reflected this trend through his statement that "just because I'm not a woman who was grabbed in an alley that doesn't mean I should be blamed for what happened to me." In part, then, these narratives arose from participants' challenges and their desire to be viewed as legitimate survivors, worthy of respect. Broadly speaking, their narratives should be understood in relation to a larger heteronormative environment that positions some queer men as blameworthy for their assaultive experiences.

At the same time, these narratives typically reproduced, and likely arose from, a larger anti-feminist context in which individuals may minimize the challenges facing women survivors. These participants' statements about women survivors were most frequently constructed around "support" or "sympathy," as twenty-six respondents used at least one of these two words. Some of these participants focused on presumable support they thought women would experience from friends or family members, while others emphasized resources devoted to violence against women or argued that the police would take rape more seriously for women survivors. Kyle, a fifty-four-year-old Black gay man, said, "Women will get more help and have people taking it super seriously. . . . Like police or doctors." Nevertheless, research has shown that women who have been sexually assaulted frequently experience unsupportive responses in many institutional settings, including from law enforcement and medical personnel.[8] In emphasizing support for women survivors, participants' comparisons reproduced a gender difference framework, with an exaggeration of differences across gender lines.[9]

Most of these respondents, twenty in total, said that survivors across gender lines experience the same or similar feelings, which then helped to underscore their perception of an unfairness that exists regarding support. Damon, a twenty-six-year-old Black bisexual man, described his perception of this difference succinctly: "The feelings are the same, but it doesn't get as much attention when it happens to a man—society doesn't view it as a big deal. Women get more support." Participants who described themselves as feminine most forcefully made these arguments that emphasized similar feelings across gender lines; almost half, fifteen, of these respondents described themselves as feminine. Ornell, for example, a thirty-seven-year-old Black gay man, stated:

Rape is rape no matter what. It hurts us all. But it is viewed differently. Women get more respect. . . . I've always seen myself as a very feminine person, and femininity as very powerful. The feelings are the same for me as they are for women, but *they get more sympathy* [emphasis added, said angrily]. When people think of rape, they think of a woman being pulled into the bushes in the park, so that's who they're going to sympathize with. Men, people won't care about, even if we're feminine.

Participants such as Ornell drew attention to an assumed gendered similarity—femininity—between themselves and women survivors to accentuate a presumed inequity in treatment. From this perspective, many women and feminine men may be associated with similar characteristics and may experience comparable feelings from a sexual violation, yet these participants drew attention to such similarities not to construct possible alliances or to express solidarity but to position these survivors hierarchically in terms of how each group is treated.

The ongoing assumption in these narratives relied on a contrast with an implicitly heterosexual survivor, as queer women did not appear in any of these narratives. Three of these participants referred to women survivors as dating or having sex "with men" and explicitly contrasted themselves with a heterosexual woman. More broadly, these comparisons with an implicitly heterosexual woman helped to accentuate respondents' anti-queer experiences, or fear over confronting such responses, given that such women presumably would not face the same discriminatory experiences rooted in anti-LGBTQ prejudice. Through a gender difference framework, femininity frequently becomes conflated with women, leading to the disappearance of feminine queer men's concerns. In this sense, a gender difference framework contributed to some of the discourse that participants used, while also being part of what they reacted against— an understanding that women's femininity may be framed as worthy of protection.[10]

Similar to Ornell, most of these participants brought up without being asked about it the stereotype of a stranger attacking a woman in a park or dark alley.[11] Respondents here typically experienced sexual assault in the context of either a relationship or a casual sexual encounter and did not have experiences that resembled stereotypical representations of rape. Instead, they used these representations to position women as receiving a lot of support and to highlight the lack of support experienced by individuals such as themselves.

Only five of these respondents said that they personally knew a woman who had been sexually assaulted, at least to their knowledge.[12] Four of the five participants who knew a woman survivor nevertheless described how others had responded unsupportively to her disclosure of sexual assault. Chad, a forty-eight-year-old white gay man, said, "Women will have people helping them more so than men because people think of a woman being grabbed in a dark alley." Later during the interview, however, he described a female friend who was raped in college and had experienced harassment after she reported the assault to the administration; some of the rapist's friends called her a "slut" and began circulating rumors about her around campus. Thus, even participants who had evidence of women encountering negative reactions did not typically use these experiences to highlight a lack of support for survivors across gender lines.

My research did not reveal race and ethnicity differences in the number of participants arguing that women receive more support than men; a similar percentage of respondents across racial and ethnic lines made these arguments. Still, while white participants focused solely on gender and sexuality, Black queer men more frequently described the effects of race. For example, Kenneth, a forty-two-year-old Black gay man, stated:

> It just pisses me off that whenever you see it, it's always some white woman who is snatched into some dark place. Her clothes are torn, really dramatic. Like it's so ridiculous; who could believe that? That's why I think it's easier for women—everyone comes running to help them, like, "Oh my god, what happened to her?" That's why I see women as being supported more so. Gay guys are seen as so sexual, so we must always want it. . . . Like Black [gay] men especially are always supposed to be there to please any man that comes along. . . . Other gay guys think that. . . . And then if you're feminine, people think you've just wasted your existence as a man, so who really cares if you've been raped? Who's gonna notice a feminine guy screaming rape? People think you brought it on yourself. People need to understand that there's nothing wrong with a guy being feminine or a gay guy wanting to sleep with other people—that doesn't give someone the right to violate you.

Black participants highlighted their unique challenges, as Kenneth here emphasized that Black queer men are especially sexualized—as "supposed to be there to please any man that comes along." Thus, it is important to account for the sexualization of Black queer men. Black participants also most frequently mentioned that others may view their femininity as a "waste," as Kenneth did when saying, "If you're feminine, people think you've just wasted your existence as a man." Black respondents who described themselves as feminine addressed this pathologizing more than other participants, as Black queer men who challenge traditional understandings of gender may be condemned for "inappropriately" representing their racial communities or for failing to live up to racialized stereotypes that associate Black men with heterosexual masculinity.[13]

Although Kenneth was the only participant to state explicitly that whiteness has been part of how rape victims have traditionally been represented, the common positioning of survivors as not only women and heterosexual but also white likely played an important role in perceptions that women receive a lot of support. If survivors were more commonly positioned as Black, these respondents may not have constructed women as receiving a lot of support as frequently as they did. Participants neglected Black women when positioning women survivors as receiving considerable support, which reflects some broader approaches toward sexual violence, in which mainstream US attention has usually focused on the experiences of white women, despite this group's lower rates of sexual assault than Black women.[14]

When white participants argued that women survivors receive more support than men, I noticed that these respondents sometimes implicated me as agreeing with their statements. For instance, Sean, a fifty-three-year-old white gay man, said, "You know what it's like" when arguing that "women, people will sympathize with—not men." The identity of an interviewer in part shapes what participants will say, and respondents, particularly other cisgender gay men, felt comfortable at times sharing arguably sexist thoughts with me more than they likely would have if I were a woman. Sean expressed the most anger during the interview when describing women survivors—which likely reflected some misogyny—but I also noticed that he seemed to become considerably less angry after speaking about how women survivors receive more support than men.

Part of his subsiding anger may have arisen from a connection he perceived himself as forming with me through this emphasis on women survivors receiving a lot of support. While interview-based research is inevitably immersed in such dynamics, it remains important to question why hierarchies of victimhood—and, more broadly, hierarchies of systems of oppression—are enticing for many individuals as a way of underscoring the severity of their own traumatic experiences or the seriousness of social inequalities that disadvantage them. I do not want to naturalize hierarchies of victimhood—in a less hierarchical society than the United States, I can imagine them being employed less frequently or not at all—yet attention also needs to be devoted to processes that encourage individuals to rank their traumatic experiences as "more severe" than those of other people. Constructions positioning women and queer men as competitors with one another reflect pressures toward adversarial relations between oppressed groups—sometimes referred to as an "Oppression Olympics"—in which marginalized individuals are encouraged to compete with one another over who is "more oppressed."[15]

Moreover, given that misogyny often operates on these grounds, with the mocking or belittling of characteristics associated with femininity, it is essential to remain attuned to pressures encouraging sexist discourse. A few of these participants spoke about women's bodies in graphic terms; for example, Sean, when emphasizing some possible reasons for his perception that women survivors receive a lot of support, began speaking about how their bodies may appear "really damaged" because "they'll have blood coming out of their [participant stopped speaking here]." This statement from Sean occurred several months after Donald Trump's infamous comments about Megyn Kelly, in which Trump used similar language during the 2016 Republican presidential primary.

I asked Sean toward the end of the interview if his comment was designed to be a takeoff on Trump's statement, and he responded as if he did not know what I was referring to, suggesting that he was not necessarily aware of this remark. Regardless, I have drawn attention to Sean's comment in the hope of taking seriously critiques of gay male misogyny.[16] The privileging of masculinity over femininity in queer male communities facilitates demeaning language toward women, including their bodies, and queer male survivors may reproduce this discourse. These responses focusing on women's bodies were atypical among participants, which means that their frequency should not be overstated, but the more common downplaying of the challenges confronting women survivors reproduced some sexism as well.[17]

These discourses, although problematic, should be contextualized in relation to not only larger dynamics of gender inequality but also participants' own struggles. When Sean made these comments, he repeatedly invoked this representation of a woman survivor who had been raped multiple times. From Sean's perspective, such a woman would be viewed sympathetically, as extraordinarily "damaged." As I probed further, Sean appeared to worry that outsiders would use his multiple experiences of assault, with different assailants, to construct him as a pathological person. He said, "Women who have been raped, people will see as the 'ultimate victim.'. . . But, me, I'll be seen as, 'What's wrong with you that it keeps happening to you?'" Survivors who have been assaulted many times or by multiple assailants may be positioned not as worthy of greater empathy, given that they have been victimized on more than one occasion, but as troubled or demented people.

The pathologizing of survivors who have been assaulted on multiple occasions certainly extends to women survivors, as I do not find it helpful to position these notions as exclusive to queer men. When interviewing Sean, however, I wondered if he would have expressed less misogyny if this pathologizing was less prevalent. More broadly, I do not want to defend or excuse gay male misogyny, yet some of this sexism might decrease if cultural understandings of sexual assault against queer men improved. Participants' perceptions that others would not recognize them as legitimate survivors occurred for a wide range of reasons that I have highlighted throughout this book—such as anti-queer prejudice, "promiscuity" discourse, racism, and attributions of blame that focus on men's strength—yet an additional reason includes frequency of victimization. Participants such as Sean who were assaulted multiple times sometimes expressed concern that others would use this repeated victimization against them, as a sign that something was wrong with them rather than their assailants.

Although participants in this section disproportionately identified as feminine, with fifteen of the thirty-one describing their gender expression in this way, the other sixteen respondents did not, which suggests that the frequency of male femininity among those outlined here should not be overstated. Still, even the participants in this section who did not identify as feminine usually criticized the stigmatizing of male femininity or queer sexual desire. Sean was one of these participants, as I was struck by how he used some aggressive language toward women survivors, but then later said, "It's hardest for feminine men because people really think they want it."

These results, especially when coupled with those in the next section, reveal a nonlinear process whereby participants' hierarchical constructions among queer men and across gender lines, in making comparisons with women, did not typically correspond. That is, the group of respondents in this section did not position some queer men as blameworthy, as those in the next section did, and generally criticized the stigmatizing of male femininity or queer sexual desire. Nevertheless, their frequent emphasis on women survivors receiving a lot of support indicates that significant barriers may exist in terms of creating alliances between women and queer male survivors. In light of larger structures of gender inequality, queer men may find it especially enticing to try and gain status through a comparison with women who have been sexually assaulted. After all, given that gender power relations encourage negative constructions of women, these participants' narratives remained largely consistent with such aspects of gender inequality.

In resisting discourse that downplays the challenges of women survivors, an important approach would involve emphasizing that gender inequality, as well as heteronormativity, structures many forms of sexual assault against queer men, in addition to responses toward this violence.[18] This emphasis on gender inequality can make it more difficult for queer male survivors to view their challenges as entirely separate from those facing women, due to some overlap in structural oppression based on gender and sexuality. Additionally, emphasizing solidarity among survivors across the lines of gender and sexuality would be useful for challenging pressures that encourage survivors to compete with one another.

Resistance to rape myths that construct sexual violence against women in relatively narrow ways—as a stranger attack, perhaps involving a brutal beating—also remain necessary, as participants in this section often drew on these notions when arguing that women receive a lot of support. Such rape myths exclude many survivors and can be used to dismiss the seriousness of many forms of assault. They also contribute to race and gender inequalities and establish stranger-based assaults as the most serious, even though research has shown that most survivors know their assailant prior to the assault.[19] Consequently, resistance to these rape myths is particularly important because such stereotypical representations are part of a larger social context in which many assaultive experiences may be minimized or positioned as inconsequential.[20]

"THERE'S A DIFFERENCE BETWEEN A GAY MAN AND A FAGGOT": CONSTRUCTING HIERARCHIES OF QUEER MALE SURVIVORS

In contrast to respondents in the previous section, another group of participants first responded to questions concerning hierarchies of victimhood not by focusing on women survivors but by emphasizing differences among queer men. These ten participants all identified as gay and did not describe themselves as feminine. Only four described themselves as masculine, yet a resistance to male femininity was consistently expressed throughout their narratives. Contrary to participants in the previous section, all of these respondents had one or more experience in which a stranger had raped them in a nonsexual context. These participants also repeatedly invoked a particular type of contrast—one involving a queer man seeking consensual sex. For instance, Tyrice, a thirty-year-old Black gay man, contrasted himself with his friend, a Black gay man who had a group of men rape him:

> The way I see it is there's the willing and the unwilling. Some go out there looking for sex, while others have it forced on them. . . . I have a hard time with consoling that friend because, to me, you asked for it, you went there to do drugs, you went there to have sex. . . . He's this feminine guy who likes to party until dawn. I don't like to hang out with men like him who consider themselves girly. . . . Everything that happened to that person that day was their fault, in my eyes. And, that's coming from a person who, I can say, is a real victim. . . . I was young, innocent. . . . I was kicking and screaming and had a gun to my head. You were willingly going there to get high and have sex. And one, two, three, whatever amount of people, had their turn with you

without your knowledge, because you were too high and out of it. I can't really sympathize, saying that you were raped, because you went there for that.

Participants constructed other queer male survivors as blameworthy in a variety of ways, but one of these ways was through this emphasis on age and force, as Tyrice mentioned that he was "young" and "had a gun to my head." He positioned himself as not having the capacity to resist or avoid the assault, while constructing his friend as more culpable and less deserving of respect or sympathy.

Hierarchies between forceful stranger attacks and sexual assaults involving some initial desire for consensual sex have a long history, as media representations have most frequently presented rape as immediately nonconsensual, even though survivors may pursue or engage in consensual sex acts before the assailant does something against their will.[21] These representations reproduce an implicit contrast between innocent and faultworthy survivors, in which the latter are constructed as responsible for their assaultive experiences or even positioned as "deserving" of the violence.[22] Tyrice's discourse, "You went there to have sex," establishes such actions, rather than those of the assailant, as precipitating the assault, reinforcing the blame that survivors with these experiences may confront.

Although constructions of "real" victims of sexual assault exist beyond LGBTQ communities, the tropes that these respondents drew upon appeared specific to queer men in some ways. Similar to Tyrice, most of these participants referred to "drugs," three of whom described a stereotypical representation of a "club kid." For instance, Danny, a thirty-one-year-old white gay man, said: "It'd be one thing if I was some club kid—dancing, doing drugs. Sashaying down the runway, looking pretty, going on Grindr at all hours of the night. . . . They open their legs for anybody. But I didn't want this to happen to me." All of these respondents positioned other, blameworthy queer men as feminine or sexual. This emphasis on femininity operated in a variety of ways, but included references to feminized activities or characteristics, such as "looking pretty" or "sashaying down the runway" here. These responses have been characterized as "femmephobia," or the systematic devaluation of femininity, in some LGBTQ research.[23]

Seven of these participants mentioned Grindr, which helped to contrast themselves with individuals seeking consensual sex. Two of these respondents said that they used Grindr themselves, explaining that they perceived a problem with habitual sex rather than with the app per se. Users of such apps may privilege dating over casual sex or may hold sex-negative views, positioning the app as ideally suited for seeking romantic partners. Most of these participants, six, also referred to the act of bottoming, as Danny did here with "they open their legs for anybody." Another one of these participants, Tario, a forty-seven-year-old Latino gay man, described queer men who are "looking for sex" as needing "to be more careful with who they let put something in them." This discourse relies on understandings that being penetrated potentially exposes oneself to negative consequences and, thus, the onus for preventing sexual assault is placed on the sexually receptive partner.

Conversely, these participants all explained that they prefer to top. Respondents were never asked about their preferred sexual activity, which led to some surprise on my part when they volunteered this information. This articulation of their preference for topping likely helped with masculinizing themselves in relation to other queer male survivors, whom they typically positioned as feminine.

Describing their preference for topping also helped these participants with establishing their experiences of anal rape as nonconsensual. That is, this emphasis helped to shield against accusations that they may have wanted, enjoyed, or been looking for, anal penetration—an accusation that other men in this study sometimes experienced, with outsiders reframing incidents of anal rape as desired sex acts. Further, constructions of a sexualized queer man may have comforted these respondents, allowing them to feel safer and to believe that they would not experience sexual assault again as long as they did not imitate this stereotype. These accounts can be understood as examples of "defensive othering"—the process whereby members of a subordinated group reinforce negative ideas about their social category by claiming that stigmatizing labels apply to others but not to themselves.[24] Instead of criticizing negative stereotypes associated with queer male survivors, these participants exempted themselves from such notions and argued that the stigmatizing ideas pertain to some other queer men.

During the interviews, it remained striking that the respondents in this section positioned other queer male survivors as blameworthy, but then usually advanced claims about the seriousness of sexual assault against women. For instance, Yamen, a fifty-five-year-old Black gay man, stated:

> You got those out there that they don't care, they're nymphos, all they care about is they look for dick.... There's a difference between a gay man and a faggot. The difference is, with a gay man, he picks and chooses who he wants to sleep with; a faggot is a doorknob where everybody gets a turn. A gay man is not going to put himself in a position to get hurt, but a faggot will put himself in the position for anything. Faggots live a dangerous life because they're sleeping with any and everybody.... They use their femininity for attention. If you carry yourself fucked up, you're going to get treated fucked up.

This narrative is consistent with a lot of the themes in this section, as this distinction between a gay man and a "faggot" relies on a positioning of the latter as more sexual, feminine, and prone to danger. In contrast to Tyrice's earlier positioning of himself as "young" and "innocent," and therefore with implicitly little or no agency to resist, Yamen here constructs a gay man as more agentic than a "faggot"; he positions the former as someone who "picks and chooses who he wants to sleep with," while constructing the latter as a "nympho" or a "doorknob where everybody gets a turn."

Later during the interview, however, Yamen described women survivors more positively: "Women don't receive a lot of support either, so I think they need more.... Gay men need to be there for women who've been raped and the message needs to go out that it's bad for us all." The main difference between these respondents and those in the previous section is that participants here did not construct women as problematically receiving more support than men. Another one of these respondents, Norman, a thirty-eight-year-old white gay man, said, "Rape against women isn't taken seriously enough."

Although the language these participants used was noticeably less harsh toward women survivors than those in the previous section, respondents here also tended to reproduce chivalrous understandings of gender. Marcus, for example, a thirty-seven-year-old Black gay man, explained his reasons for believing that sexual assault against women needs to be taken more seriously: "Women who've been raped are treated so badly, too, when you'd think they would be treated with the most love—because women are holy creatures, who should always be respected." Marcus's positioning of women as "holy creatures" reproduces chivalrous approaches toward women, in which they are elevated to an exalted status but are treated protectively and prevented access to the same domains as men. These more benevolent forms of sexism may construct women as deserving of love or kindness but nevertheless contribute to gender inequality by advancing a paternalistic, protective view of women.[25]

Most of these participants, in contrast to those in the previous section, also supported stereotypical representations of rape, in which a woman is forced into a location such as a park or a dark alley. For instance, Jayden, a forty-five-year-old Black gay man, said, "The raping of women is a big problem, too. They need to be protected. That 'woman being snatched into a dark alley' shows what it's like for all of us. . . . Because there's a lot of sickos out there. I had a group of guys attack me from behind—how was I supposed to do anything? They overpowered me; so, it's kind of similar in some ways—I was defenseless. . . . I just don't like the 'aren't you strong enough to defend yourself?' I couldn't!" The difference between participants here and those in the previous section arose in part from these respondents all having at least one experience that more closely resembled traditional understandings of sexual assault, in which a stranger had raped them in a nonsexual context. Participants in the previous section with assaultive experiences in the context of a hookup may have also had a stranger as their assailant, but those respondents did not view their assaultive experience as aligning with traditional representations, given that the encounter began with some understanding that consensual sex might occur.

In addition, some of the challenges facing the ten respondents in this section appeared particularly pronounced for Black queer men. Although racial differences did not exist regarding the frequency with which participants constructed other queer male survivors as blameworthy, the Black gay men in this section, as outlined in chapter 1, were more likely than other respondents to describe struggling with perceptions of themselves as strong. Jayden, for example, said, "I just don't like the 'aren't you strong enough to defend yourself?'" These statements need to be understood in relation to a broader context, in which some male survivors, particularly Black gender-conforming men, may have their experiences dismissed as something they should have been able to prevent through physical strength. Struggling against such notions, these respondents constructed themselves as incapable of preventing the violence and contrasted themselves with other queer men, positioned as responsible for the assault.

This second group of participants, all of whom identified as gay, may reflect a more common response among gay cisgender men than among other queer men, such as those who are bisexual. Further analyses also remain necessary to account for the perspectives of transgender and nonbinary individuals, as the hierarchical constructions outlined in this chapter were most common among cisgender queer men. Overall, respondents' narratives in this section revealed the limitations of perspectives, at least among queer male survivors, that emphasize the seriousness of sexual assault against women and the importance of traditional representations of rape. While retaining their emphasis on taking sexual assault against women seriously, further critiques of their negative constructions of sexual desire and male femininity remain necessary.[26]

ADVANCING A SEX-CRITICAL POLITICS

Based on the narratives of this second group of participants, a particular stereotype of queer men who have been sexually assaulted appears to exist—one of a feminized man seeking consensual sex, on a place such as a hookup app. Although none of the participants in this second group experienced an assault after looking for consensual sex, other respondents encountered this violence. On the one hand, such experiences must not be used to pathologize consensual sex more broadly. On the other hand, queer men experience assault in these contexts of meeting for consensual sex, and my results indicate that other queer male survivors may be the most likely to blame such men for the violence enacted against them. The frequency with which participants invoked this stereotype of a queer man seeking consensual sex points to its power and to the continued need for queer and feminist work adopting a sex-critical approach—a theoretical perspective that avoids pathologizing consensual sex and examines the ways sex and power relations intersect.[27] A sex-critical perspective, while overlapping in some ways with a more mainstream "sex-positive" approach, nevertheless contends that not all expressions of sexuality are "positive" and avoids neoliberal notions of self-empowerment.[28]

Given that queer men are often disparaged through sexualizing and femininizing stereotypes, this group is at a unique position in some respects to challenge discourse that constructs consensual sex as the basis for rape and that situates male femininity as leading to sexual violence. This second group of participants, however, did not respond in this more critical way. Feminist, sex-critical scholarship can help to reposition this violence as the product of social inequalities, not survivors' behaviors or attributes.[29] Resistance to the naturalizing of male femininity as the site of sexual assault against men seems particularly important in this regard, given that gender inequality frequently establishes male femininity as setting the stage for negative consequences.[30] Of course, queer male survivors with masculine gender expressions will face many of their own challenges, but participants denounced other survivors by drawing attention to feminine attributes more frequently than masculine ones.

In addition to reframing male femininity in more positive terms, sexual assault advocacy and scholarship could benefit more survivors by emphasizing the value of queer sexual desires and practices. Casual sexual encounters must not be positioned as inevitably leading to negative consequences such as sexual assault, given that this understanding arises out of sex-negative discourse. I can imagine a utopic world in which every time individuals seek consensual sex, they are not sexually assaulted. Eliminating Grindr will also not end sexual assault against queer men, as some of the men in this chapter suggested; broader approaches that challenge ongoing inequities remain necessary. Online interactions and subsequent in-person meetings reflect broader patterns of behavior, rooted in systems of inequality, rather than existing independently of them. Thus, power relations remain more important than hookup apps in producing forms of sexual assault, indicating that attention should be devoted to changing the former.[31]

LINKING ASSAILANTS' MOTIVATIONS WITH THEIR SEXUAL DESIRE

Related to these concerns with focusing on survivors' sex practices prior to the assault, assailants' motivations may also be linked with their sexual desire. Examining sexual assault in relation to such desire can reinforce rape myths that assailants are motivated to commit violations primarily due to their sexual proclivities. Research indicates that this understanding of sexual assault remains widespread in the United States.[32] A long line of feminist scholarship has addressed the problems with understanding sexual violence in this way, given that a desire for power and dominance may play a more central role in precipitating the assault.[33] From this perspective, assailants would be having consensual sex, not harming another person, if sexual desire was the sole motivating factor.

Conversely, other research has emphasized that sex cannot be separated entirely from rape, given that sex and sexuality in the United States are fundamentally linked with aspects such as power, violence, and control.[34] As a result, clichés such as "rape is about power, not about sex" simplify too much. Some assailants become sexually aroused during an assault and survivors frequently feel as if they have been violated in a sexual way, which differs from most other forms of violence.[35] In general, this body of scholarship has argued for a more complex understanding of sexual assault in which it is reduced to neither sex nor power, but instead is examined in ways that account for how these aspects overlap.[36]

Obviously, I do not have data on assailants, only participants' perceptions of them, yet cases in which heterosexual cisgender men had sexually assaulted a cisgender queer man revealed some additional problems with attributing sexual assault to an assailant's desire. For example, Jayden, a forty-five-year-old Black cisgender gay man, told his mother about his assaultive experience, in which two male heterosexual friends of his cousin had raped him. His mother did not believe him, asking, "How could they do that? They're straight." The association of sexual assault with desire can be used to dismiss experiences such as Jayden's in this way. Heterosexual men can commit sexual assault against other men, queer or otherwise, because these violations are not solely acts of sexual desire.

I am not interested in determining whether the men who assaulted Jayden are "really" heterosexual or not, but instead interested in critiquing assumptions that these men must be gay or bisexual, as well as assumptions that they could not have committed the assault due to their heterosexual identity. If a gay man was accused of sexually assaulting a woman, it remains worth asking if others would similarly say, "How could they do that?

They're gay." An unwillingness to see negative outcomes as arising from heterosexuality likely undergirds what Jayden's mother asked. In contrast, when queer men commit sexual assault their actions are sometimes viewed as reflecting a larger pathological problem with this group of people.

Despite these concerns with examining sexual assault through the lens of desire, it is still important to discuss queer men's participation in casual sexual encounters. Participants' experiences may not be representative of queer male survivors more broadly, but the context of a hookup was the second most common, behind relationships, in which respondents experienced a sexual assault as an adult. Although a lot of feminist work has pointed out that most forms of violence occur between two or more people who know each other—an important point to combat the idea of "stranger danger"—this argument can obscure some forms of assault, such as those in the context of a hookup, in which the two individuals may be relative strangers before that moment in time.[37]

TOPPING AND BOTTOMING: CONSTRUCTING HIERARCHIES OF SEXUAL PRACTICES

Overlapping with participants' narratives that negatively positioned sexual desire and male femininity, some of the men who described their preference for topping spoke about bottoming in punitive or pathologizing ways. For instance, Jontray, a fifty-eight-year-old Black gay man, said, "It's not just bottoms who are raped. . . . It's worse for a top, because bottoms know what [anal intercourse] feels like—[a penis] has been in them before. While for someone like me it's painful." Six participants made this type of argument, where they focused on how a man's history with bottoming during consensual anal intercourse could make an experience of rape less traumatic. These histories may lead to some differences, but this discourse too bluntly compares consensual anal intercourse with rape. Another one of these participants, Yamen, a fifty-five-year-old Black gay man, stated, "Bottoms have had that inside of them before, so they're going to be better prepared for it."

These statements involve a downplaying of the traumatic consequences that rape typically has for men who prefer to bottom, extending from discourses that minimize the severity of some forms of sexual assault. Yet this discourse also extends from a social pathologizing of bottoming, as rape must be understood as harmful to a survivor regardless of their sexual history with anal intercourse. A more useful approach would underscore that survivors generally experience harm from their assaultive experiences, avoiding frameworks that undermine the severity of this violence.

An even larger number of participants, thirteen, emphasized that after an experience of anal rape, they subsequently only engaged in the sexual practice of topping, not bottoming. In most cases, participants explained that their experience of anal rape then made the act of bottoming unpleasant or frightening for them, as it reminded them of the assault. Across these narratives, however, I was struck by how participants described this shift from bottoming to topping as a change that would prevent them from experiencing sexual assault in the future. Vondell, a twenty-nine-year-old Black gay man, stated this idea succinctly: "I only top [after I was raped] so that it won't happen again." Participants also typically framed this action in agentic terms, as a sign of their agency or their capacity to act. For instance, Jeremiah, a twenty-two-year-old Black gay man, whose violent experience took place in a relationship, explained his shift from bottoming to topping in the following way: "That situation made me know that I wanted to be 'a top' full time. . . . It wouldn't happen again, and it hasn't, because I won't be in that situation again. . . . I stopped it."

When I heard these statements, I often thought of the men who preferred to top and who had been raped. Certainly, topping does not exempt one from the possibility of experiencing sexual assault. Participants experienced a range of assaultive experiences, and men who preferred to top experienced these forms of violence, including sometimes from men who preferred to bottom. In this sense, the discourse of switching from bottoming to topping can be viewed in part as a defense mechanism, enabling participants to feel safer and to understand their efforts as contributing to this safety.

Jontray, quoted earlier in this section, was one of these participants who preferred to top and experienced an assault from a man who preferred to bottom. His assaultive experience occurred on a night when he went over to the apartment of a former friend, Colin. Jontray said that the two of them often met for casual sex and he described Colin as "gay and very feminine." Jontray said that this evening began in a similar way as usual in terms of their meeting for sex; Colin reached out and then Jontray went over to Colin's apartment. The night of the assault nevertheless differed because Jontray said that Colin did not seem at all interested in sex, as they began to argue with one another instead. After a while, Jontray became "very drunk" and passed out. He thought that one of his alcoholic drinks had been spiked with a narcotic or sleeping pill, although he could not be certain, since he may have passed out from the alcohol. Regardless, Jontray woke to Colin penetrating him anally with an object, while Jontray went in and out of consciousness. Jontray went to the hospital the next day, but had otherwise not told anyone else about the assault.

In part, this experience reveals that queer men who prefer to bottom should not be naturalized as representing all queer male survivors, as such a positioning excludes some queer men who have been sexually assaulted. At the same time, other respondents viewed the act of bottoming as more dangerous than the act of topping, which is why they switched from the former to the latter. This perception has everything to do with inequalities based on gender and sexuality, not some "natural" vulnerability of the anus in comparison to the penis. As some feminist scholarship has highlighted, the penis is in some ways a quite vulnerable sex organ, and yet, because of unequal gender norms associating it with prowess and strength, it has been understood as an instrument for perpetrating sexual assault more frequently than an organ that could experience this violence.[38]

While queer men who prefer to top experience forms of sexual assault, it seems likely that queer men who prefer to bottom experience this violence disproportionately, due to social understandings of this latter sexual position. Given gendered notions that associate topping with a variety of characteristics—dominance and aggression, for example—some men may commit sexual violence due in part to these associations. Indeed, other respondents sometimes critiqued their assailants' understanding that topping involves aggressiveness. For instance, Gene, a fifty-year-old Black gay man, argued the following after being asked why he thought his ex-boyfriend had been abusive in their relationship:

A lot of times, when an assault happens someone is trying to assert power and trying to release anger or control. . . . [My ex-boyfriend] is a controlling type, yes, because he feels that he's the top. Just the concept of, "I'm more masculine, and I'm the top—I'm supposed to be more aggressive and you're supposed to be more submissive." . . . That's probably their thought, "I'm going to get off, I'm going to ejaculate, I don't care what you say." And, I'm thinking that's probably what was going through his mind, "I'm already there, I'm already into it, I'm almost done, so I don't care what you say. I don't care that you're saying 'no,' I'm going to finish." . . . In a Neanderthal sort of way, "I'm the top and you're going to do what I say" sort of thing. I'm assuming; I don't know. I haven't thought about that. I don't have concepts around this.

Gene addressed a sense of ownership that some men who prefer to top may have, as a sexual assault may be justified under assumptions that the man who is bottoming "owes" his sexual partner an orgasm and should therefore consent to sex acts even if he does not want them. From this perspective, if the man who prefers to top wants sex, he may then view it as his sexual partner's "duty" to consent. These assumptions can then lead to a dismissal of the pain or discomfort on the part of the man who is bottoming, as reflected by Gene's description of assailants who discount "no."

These findings indicate that critiques of masculinity in queer male communities remain necessary, as it would be helpful for further work to break down associations of topping with masculinizing, and potentially abusive, characteristics. Even though topping and bottoming are sexual acts, in which there's nothing inherently masculinizing or femininizing about them, gendered dichotomies are often attached to these positions, including strong/weak, active/passive, and dominance/submission. Undoubtedly, these associations reduce a lot of complexity; individuals who bottom, for example, may be dominant and command another individual to submit to penetrating them. The association of topping with masculinity is socially produced, not "natural," and these forms of abuse should be understood as arising out of particular dispositions—such as control and aggression—not the act of topping or even the identity of "a top" per se. After all, many queer men who identify as "a top" are unabusive. While being careful not to pathologize individuals who may take on identities such as "top" or "bottom," it remains important to address the cultural pathologizing of bottoming and the social conditions that link topping with aggressive characteristics.

Given that Gene here said, "I don't have concepts around this," queer and feminist scholarship can help in this regard, by further critiquing the gendering of these sexual positions. The association of topping with power and control and bottoming with weakness and passivity—the latter of which are disparaged characteristics in the US cultural imagination— seems especially necessary to challenge. Nevertheless, this work has to be careful about attempts to recuperate bottoming through masculinity.[39] In queer male communities, the term *power bottom* is often used in this way, to disassociate bottoming from passivity and link it with power. This type of discourse leaves in place the privileging of gendered characteristics associated with masculinity—such as "power"—over those associated with femininity, such as passivity. Indeed, the term *passive top* does not have the same cultural currency as *power bottom*, as some assumption exists that power is preferable to passivity. Even the term *service top* does not imply passivity, but draws on notions of activity, as well as masculine or gentlemanly courtship.

One way forward in challenging the gendered essentializing of these positions involves resisting their construction as mutually exclusive "opposites." An emphasis on "versatility," or a preference for topping and bottoming, brings more complexity to this binary, but does not necessarily break down the gendering of these positions. I was surprised by how little "vers" or "versatility" came up during the interviews—it was never mentioned or even implied—while topping was overtly discussed and included in participants' descriptions of their self-identification. Although respondents did not overtly identify as preferring to bottom, this sexual practice was sometimes implied as an act they enjoyed and was also mentioned more frequently than versatility, albeit at times in more negative ways than topping. It would be helpful for research and advocacy to avoid privileging versatility over bottoming, as the former may be constructed in some queer social circles as the ideal—the "most fluid" or "least heteronormative"—practice, thereby creating normative pressures and potentially reinforcing the cultural pathologizing of bottoming.

Here, I am interested less in drawing attention to sexual practices such as versatility that were unspoken and more in the gap between what participants' assaultive experiences revealed and what they advocated for in terms of solutions. One example of this gap is that respondents sometimes experienced violence that appeared rooted in the cultural stigmatizing of bottoming, and yet the solution they advanced focused not on destigmatizing it, but on no longer doing it. For instance, Latrelle, a forty-nine-year-old Black gay man, had a former partner rape him; this man said "you know you want it" while committing the assault. Latrelle critiqued this man in a similar way as Gene, saying, "Sometimes tops think they can just take what they want—doesn't matter what you say." Later, Latrelle stated that he "became a top," describing bottoming as "too difficult," and he argued that this change will "make [an assault] not happen again."

This focus on switching away from bottoming may have arisen in part from these participants' lack of social power, as they may have felt as if they had little ability to destigmatize bottoming on their own or as if a commitment to destigmatizing it would not be supported by others. As a result, they may have felt as if they could not control the cultural stigmatizing of bottoming, but that they could control their having sex in this way. Abandoning the practice of bottoming, then, may have helped these participants feel a renewed sense of control over their lives and over events that may happen to them in the future.

While understanding and taking seriously survivors concerns with not wanting a sexual assault to occur again, I hope to advance some more social considerations when thinking about ways to reduce this violence. Proposing a solution to sexual assault against queer men that calls for the abandonment of bottoming seems not only unrealistic but also problematic in potentially further stigmatizing this sexual practice. Asking queer men to change sexual behaviors they enjoy also represents the opposite of the approach I am arguing for in this text, in which work focusing on sexual assault does not pathologize consensual sex.[40] Alternatively, it would be helpful for scholarship and advocacy to continue to destigmatize bottoming to the point where it is no longer seen as exposing oneself to violence or as consenting to whatever another sexual partner wants.

The construction of a shift from bottoming to topping as agentic behavior also needs further contextualizing. Some research in gender and sexuality studies has emphasized how individuals, including LGBTQ people, may modify aspects of their gender expression, such as their style of dress or manner of speech, to avoid experiencing harassment.[41] In this sense, forms of social control largely encourage gender conformity. This modification of gender expression may occur after individuals have experienced violence or harassment; queer men, for example, may adopt more masculine gender expressions after being harassed for gender expansiveness.[42] However, less work, as I am showing here, has emphasized that queer men may alter their sexual practices after a traumatic experience.

One problem with positioning a shift from bottoming to topping as agentic is that it relies on notions of an autonomous subject, separated from cultural conditions. A central idea of queer theory and poststructuralist thought more generally is that the self and the discourses that exist in our culture cannot quite so easily be detached from one another.[43] Instead, these cultural discourses are part of us, at least to some degree, as our identities are much more intertwined with cultural conditions than common media narratives in the United States encourage individuals to think.[44] Consequently, in terms of switching away from bottoming to avoid sexual assault, it is not necessarily an agentic move to do so, given that cultural conditions already grant more esteem to topping. Approaches designed to reduce sexual assault have to be careful about establishing this shift as a positive one. In relation to bottoming, the problem is with how it is culturally framed and interpreted, not with the practice itself. Thus, what remains necessary is more work that points to the stigmatizing of bottoming and then further attempts to rectify this pathologizing.

SOCIAL INEQUALITIES AND THE LIMITATIONS OF SURVIVOR-CENTERED APPROACHES

Conducting research on this topic has made me think more deeply about some possible limitations of survivor-centered approaches, including my own. Linda Martín Alcoff, in her important book *Rape and Resistance*, has stated, "I will argue, it is the voices of victims that need to remain at the center of the fight for cultural change."[45] My text here would not have come to fruition had I not believed this statement to a certain extent; survivors' voices are too frequently marginalized. Still, while a lot of value may reside in focusing on survivors' perceptions and experiences, I also see some potential shortcomings with this approach. Individuals who have not been sexually assaulted need to take on some of the work of combatting sexual assault as well; such advocacy must not remain entirely the responsibility of survivors. In addition, as I have shown, individuals who have been sexually assaulted sometimes reinforce social inequalities themselves.

Survivors subsist in a US social context structured by patriarchy, white supremacy, and heteronormativity, as well as a culture that advances some negative ideas about individuals who have been sexually assaulted. It seems potentially dangerous to elevate survivors to an exalted plane, as if race, gender, and sexuality hierarchies do not sometimes inform this group's thinking and behavior as well. Instead, as I have revealed, queer male survivors may reproduce sexist discourse and draw on rape myths focusing on stranger-based violence, as participants were more likely to reinforce than challenge these myths. This focus on survivors' potentially harmful narratives provides a more nuanced representation than one that avoids any potentially problematic discourse from this group. An important path forward is to advance complex representations of survivors, taking seriously their concerns, while also avoiding romanticized or unrealistic portrayals that position this group as "above" social inequalities.

6 Outing, Disclosing Marginalized Identities, and Navigating Multiple Stigmas

Previous scholarship on sexual assault has emphasized LGBTQ survivors' challenges with regard to outing, or disclosing an LGBTQ person's sexuality or gender identity without their consent.[1] In particular, assailants may threaten to out LGBTQ survivors as a way of coercing them into having unwanted sex or ensuring their silence about a sexual assault.[2] With participants in this study, although their concerns often overlapped with those of other survivors, their experiences of outing revealed that LGBTQ survivors may encounter unique challenges in this regard. For instance, Marteese, a sixty-year-old Black gay man, dated and had sex with a man, Christopher, in his neighborhood when he was in his late twenties. Marteese was not out at the time and said that he was scared about his family learning that he was gay due to his concern that they would cut off contact with him. After the two men had gone on several dates and had sex a few times, Christopher began to threaten Marteese.

Christopher threatened to tell Marteese's friends that he was gay if Christopher did not receive money from him. This financial blackmail took place before the advent of cellphones or answering machines, but Marteese said that he would receive phone calls at his apartment, in which Christopher would say, "I know where you live." Marteese became fearful during this time, both for his safety and over his friends and family members learning that he was gay. If any of his friends discovered this information, he said that it would only be a matter of time before his family also learned about his homosexuality. Marteese explained that he disclosed his sexuality to most of his family members years later, but that he wanted to "do that when I was ready, not have it forced on me."

The stalking mostly occurred via telephone, yet Christopher would also spend time outside of Marteese's building, which Marteese viewed as designed to make him more fearful and more likely to pay the money. The harassment ended when Marteese threatened to report Christopher to the police. At the same time, Marteese said that after telling Christopher about potentially calling the police, he became more fearful for his safety, as he worried that Christopher's threats would escalate into physical violence. Marteese's experience reveals the importance of including many forms of stalking as part of the landscape of sexual victimization. He spent the most time emphasizing that the threats made him fearful of being physically hurt and of losing contact with his family, yet he also mentioned how hard it was on him because he did not have anyone he could speak to about it, given that "I would have had to tell [them] that I was gay then."

Certainly, queer survivors may keep an experience of sexual assault or harassment hidden because revealing it would require them to disclose a sexuality they do not want to make known. Rumor-spreading about queer people who are not out may also cause them to feel as if they will not be believed about an assaultive experience, given that outsiders may interpret these survivors as "not being honest" about their sexuality and therefore as unlikely to be telling the truth about an assault. These concerns become particularly significant when considering the challenges of LGBTQ people who are stereotyped as deceitful, such as bisexual and transgender people, as well as those who are HIV positive.

While most attention with regard to outing has focused on these issues in relation to a survivor's LGBTQ identity, it is also useful to understand how outing may involve other forms of nonconsensual disclosure.[3] In this study, almost one-third of the participants connected past experiences of coming out as queer with concerns over disclosing an assaultive experience. David, for example, an eighteen-year-old Black gay man, described this dynamic succinctly: "You have to 'out' yourself all over again." He spoke about how his coming out experience as gay was not particularly positive, which led to some hesitancy in disclosing his status as a survivor. In this sense, anxieties around identifying as a survivor may be compounded by queerness. When individuals have had negative experiences with disclosing their sexuality or gender identity, they may be reminded of these events when deciding whether to tell others that they have been sexually assaulted.

Of course, even if queer survivors did not have negative experiences with coming out, the uncomfortableness they felt at the time may lead to more fear or hesitancy in terms of disclosing an assault. Another participant, Latrelle, a forty-nine-year-old Black gay man, said that other queer men may have had bad experiences with coming out, and then react negatively to another queer man such as himself identifying as a survivor: "They've had to tell others about their sexuality, so then they get uncomfortable seeing someone do that with rape." This process of disclosing sexual assault to another queer person may be fraught with particular tensions, in which the survivor worries that the other individual will project their anxieties in terms of coming out or experiencing a sexual violation onto the person who has disclosed their status as a survivor.

Latrelle also spoke about the difficulty with telling romantic partners about an assaultive experience, as he described how this disclosure can change the relationship. Specifically, he said that romantic partners will frequently react in a way where they become overly gentle, cautious, or protective. He explained that he did not like this reaction, as he did not want to be "protected," but instead, he just wanted "to be treated like the same person." Another, although less common, reaction that Latrelle pointed to from romantic partners involved them becoming more distant, as he felt that they "do not know how to handle hearing about it" and may therefore begin to withdraw from the relationship. In some ways, these two responses are opposites, as the former involves a greater attachment—too much, from Latrelle's perspective—while the latter consists of a detachment.

Beyond these relationship concerns, most participants described anxieties about being outed as a survivor; a few even detailed experiences in which this had happened. For instance, Kemal, a thirty-seven-year-old Black gay man, described how he had told a few friends about an ex-boyfriend who sexually assaulted him. Several weeks after telling these friends, he received a threatening voicemail from his former partner, who told him to "stop spreading lies." Kemal said that mutual friends began to "take sides" and that he was most upset with the friend or friends who had betrayed his confidence by telling others about the assault, since he had told them under the assumption that they would keep it private. However, because Kemal had told several people, he was unsure exactly who had betrayed his confidence. Participants with such experiences spoke about this betrayal as an additional form of victimization, in which they felt as if their trust or bodily integrity had been violated through the assault and then again through this violation of their privacy. Similar in some ways to outing based on sexuality, these participants emphasized that they wanted to be able to tell others about an assault on their own terms rather than having it disclosed for them.

Further, being outed as a survivor may remind some queer men of outing they faced in relation to their sexuality or gender identity. Kemal here, for example, had been outed during high school by a classmate who went through his personal belongings and found pictures of men Kemal found attractive. When I noted that the outing of him as a survivor was then the second time a nonconsensual disclosure had happened to him, he said, "Yes, it brought back that anger." Some other participants had not been outed against their will as queer, but spoke about how their negative experiences with coming out led them to worry about having another bad experience when disclosing the assault. In short, these concerns around outing—as a survivor or as queer—appeared to magnify one another for many respondents, as anxieties or experiences around one of these forms of outing increased tensions around the other.

Conversely, a few participants explained that disclosing their sexual identity had led them to see the importance of coming out as a survivor. For example, Marcus, a thirty-seven-year-old Black gay man, said, "You see the power of coming out [as gay] and then you can use that to come out as a survivor." These statements were atypical, given that a significant minority of participants had never told anyone about their assaultive experiences and given that most of those who had told others did not frame disclosure in these terms. Nevertheless, it is not always the case that coming out experiences will decrease a queer survivor's likelihood of telling others about an assault. It is certainly possible that even negative experiences with coming out could make an LGBTQ survivor more, not less, likely to disclose their status as a survivor. Coming out experiences should not be framed as inevitably emancipatory, but it is also the case that previously identifying as queer may lead some survivors to reveal that they have been sexually assaulted.

In this chapter, I argue for expansive understandings of outing, given that participants described various forms of nonconsensual disclosure simultaneously. Moreover, respondents' narratives did not always focus principally on outing related to their sexuality or gender identity. Accounting for other forms of outing not focused on queerness, such as those related to being a survivor, revealed the importance of conceptualizing outing in expansive ways. Beyond queerness and survivorhood, participants spoke about some other important forms of nonconsensual disclosure as well.

OUTING CONCERNS RELATED TO HIV

While concerns with outing may affect a wide range of queer men, it is important to remain attuned to other factors, including HIV status, that may shape a survivor's willingness to disclose a sexual assault. Participants living with HIV were particularly attuned to these concerns around outing. Ten respondents said that they were HIV positive; six of these participants had acquired HIV from their assailant. Most of these respondents described privacy concerns that they had regarding their HIV status and their status as a survivor. For instance, Marcel, a twenty-seven-year-old Black gay man, said, "Like I know how important my [HIV] status is to keep private. So it's like with that and being gay, you learn there's certain things that only you should be able to share. And [being sexually assaulted] is another one of those things." Most of these participants living with HIV did not mention their sexual identity in the way Marcel did here, yet a majority drew parallels between the privacy they thought should be accorded to their HIV status and the privacy they wanted in terms of sexual assault.

These participants differed in arguing whether their HIV status made them more or less likely to tell others about the assault; respondents were fairly evenly split on this matter, as I heard arguments in both directions. Marcel, for example, experienced rape in the context of an internet hookup, where the male assailant did not wear a condom during the assault; Marcel acquired HIV from this experience. He argued that if he tells someone about being sexually assaulted, he often feels compelled to disclose his HIV status, since the assault is what led to him living with HIV. When explaining this process, he said, "So I have to figure out if I want someone to know that I'm positive before I talk about [the assault]." Other respondents framed this decision-making process in the opposite direction—that they would not reveal their HIV status because it meant that they would then feel compelled to describe the assault—but the important point here is that these concerns around outing oneself as a survivor or as HIV positive often intensified, and overlapped with, one another.

Some other participants, however, spoke about their HIV status as leading them to feel more comfortable with disclosing an assaultive experience. For instance, William, a thirty-six-year-old white bisexual man, acquired HIV from an ex-boyfriend who had sexually assaulted him. He said, "You have a lot of practice at saying 'I'm positive,' so then when you say, 'I was sexually assaulted,' it's a little easier because you've already come out as positive before." Although he thought that his history with disclosing his HIV status had made him more comfortable with speaking about his assaultive experience in most situations, William said that other queer men are the most likely to respond negatively when hearing that he contracted HIV from a sexual assault. In particular, he said that some queer men will "blame you [for a sexual assault] when they find out that you got HIV from it."

A few other HIV-positive participants described experiences in which this blame had been directed toward them by other sexual minorities. HIV-negative queer men may be especially likely to respond in this way because it may be comforting for this audience to believe that queer men living with HIV deserve some blame for their positive status, rather than this group thinking about their potential vulnerability to sexual assault and to sexually transmitted infections. Of course, heterosexual, cisgender people may also view HIV positive people as blameworthy for their status, yet participants living with HIV most frequently described worrying about these reactions from other queer men.

In addition to these attributions of blame, outsiders may perceive HIV-positive people as deceitful, given stereotypes of this group as untrustworthy.[4] Mendez, for example, a twenty-seven-year-old Black and Latino bisexual man, had a man rape him in the context of a hookup, where he acquired HIV from this assault. When explaining the effects of his HIV status, he said, "People think you're lying about how you got [HIV]. . . . Like, 'Oh, honey, you just don't want to admit that you got it because you're a hussy, so you gotta make up this story about you being raped.'" In this sense, a survivor's HIV-positive status may be used to dismiss the legitimacy of an assaultive experience. Hierarchies of an "innocent" versus "blameworthy" HIV-positive person sometimes rely on a contrast in which the former has acquired HIV in a romantic relationship, while the latter has contracted HIV from a casual sexual encounter. These hierarchies pathologize consensual sex and point toward the need to decouple HIV from discourses of blame. They also overlap with some hierarchies of victimhood, described in the previous chapter, in which individuals may construct blameworthy survivors as extraordinarily sexual.

While in most cases Mendez thought that HIV-positive people are disbelieved about a sexual assault, he argued that if they are believed, then others will think "well, why'd you get with him? . . . Like he has a sign on his head." This notion also overlaps with victim blaming outlined in previous chapters, resembling the pathologizing of "dangerous" DL men described in chapter 1. Yet, the stigmatizing of individuals living with HIV is unique in some important ways as well. Assumptions exist that individuals living with HIV can be easily identified. Additionally, media representations of a "dangerous" HIV-positive person have a long history in the United States, with constructions such as a heavily pathologized stereotype of someone purposely looking to transmit the virus to others.[5]

Media discourse during the AIDS crisis of the 1980s routinely scapegoated gay and bisexual men in these ways, which helped to justify widespread indifference to the epidemic. During this time, media representations, such as the famous "Patient Zero" one focusing on a gay male Canadian flight attendant, Gaëtan Dugas, were often presented as white gay men, since homosexuality was understood largely as a threat to the white family.[6] Thus, homophobic representations at the time frequently operated on these grounds, as LGBTQ people of color were generally excluded from mainstream media.[7]

Nevertheless, the "Patient Zero" representation historically and media portrayals now sometimes focus on foreign-born HIV-positive people who are positioned as coming to the United States and deliberately transmitting the virus to others. In this sense, these stereotypes of HIV-positive people may strengthen xenophobia by positioning migrants and immigrants as manipulative or untrustworthy. Indeed, Herman, a thirty-six-year-old Black gay man who immigrated to the United States from Jamaica said that he only tells medical personnel he trusts about his HIV status, since he worries about others viewing this matter through a xenophobic lens, in which he would be perceived as "bringing HIV here." Although in this book I have focused more on race, gender, and sexuality as significant power relations for understanding sexual assault, these findings indicate that HIV status also needs to be more fully understood as an important dimension of social inequality, including how it may overlap with other inequities such as those based on immigration status.

Herman also experienced housing discrimination, in which a landlord saw his IIIV medication with his mail and then subsequently demanded that he leave the apartment complex. Even though this practice is illegal, Herman felt that he had little recourse in terms of the law, since "it was my word against his." He thought that his landlord must have seen the medication because other people in his building became aware of his HIV status, but he did not have any proof or documentation that he could provide to a judge or lawyer.

While the landlord did not know Herman's status before looking through his mail, the subsequent outing of him as HIV positive to others in the building is another example of a nonconsensual disclosure. More broadly, formal and informal surveillance practices target HIV-positive people more frequently than their HIV-negative counterparts.[8] When describing the negative stereotypes of people living with HIV that may have led to his landlord's actions, Herman said, "I'm a 'disease carrier' then— that's how a lot of people think." These issues must also be understood intersectionally, as Black, transgender, and queer HIV-positive people may be perceived in especially negative ways. To be sure, after his landlord found his medication, Herman was called a "monster" by one of his neighbors, a white heterosexual woman.

Although white and heterosexual people living with HIV are frequently stigmatized, empathetic representations of people who have died
from AIDS-related complications have more frequently been presented
as white or heterosexual than Black and queer.[9] Only a small number of
HIV-positive respondents participated in this project, making comparisons across social groups difficult, yet white gay men did seem more comfortable than queer men of color with being out about their HIV status.
Inequalities experienced by HIV-positive people often rely on a division
in which some individuals are positioned as "sympathetic" or not at fault
for their contraction of HIV, while others become constructed as blameworthy and not sympathetic at all, as Herman's experience of being called
a "monster" indicates; these divisions are likely structured in part based
on race and sexuality. A positive status will generally increase the amount
of discrimination queer men experience regardless of racial identity, yet
others may also perceive HIV-positive people differently based on race.

Given the challenges outlined thus far, and given widespread structural
oppression facing people living with HIV, it is vital not to downplay these
challenges. At the same time, it remains important to account for discourses of HIV-positive people that mobilize support or empathy. I was
surprised that as many as six out of the sixty participants had an assaultive
experience in which their assailant was HIV positive and had transmitted
the virus to them. All of these participants thought that their assailant
was purposely trying to transmit the virus, since the assailant had made a
point of not using a condom during the assault.

My concern here is that sexual assault against queer men may become
positioned as disproportionately serious when an assailant purposely
transmits HIV to the survivor. An implied contrast could operate here, in
which other, "regular" forms of assault that do not involve the purpose-
ful transmission of HIV may be constructed as comparatively inconsequential. Pressures undoubtedly exist on people living with HIV who have
become positive from a sexual assault to construct their assailant as in-
tentionally transmitting the virus to them—given the cultural currency of
this stereotype—yet it remains important to be mindful of HIV-positive
people who cannot rely on this narrative. The deceitful part of the stereotype can also have negative consequences for HIV-positive survivors,
as their disclosure of sexual assault may be dismissed under assumptions
that this group is untrustworthy. In short, research on sexual assault must

avoid perpetuating this stereotype and reinforcing notions of HIV-positive people as conniving or malicious.

OUTING ISSUES RELATED TO BDSM

Respondents who spoke about their participation in BDSM described concerns around outing as well. For instance, Allen, a thirty-eight-year-old white gay man, was sexually assaulted by a male sex partner at a BDSM-themed party. The BDSM scene or encounter began with a verbal contract in which Allen said to the man, "I want you to be rough with me, but if I tell you to stop or if I tell you that it's hurting, I will expect you to stop." They agreed on a safeword, which Allen did not remember at the time of the interview but said that it was "something unusual," since words such as "stop," "no," or "don't" are not always appropriate in a BDSM context, in which part of the erotic charge may come from the illusion of non-consent.

The agreement involved participation in watersports—a slang term for sexual activity that usually involves urinating or being urinated on by others—but Allen said that the man did not stop when Allen used the safeword. The assault involved the man forcibly urinating in Allen's mouth. During the interview, Allen described how him telling others about the assault meant not only revealing his experience as a survivor but also disclosing his interest in BDSM: "There's not a lot of people who know that about me, so I first have to get over telling them about me liking rough sex, humiliation. . . . It's an extra barrier to get through." He explained that his romantic partner knew about his interest in BDSM as well as the assault; a few close friends were also aware of his participation in kink, but he had not told them about his assaultive experience.

When I asked Allen his reasons for not telling these close friends about the assault, given that they knew about his interest in BDSM, he said, "They are very supportive, but I don't want them to think like, 'Oh, this happened because you're into kink.'" I have noted many examples throughout this book in which participants worried about their assaultive experiences being used in this way—by connecting their sexualities with the assault. This type of discourse is undoubtedly pathologizing, as it relegates sexual assault to particular sexualities. Although queer men who were not interested in BDSM frequently worried about these reactions, some differences also existed in this regard.

The association of BDSM with sexual abuse remains deeply engrained in the U.S. cultural imagination, as media representations have regularly presented kink as arising from sexual abuse.[10] For example, the popular book and film *Fifty Shades of Grey* includes a sequence in which the central male character who engages in some BDSM practices is revealed to have been sexually abused when he was young.[11] These narratives serve to "explain" sexualities that a mainstream audience likely perceives as taboo or pathological, as the assumption is that harmful events lead to purportedly negative sexual behaviors or identities. In contrast, more progress has occurred over the past several decades with regard to stereotypes linking homosexuality with sexual abuse.

Now, when I show historical documentaries in my classes in which gay men are positioned as pedophiles, or homosexuality is debated in relation to child molestation, my students largely view these debates as outdated relics of the past. These ideas undoubtedly continue to affect transgender people, and they have not disappeared, even with regard to homosexuality, as my students sometimes describe individuals such as their parents believing these stereotypes of gay men as child molesters. Still, being out with regard to BDSM does not carry the same cultural weight in the United States as being out with regard to homosexuality; these differences may lead to some important disparities for survivors. Homosexuality and BDSM are not mutually exclusive, yet I was struck by how little Allen described concerns over discrimination for being gay, since most people already knew that information, and since he viewed BDSM as the more central barrier in terms of disclosing his assaultive experience.

Regarding BDSM, Allen detailed multiple concerns with disclosing the assault, as he thought that some people would say "that's just rough sex, not assault" and he worried that others would view nonconsensual sex acts as intrinsic to BDSM. Indeed, BDSM is often interpreted as assaultive by outsiders, regardless of what happens, since discriminatory understandings link it with abuse.[12] For this reason, BDSM communities have often gone out of their way to emphasize the consensual nature of kink, as the commonly known "safe, sane, and consensual" (SSC), as well as the more recent "risk aware consensual kink" (RACK), draw attention to how BDSM sexual practices are consensual.[13] Research indicates that BDSM practitioners are no more likely than the general population to experience sexual assault or to have to go to the hospital for physical injuries.[14] Thus, this discourse that links BDSM with abuse needs to be understood as mistaken and prejudicial.

Of course, sexual assault occurs in BDSM communities, as it does in others, and when individuals involved in BDSM have been sexually assaulted, they have sometimes experienced pressures to remain silent, due to notions that they should not reinforce stereotypes of these communities.[15] Allen explained that he had told other BDSM practitioners at the party about what had happened to him, and they responded angrily toward the assailant, attempting to find him and ban him from the premises. In this sense, BDSM-community norms frequently facilitate consent, even though the non-BDSM public may be unaware of the rules and practices in these communities designed to produce consensual activity.

Moreover, a lot of work in BDSM communities has helped to establish nuanced understandings of consent.[16] In comparison with mainstream approaches, BDSM encounters typically involve not only more discussion and negotiation of consent prior to and during sex but also greater consideration of risk. While mainstream understandings of consent often demand "safety," BDSM approaches more commonly suggest that no sexual activity is truly safe or free of risk. From this perspective, it makes little sense to distinguish between "safe" and "unsafe" activities, as only "safer" and "less safe" sexual practices exist. A model of consent that insists on "safety" can be used to pathologize forms of BDSM, since kink may achieve its erotic charge from practitioners engaging in sexual practices frequently considered "unsafe." Thus, rather than positioning safety as paramount, BDSM models of consent encourage sexual participants to accept and negotiate the risks that accompany sex acts.

In addition to consent, race remains important to consider in these accounts, as I noticed some intra-racial differences among queer men involved in BDSM and those who were not. White queer men, for example, may differ intersectionally in some significant ways based on whether they belong to BDSM communities. Only two white queer men spoke about their participation in BDSM-related sexual activities or communities, but Allen, as well as the other white participant, placed more emphasis on community-based concerns than white respondents who were not involved in BDSM. Allen said, "I don't want to give people more ammo" when describing how others may use an assault that occurs during kink to stigmatize BDSM to a greater extent. He viewed these notions as misguided—after all, when more vanilla forms of sex, or sexual behavior that does not involve kink, are assaultive, these sex acts are not usually pathologized more broadly.

Although several people in Allen's life knew about his interest in kink, another one of these participants, Darius, a thirty-four-year-old Black bisexual man, had told only one other person, a former partner, about his interest in BDSM.[17] Darius never experienced sexual assault in the context of a BDSM encounter. However, an ex-boyfriend of his, after they had broken up, threatened to send nude pictures and video of Darius performing BDSM-related activities to Darius's friends. He had engaged in kink with his former partner during their relationship and they had recorded and taken pictures of some of their sexual activities together. His ex-boyfriend still had possession of most of this imagery. The threat or practice of releasing sexually explicit images without a person's consent—sometimes colloquially known as "revenge porn"—caused Darius considerable distress, as he described not being able to sleep for several weeks after the threats had occurred. His ex-boyfriend never released any of this imagery, at least not to Darius's knowledge, yet the threats still seemed to have an effect on him two years after they had occurred, given that he still worried at times about the images circulating.

While mainstream media have often focused on these "revenge porn" cases in relation to heterosexual women, my results here indicate that queer men have these experiences as well.[18] Further, Darius's experience reveals that outing should be understood in expansive ways. He said that he was "out to everyone" in terms of his bisexuality, but he worried about friends and family members "looking at [him] differently—like a 'sick person'" if they learned that he was involved in kink. Undoubtedly, aspects of biphobia may overlap with and amplify these concerns of being viewed as a "sick person," yet queer men may also be out with regard to their gay or bisexual identity, but not in terms of their involvement in BDSM. In short, it is important to understand outing as involving sexual practices and identities that are often included under the "queer" part of the LGBTQ acronym. Individuals who are out to a greater extent regarding their participation in BDSM may have different experiences than the respondents in this study, yet my overall point here is that research and advocacy focusing on sexual assault would benefit from further considering the perspectives of survivors who engage in kink and, more broadly, who challenge conventional approaches to sex.

EXPANDING UNDERSTANDINGS OF OUTING

Overall, participants experienced and worried about multiple forms of outing. These nonconsensual disclosures may occur in the traditional way that the word "outing" is meant to signify—the revealing of someone's LGBTQ identity without their consent. That concern may interact with and magnify other forms of outing, such as nonconsensual disclosure of sexual assault. Participants frequently had negative experiences with coming out as queer in the past—some of which involved them being outed by others—which then usually made them more fearful about disclosing an assaultive experience.

These concerns became even more complex and weighty when considering HIV or BDSM, as participants who discussed these matters spent the most time describing concerns around outing. All of these forms of outing need to be understood as harmful, and scholarship on sexual assault as well as work in sexualities studies would benefit by using expansive understandings of outing to include aspects beyond LGBTQ identity. When accounting for participants' experiences of disclosing multiple stigmatized identities, I found that this process is fraught with overlapping tensions and issues, as these identities generally intersected with one another to heighten anxieties over coming out as someone who belongs to a marginalized group.

Conclusion

FUTURE CHALLENGES AND POSSIBILITIES

In terms of productive paths forward, scholarship and advocacy would benefit by continuing to shift away from an individualistic framework, in which attention is devoted to singular assailants, and toward a broader, more social, approach in which greater consideration is given to the social conditions that facilitate sexual assault.[1] Dominant constructions of masculinity are undoubtedly one area in which such social changes are needed, but they are not the only one; as I have argued throughout this text, challenges to heteronormativity and racial inequality should be more deeply incorporated into work combatting sexual violence. One reason a shift toward more social approaches remains necessary is because many participants, particularly those who were Black, had experiences in which their assailant was constructed in quite negative terms—for example, as "dangerous" when perceived as a masculine man—to position the survivor as someone who "should have known better" than to become involved with the assailant. These survivors, then, do not benefit from narratives that pathologize assailants in this way.

The word *rapist* may even bring to mind notions of assailants as extraordinarily troubled or demented. Mainstream media have often presented men who rape as "bad apples," or isolated cases, while a lot of feminist work has framed men's violence as connected with, rather than existing in opposition to, hegemonic forms of masculinity.[2] Feminist research has challenged traditional understandings that "most men"—at least who are white and middle class—would never commit sexual assault. Instead, this line of work has revealed the links between normative masculinity and sexual assault perpetration, as male assailants may attempt to assert or maintain a masculine sense of self through their assaultive behavior.[3]

With regard to survivors, my findings throughout this book, on the one hand, are consistent with a lot of sexual assault scholarship and advocacy that has highlighted the prevalence of victim blaming and the minimization of survivors' experiences.[4] Participants across the lines of race, sexuality, and gender identity had negative experiences disclosing a sexual assault or reporting it to the police, although important differences existed here as well. I have also shown that many queer male survivors—like women who experience this violence—blame themselves for the assault.[5] Additionally, some respondents blamed other survivors and reproduced hierarchies of victimhood by pathologizing consensual sex and by constructing feminine survivors as more blameworthy than masculine ones. Thus, this research adds to existing theories of sexual assault that have emphasized the pervasiveness of anti-survivor discourses in a US context, which even some survivors may reproduce.[6]

On the other hand, while survivors across the lines of race, gender, and sexuality confront many pathologizing notions, I have also revealed that queer male survivors' challenges differ based on their social position. For this reason, theories of sexual assault would benefit by continuing to destabilize uniform understandings of survivors and their experiences. Many survivors struggle with stigmatizing ideas, but it is also the case that stereotypes of marginalized groups intersect with these notions to disadvantage some survivors more than others.

Understandably, sexual assault scholarship and advocacy has frequently drawn attention to the scope of the social problem of sexual assault and, in doing so, has sometimes presented survivors' challenges broadly. Emphasizing the degree to which many survivors are not supported in a US context remains necessary, yet this broad emphasis can obscure important differences and conceal the experiences of more marginalized survivors. For instance, previous research has shown that outsiders may blame male survivors for not physically preventing their assaultive experiences, due to hegemonic understandings of masculinity.[7] My work here has revealed that queer male survivors face these notions, yet I found that racialized stereotypes led to some important differences in this regard.

In particular, Black participants were the least likely to be able to rely on constructions of themselves as physically weaker than their assailants, given stereotypes associating Black men with strength or aggression. Consequently, in centering the experiences of Black queer men, strength becomes a particularly problematic point of emphasis, as outsiders may read the bodies of Black men as especially strong and therefore blame them most harshly for not physically resisting a sexual assault. In this sense, it is not that masculinity is irrelevant for understanding male survivors' experiences, but that it intersects with race to such an extent that theories of sexual assault would improve by accounting for both of them simultaneously.

Focusing solely on gender or masculinity can obscure these complexities or even reinforce aspects of racial inequality. Another example from this study is how participants of color did not perceive their assaultive experiences through the lens of emasculation, revealing that this response should not be understood as a universal one for male survivors, but may instead be linked disproportionately with whiteness. By adopting an intersectional approach, research can expose these differences, helping to not only move beyond monolithic representations but also account for the experiences of survivors who are marginalized by more mainstream discourse.

With this research project, I obviously do not have data on assailants or their motivations, only participants' perceptions of them, but future work in this area would benefit by drawing further connections between the enactment of sexual assault and other systems of oppression, beyond institutional sexism. Understanding sexual assault in relation to multiple dimensions of inequality helps with explaining and drawing attention to high rates of assault experienced by multiply marginalized individuals, such as Black women and LGBTQ people of color.[8] Further, conceptualizing sexual assault as a violent practice rooted in multiple systems of oppression facilitates a better understanding of how it operates, allowing feminist and intersectional work to account for forms of assault in which gender inequality may be less apparent and to examine how assailants' actions can reproduce, or emerge from, several social hierarchies.

If sexual assault is understood as arising out of multiple systems of inequality, then the importance of simultaneously challenging several of these systems becomes more apparent as well. Of course, forms of sexual assault may involve different factors than violence or even force, as some violations may not feel particularly "forceful" to survivors, many of whom do not experience any visible signs of physical injury.[9] The "violence" in this conceptualization of sexual assault should thus be understood broadly, as something that causes harm, not as an act that necessarily produces outward physical consequences, such as scarring or bruising.

FURTHER INTERSECTIONAL COMPLICATIONS

In further incorporating intersectionality, sexual assault scholarship can help with shifting away from a focus on marginalized assailants, especially those who are oppressed based on race or class. Research has shown that media overrepresent the amount of crime that Black men in particular commit, both in terms of the news and in fictional representations such as film and television.[10] Consequently, many consumers of media become socialized into understanding crime through a racialized lens. Even when an assailant's race or ethnicity is not identified in such reporting, the concern is that viewers will imagine an already-marginalized assailant as committing the violence, given the predominance of this cultural narrative around crime.

Historically, the racializing of sexual assault has led to an interracial positioning of not only Black assailants but also white victims.[11] Highlighting the experiences of multiply marginalized survivors can help to rectify some of this traditional emphasis. Changing representation remains important to a degree, as greater attention has been devoted to racially marginalized assailants than racially marginalized survivors. As I have argued, stereotypes of Black men, linking this group with masculinizing characteristics, may prevent individuals from thinking about Black men as survivors.

While critiquing masculinizing stereotypes of Black men remains important, sexual assault scholarship and advocacy—and, more broadly, men and masculinities research—would benefit by breaking down assumptions that link male femininity with whiteness. In considering the experiences of Black queer men with feminine gender expressions, a whitening of male femininity contributes to the exclusions facing this group of men. Survivors, including those who are male, have traditionally been gendered feminine, and yet because of stereotypes of Black and Latinx men, and because of a whitening of male femininity, queer men of color with feminine gender expressions have typically not figured into representations of survivors.[12] The particular dynamic that deserves further critique or consideration is how white queer men's femininity may be viewed as the most authentic enactment of this gender expression, while Black and Latinx queer men may have their femininity perceived as contrary to racialized, masculinizing stereotypes and, therefore, as "less authentic" expressions of male femininity. These differences can then affect how vulnerable to sexual assault others may perceive these groups, with outsiders viewing white queer men who have feminine gender expressions as more "natural" survivors than their Black or Latinx counterparts.

In this text, while I have advanced an intersectional approach for understanding sexual assault against queer men, it would be beneficial to utilize this approach further to complicate traditional understandings of men and masculinities more broadly. Scholarship on men and masculinities has drawn important attention to comparatively privileged men, such as those who are white, heterosexual, and middle class, yet intersectional silences can occur when more marginalized groups of men are not incorporated into this line of research. Other areas of study regarding men and masculinities would benefit by further centering the experiences of more marginalized men, as sexual assault scholarship is not the only area in which groups such as Black queer men have received relatively little attention.[13]

EXAMINING GROUP-BASED DIFFERENCES AND
EXPANDING REPRESENTATIONS OF SURVIVORS

Sexual assault scholarship concerned with race and gender is in a difficult position in some respects, as this work may want to emphasize different victimization rates for various social groups while also avoiding an essentializing of male assailants and female victims. A desire not to lose sight of the gendered enactment of sexual violence has led scholars such as Joanna Bourke to call for a "reinterrogation of the masculine," since "men act in sexually aggressive ways much more frequently than women."[14] Concurrently, naturalizing men as rape offenders or women as rape victims can marginalize experiences that fall outside of this framework and can reinforce binary gender notions of "passive" women and "active" men.[15] As a result, managing these tensions requires being attuned to power structures that shape the unequal distribution of sexual violence across social groups, while also resisting dichotomous, essentialist frameworks that position women as powerless and men as agentic.[16]

A history of anti-feminist "men's rights" discourse has also created a false equivalency between men's and women's violence in heterosexual relationships.[17] In taking this history seriously, feminist analyses of sexual assault such as mine here need to be careful about making it seem as if all social groups commit and experience equivalent rates of assault.[18] At the same time, in attempting to push beyond the common media focus on white women survivors, scholarship has often emphasized group-based differences showing that white women do not experience most of this violence.[19] While it would be beneficial to broaden understandings of survivors in more intersectional directions, group-based differences in terms of victimization rates are not always exactly knowable, given that various data sets reveal different trends.[20] Moreover, as most of these data reveal sexual victimization rates for white women that are still quite high—and they generally appear even higher for Black and Latinx women—perhaps the more important point is that many social groups in the United States continue to experience sexual assault at rates that are far too high.[21]

While avoiding hierarchies of survivors across gender lines, I similarly want to avoid a debate that ranks the experiences of queer men and heterosexual, cisgender men, as I have written this book in the spirit of solidarity for survivors across the lines of gender and sexuality. Still, these groups face some different challenges, and it remains troubling to me when I hear individuals construct queer male survivors as more privileged or respected than their heterosexual, cisgender counterparts. I have heard these arguments in light of evidence that queer men may figure most prominently in representations of male survivors.[22] Heterosexual, cisgender men certainly face challenges that queer men do not, as research shows that the former may have their sexual identity dismissed or questioned, becoming labeled as bisexual or homosexual when disclosing that they have been sexually assaulted by another man.[23]

However, other research indicates that outsiders tend to perceive male-perpetrated sexual assault as "worse" when it is experienced by heterosexual men than by queer men, since the former group of survivors can more easily be understood as not desiring or not consenting to have sex with a male assailant.[24] That is, outsiders may view queer men as consenting to assaultive acts—or as "asking for it"—when the assailant is a man, while understanding some heterosexual men with similar experiences as not consenting, given their attraction to women. Conversely, more research remains necessary on the experiences of male survivors with female assailants, as some studies indicate that rape myths for men operate most intensely when the assailant is a woman, with others minimizing the assault as "pleasurable" for men who are, or are assumed to be, heterosexual.[25] It would be helpful for future work on male survivors to remain attuned to these different challenges and experiences, without reinforcing simplistic debates over which group of survivors "has it the worst," since that discourse prevents solidarity and coalition building.

Some solidarity among survivors across the lines of race, gender, and sexuality remains important, yet a continual push to diversify and expand representations of survivors is also needed. Intersectional representations have begun to increase in media as of late, as the recent HBO show *I May Destroy You* features a Black queer man's assaultive experience and the HBO documentary *On the Record*, from the makers of *The Hunting Ground*, shines attention on Black women's assaultive experiences. Complicating traditional narratives is important and can certainly be accomplished in other ways than I have done in this text, as a wide range of survivors—including queer women of color, immigrants, and asexual people—have received relatively little attention in sexual assault scholarship, despite some notable exceptions.[26]

Although my argument is in part that the inclusion of a wider range of survivors into feminist theorizing on sexual assault would likely improve understandings of this social problem, focusing even on Black queer men's assaultive experiences is not inevitably intersectional or forward thinking. Changing portrayals of survivors in more intersectional ways is part of what remains necessary, yet simply reducing intersectionality to this notion is counterproductive, as representations focusing on multiply marginalized groups can still be unhelpful, and intersectional approaches demand more substantive or transformative changes. Situated in an interdisciplinary Women, Gender and Sexuality Department, I find myself increasingly interested in academic work that speaks to real-world social problems. Thus, in the remainder of this conclusion, I outline some tensions and possibilities between work devoted to combatting sexual assault and to challenging mass incarceration, ultimately advancing an anti-punitive or anti-criminalization approach for reducing sexual violence.

ADVANCING AN ANTI-CRIMINALIZATION APPROACH FOR COMBATTING SEXUAL ASSAULT

While tensions undoubtedly exist between advocacy against mass incarceration and work attempting to reduce sexual assault, moving forward, scholarship can do more to connect these forms of advocacy with one another. That is, movements working to combat mass incarceration can be understood as benefiting survivors, and attempts to reduce sexual assault can be further linked with anti-criminalization work. For instance, research reveals that Black women experience high rates of sexual assault in jails and prisons, often at the hands of the guards.[27] Latinx women, especially those who are migrants and immigrants, have also increasingly been subjected to sexual assault by state actors in detainment camps and carceral settings.[28] Work, then, that reduces the number of Black and Latinx women in carceral institutions can be understood as a practice that helps to diminish some forms of sexual assault.

LGBTQ people, especially those who are bisexual or transgender, also experience high rates of sexual violence in carceral settings, and yet the mainstream part of the LGBTQ-rights movement has not prioritized reducing the number of LGBTQ people in penal institutions.[29] Further, prior to their time spent in jail or prison, LGBTQ inmates experience high rates of sexual assault.[30] Even though research has focused on the sexual victimization experiences of incarcerated women more than men, a recent review of this body of scholarship showed that 56–82 percent of women in carceral settings have experienced sexual assault during their lifetime.[31] Consequently, sexual victimization and incarceration are highly correlated in the United States, at least for some populations, and advancing processes of criminalization would likely lead to the imprisonment of more survivors. Connections between anti-criminalization and anti-sexual assault advocacy already exist, as many survivors have engaged in activism opposed to mass incarceration, and social justice groups—such as the Black Youth Project 100 and Critical Resistance/INCITE!—have combatted sexual assault through an anti-punitive lens.[32]

Although the aim of an anti-criminalization approach to sexual violence is not to shame or condemn survivors who pursue criminal charges against their assailants, as this response may be understandable in many cases, this approach nevertheless insists that incarcerating more individuals for assault will not help reduce this violence and will make many social problems worse.[33] Moving away from criminal-legal approaches to solve sexual assault is not currently a mainstream position, even on the US political left, yet I hope through my writing of this book, that more individuals will at least give this perspective deeper consideration. I will leave how advocacy designed to reduce sexual assault operates without the criminal-legal system to those individuals more adept at organizing and building activist coalitions, but I hope this book contributes in some small way to these ongoing efforts.

While the changes I am arguing for here are certainly difficult and complicated to bring about, I believe that my position is consistent with the intersectional aims of this book and that ending mass incarceration requires ambitious goals or radical solutions. Accepting that the effects of mass incarceration have been abhorrent—ruining many lives and communities—necessitates resisting ideas that have justified carceral systems for this long. Incarceration has increased tremendously since the early 1970s, as 2.3 million people are currently in US prisons and jails, with an additional 4.4 million on probation or parole.[34] Additionally, with the increasing presence of militarized police and the greater use of tear gas and artillery equipment, funding for the criminal-legal system has taken on an outsized role in the United States.

Participants in this study did not generally express punitive or vengeful sentiments toward their assailants, which is consistent with some national survey data showing that most victims of crime prefer social spending to address the root causes of violence rather than to invest in carceral systems.[35] As a result, the current criminalization approach is not even necessarily what most survivors themselves would like to see implemented. In part, an anti-criminalization approach involves shifting away from a reliance on policing—which largely serves a reactive role, after a crime has occurred—toward more preventative measures, which address factors, such as economic ones, that lead to high rates of violence.[36] This part of anti-carceral work involves reducing economic precarity rather than investing in the criminal-legal system.

Notions of an extraordinarily violent or dangerous person, popularized through crime shows and serial-killer movies, imply that individuals who commit violence should be imprisoned for the sake of public safety. However, analyses of violence have shown that most of its forms can be understood as the product of contextual factors more than pathological personalities.[37] In this regard, the idea of "bad people" predisposed to crime is largely a media-generated myth, as it remains important to avoid constructions of assailants as warped or irreparable.

When discussions of prison abolition arise, a common refrain I hear is that "rapists and murderers" are the ones who should be incarcerated. Several years ago, I held some of these beliefs myself, although I now view this perspective as inadequate. I understand where it comes from—a desire to make the criminal-legal system more equitable and to reorganize priorities in a way that more accurately reflects the amount of harm caused by sexual assault. It indeed seems odd or unfair that many people are currently serving jail time for low-level, nonviolent criminal offenses such as for drugs charges, unpaid fines, and missed court dates when many survivors cannot even get their cases to proceed beyond an initial report to the police. This warped sense of priorities, however, does not mean that greater investment in the criminal-legal system will help improve conditions facing survivors.

One problem with the notion that priorities should be adjusted to focus on acts such as rape and murder is that assumptions are built into it that we can build an equitable or race-neutral criminal-legal system. I no longer think this type of reform is possible, as any society in which "danger," "guilt," and "criminality" are racialized will lead to unequal criminalizing practices based on race. Connections between policing and racial inequality have deep historical roots in the United States, as the first municipal police departments, with origins in slave patrols, were instituted to control a "dangerous underclass."[38]

In considering social class, the very nature of the criminal-legal system perpetuates inequality because policing and prosecution in this country disproportionately affect people living in poverty. Making sexual assault law more punitive may result in a greater number of high-income assailants becoming incarcerated, but it would much more significantly expand the imprisonment of low-income Americans. Assailants who can afford high-paying lawyers would disproportionately continue to evade imprisonment. Since race affects class in this country, these power relations compound one another to disadvantage low-income people of color in particular. In short, the criminal-legal system contributes to, rather than reduces, social harms, and those committed to combatting sexual assault should look for alternatives outside of this apparatus.

ALTERNATIVES TO INVESTING IN CARCERAL SYSTEMS

Scholarship has emphasized how the prison system of today, in which imprisonment is the main punishment for many crimes, is a relatively recent historical development, as incarceration was unusual in Europe and America at the beginning of the eighteenth century.[39] During and before this time, offenders were typically only imprisoned temporarily, until the actual punishment was carried out.[40] In this sense, it remains important not to naturalize the current criminal-legal system and the ubiquity of long-term imprisonment as having always existed. Alternatives to incarceration abound in feminist scholarship critical of mass incarceration.[41] Restorative justice and transformative justice are two of the more common alternatives proposed, although these practices have produced a considerable amount of debate and disagreement among prison abolitionists as well.[42]

Although restorative and transformative justice differ, both involve a more community-based approach to justice, departing from a retributive model of punishment and involving a collaborative process that seeks to enable repair.[43] Community members work together to hold offenders accountable and to help survivors.[44] In this sense, offenders are not typically incarcerated or excluded from the community, and victims are given access to justice without being required to utilize the criminal-legal system.[45] By involving community members, these approaches aim to increase public awareness of the harm caused by various forms of violence, improving attitudes regarding the permissibility of these acts, and decreasing the likelihood they will be committed again in the future.[46]

Restorative justice may involve organized face-to-face meetings between the victim and offender that are supervised by a trained professional, in which survivors may speak with their assailants directly to articulate the pain caused to them and to work toward a consensus concerning how the assailant can repair harm.[47] Aims of restorative justice programs include giving survivors a more active role after the offense and providing them with therapeutic benefits. An additional goal is to help assailants acknowledge the harm they have caused, ultimately aiming to decrease their likelihood of reoffending.[48] Scholars such as Mimi Kim and Chloë Taylor have expressed concern that restorative justice approaches are being co-opted by the criminal-legal system, as they may be used as a court-sanctioned alternative to imprisonment, still with ties to sentencing and with the process sometimes taking place entirely within a jail or prison.[49] Other, albeit limited, research indicates that some restorative justice programs have been effective for both the survivor and assailant; victims have reported higher levels of approval with the process and offenders appear less likely to reoffend in comparison to incarceration.[50]

Scholars who prefer transformative justice have argued that this approach helps with altering structural conditions and addressing the root causes of violence.[51] This approach, which may be viewed as somewhat imprecise given its insistence on pushing for far-reaching structural transformation, tends to emphasize the importance of collective organizing.[52] Mimi Kim refers to transformative justice as "community accountability" and "community-based responses to violence," in which social justice groups have worked outside of state-run institutions to reduce both interpersonal and state-sanctioned forms of violence.[53] Most directly, this process operates through community accountability, in which individuals trained in violence reduction engage directly with the person who has caused harm, striving toward a scenario in which the assailant takes accountability for the harm they have caused, apologizes to those adversely affected, and commits to changing their behavior.[54]

These strategies are designed to "transform" those who caused harm and to cultivate beneficial dynamics, such as healing, justice, and accountability, rather than reproducing aspects of the criminal-legal system, such as shame, revenge, and isolation, that continue oppressive social conditions.[55] In this broader sense, transformative justice groups challenge systems of oppression, addressing sexism, racism, and anti-LGBTQ prejudice within communities.[56] These groups also tend to be anti-capitalist and anti-imperialist, organizing through an intersectional social justice lens and facilitating strong community building to prevent future forms of abuse.[57]

Other scholars and prison abolitionists have argued against both restorative and transformative justice, as considerable debate exists among anti-criminalization advocates regarding the extent to which they should engage with the state.[58] Some approaches, which may be linked with transformative justice, favor working outside of state apparatuses, while others demand a change to state funding priorities.[59] These tactics are also not mutually exclusive, given that prison abolitionists may simultaneously attempt to create non-state alternatives and to alter the state's resource allocation for social service programs vis-à-vis the criminal-legal system.[60] Regardless of the favored approach, the larger, more important point is that resistance to the carceral state takes on many forms and encompasses a wide range of practices, as the goal of much of this work is to expand the availability and acceptance of non-carceral frameworks.[61] Divesting from carceral institutions generally remains an important goal of this work, with the reallocation of funding from the criminal-legal system to more productive causes.

Broadly speaking, this process of divesting from the criminal-legal system and investing in programs designed to reduce the enactment of sexual assault aligns with leftist social justice causes that involve economic redistribution.[62] For example, greater funding for social programs designed to reduce sexual assault may include anti-poverty measures and more resources for education, housing, and health care, as well as racial justice policies such as reparations and greater investment in Black communities.[63] Given that many forms of sexual assault occur in relationships, rectifying economic stressors that contribute to intimate partner violence and keep survivors entrapped in violent relationships remains particularly important in this regard.[64] Sexual assault and intimate partner violence frequently overlap and cannot be understood as entirely separate phenomena, even if some survivors experience sexual violations in other contexts. Moreover, evidence indicates that police officers commit intimate partner violence at higher rates than the general US population.[65] This trend points to the possibility of abusive officers being called upon to help survivors and further reveals a need for alternatives to policing.

TROUBLING CRIMINALIZATION AND PREVENTING SEXUAL ASSAULT

In many rural locations, strong community cohesion correlates with high rates of sexual assault and intimate partner violence; in such locales, expectations regarding privacy and patriarchy discourage victims from speaking about their experiences and contribute to the social acceptance of gender-based violence.[66] As a result, the relationship between social conditions and the enactment of sexual assault does not always operate similarly to other forms of violence. Low community cohesion tends to produce high rates of many other forms of violence, while a large amount of this cohesion can result in elevated frequencies of sexual assault.

Despite these complexities, the debate over criminalization as a strategy for reducing sexual assault focuses in part on the effects of incarceration. Investment in the criminal-legal system directs resources away from structurally marginalized communities, increasing the number of incarcerated people from those neighborhoods and fueling community economic instability, which is highly correlated with elevated levels of intimate partner violence in many areas.[67] Leigh Goodmark has characterized the current US reliance on prisons and jails as one in which "criminalization creates the very conditions that spur the violence that it seeks to remedy."[68] Greater investment in criminalization than in anti-poverty social service programs generally results in high rates of both violence and incarceration.[69] Historically, increases in criminalization have occurred along with cuts to social welfare programs, as cultural changes with neoliberalism have positioned punitive approaches toward poor communities as preferable to governmental aid.[70] Anti-carceral work is in part about reversing these patterns and priorities, by instead investing in a wide range of prevention and social service programs rather than the criminal-legal system.

Feminist scholarship has pointed out that some forms of violence such as sexual assault are not necessarily primarily committed in low-income communities, as rates of sexual victimization remain relatively high in places such as college campuses, where individuals are disproportionately middle class.[71] Consequently, social programs devoted to diminishing sexual violence need to extend beyond those designed to reduce poverty. Goodmark has suggested further funding for educational media and has provided many examples of programs, largely with boys and men, that challenge associations of masculinity with abusive behavior, such as the MenCare campaign, Fathers for Change, and Fourth R: Strategies for Healthy Youth Relationships; some of these programs have shown to be effective in reducing gender-based violence.[72]

With these programs, the primary emphasis on gender and masculinity, but not heteronormativity and racial inequality, indicates some possible shortcomings, especially in terms of benefiting LGBTQ people, racial minorities, and others who experience structural oppression beyond institutional sexism. Accounting for racial inequality and heteronormativity in sexual assault programming may appear daunting, but such a shift remains necessary given the high rates of sexual violence experienced by Black men, women of color, and LGBTQ people of color. Scholarship has pointed out that much of the programming devoted to sexual assault on college campuses remains heteronormative, revealing a strong need to integrate LGBTQ issues into curricula, policies, and programs.[73] Since LGBTQ-specific workshops have more frequently focused on lesbian and gay issues than on bisexual, pansexual, or transgender ones, integrating a wider range of LGBTQ matters remains particularly important. Bisexual, pansexual, and transgender students' abusive experiences may overlap in some ways with those of lesbian and gay students, yet the former groups confront unique structural barriers and forms of assault, as their experiences cannot be collapsed with those of the latter groups.[74]

Beyond college campuses, more broadly anti-carceral advocacy involves concentrating on preventing sexual violence before it happens.[75] As it stands, the current approach to curbing sexual assault in the United States is not benefiting most survivors. The more marginalized survivors are, the less current approaches appear to work for them. What would benefit survivors is for their assaultive experiences not to occur in the first place. The criminal-legal system establishes itself as playing a role in prevention, but this myth is one that queer and feminist work can help to dispel, as much of this scholarship has underscored evidence that criminalization does not reduce gender-based violence.[76] In this sense, anti-carceral work involves decoupling "safety" from policing and criminalizing.

COMMUNITY-BASED AGENCIES AND SURVIVOR-CENTERED SERVICES

A shift toward more community-based forms of accountability could reinforce problematic processes, as modern calls for "rehabilitation" have sometimes brought greater surveillance—for instance, "rehabilitating" offenders through extensive monitoring, including the use of ankle bracelets.[77] As currently established, the criminal-legal system expands well beyond incarceration, as burdensome surveillance requirements lead to many forms of criminalization, often for minor infractions such as breaking curfew or failing to pay court-mandated fees.[78] Expanding community-based supervision, then, while seemingly less harsh than imprisonment, is not the best way to reduce mass incarceration.[79]

Despite these concerns, a shift of resources away from the criminal-legal system could help produce greater aid not only for measures designed to reduce sexual assault but also for survivor-centered services. As survivors often need access to places that provide care, as well as possibly housing and employment, greater funding for organizations that do this work would be considerably better than continuing to use this funding for the criminal-legal system. The Violence Against Women Act (VAWA), while previously supporting many important programs outside of the criminal-legal system, including many for survivors, has been criticized by anti-carceral feminists for devoting too much of its funding to punitive institutions and organizations.[80] The most recent version of this Act, which was reauthorized in 2013, included approximately 85 percent of its funding for police, courts, prosecutors, and community-based agencies supporting law enforcement; this percentage has also increased over time.[81] Thus, it remains a continuous problem in which the criminal-legal system has been established as the primary mechanism for addressing gender-based violence, with more funding being channeled into this system than into social service programs.

CREATING ALTERNATIVES TO CALLING THE POLICE

As some participants' experiences revealed, survivors need non-policing agencies to contact when they are in immediate danger or in need of assistance. Community hotlines have taken hold in some locations for survivors and others to call, in which individuals with training in areas such as mental health or violence reduction show up without guns to help decrease harm and provide care.[82] Transformative justice groups may engage in this work, as it can be part of how advocates help to move away from carceral frameworks. These trained individuals may be referred to as "violence interrupters" or "crisis intervention specialists" who deescalate conflict and assist victims with executing a plan for enhancing safety.[83]

Groups striving to work outside of a criminalization framework frequently question why so few options exist for survivors in many locales beyond calling the police.[84] Thus, these groups may develop, or put survivors in contact with, non-policing agencies to call in cases of violence, as well as places in which survivors can access medical or therapeutic aftercare.[85] Native American feminist scholar Sarah Deer has argued for a process in which survivors can file for protection from their assailants with a tribal or local government, while also arguing that these immediate concerns need to be accompanied by a more long-term vision of social change that involves community activism.[86]

Additionally, it would be beneficial if alternatives to calling the police were more deeply internalized by outsiders, as some participants in this study had neighbors who contacted law enforcement after hearing an argument or listening to abuse; this contact resulted in police officers then traumatizing the survivor further. In the United States, a default position of calling the police frequently operates when individuals perceive others as troublesome or dangerous. This approach disproportionately harms marginalized groups, especially those who are Black or gender expansive, and points to the necessity of a cultural shift in which that default position is viewed as potentially harmful rather than necessary or beneficial. Other groups or individuals beyond the police can then be understood as more appropriate to serve as first responders.

Of course, some communities may discourage survivors from reaching out to others or even speaking about their assaultive experiences, due to expectations of silence and secrecy.[87] The ongoing challenge involves changing cultural expectations that demand survivors remain silent, while also not instituting the police as the most appropriate agency to contact when overhearing or witnessing abuse. "Intervening" to reduce sexual assault should be understood in relation to practices that challenge social inequalities rather than those that rely on reporting to police officers or authority figures. A survivor-centered approach necessitates shifting from outsiders' favored forms of intervention to what the survivor themselves would like to see done. Some survivors may want retribution through criminalization, but the broader political question concerns how we want to move forward in dealing with harm.

COMPLICATIONS WITH ANTI-CRIMINALIZATION FRAMEWORKS

Although I view an anti-punitive approach for combatting sexual assault as essential, this position nevertheless provides some of its own challenges. In particular, this approach can potentially contribute to a minimizing of the severity of sexual assault, as media representations have often downplayed its seriousness.[88] Some rape jokes are part of this social context, as are responses that accentuate how much an assailant's life will be harmed after an assault becomes public knowledge without considering the effects on the survivor. Indeed, cultural expectations in some contexts may establish the naming of an assailant as worse or more harmful than the assault itself. Survivors may be condemned simply for identifying their assailant because some assumption exists that they should remain silent or deal with the assault on their own.

An undermining of the severity of sexual assault has also been shown in some cases that have received media attention. Judges, for example, in some high-profile cases have expressed more concern for the well-being of alleged assailants than for their survivors, with one widely reported case involving a judge downplaying evidence of assault as "just a 16-year-old kid saying stupid crap to his friends."[89] Another example involves the case against Brock Turner, a nineteen-year-old Stanford University swimmer whose six-month jail sentence for sexually assaulting Chanel Miller, who was unconscious, sparked widespread outrage; this case included his father famously referring to the possibility of his son receiving jail time, as "a steep price to pay for 20 minutes of action."[90]

These examples reveal how sexual assault may be trivialized in terms of its severity. With such responses, priorities undoubtedly seem misplaced, with attention shifting away from the survivor's experience of harm. Work devoted to combatting criminalization could reinforce these notions by downplaying the seriousness of sexual violence. As I have shown in this text, multiple forms of blame exist in relation to sexual assault; survivors' self-blame, outsiders' negative responses, and survivors' blame directed toward one another have all been addressed throughout this book. Outsiders' victim blaming remains a significant problem, but survivors' undermining of their own and others' painful experiences is also important to discuss or challenge, as these types of blame can prevent coalitions from forming among survivors.

The enduring challenge is to continue to underscore the extent of the social problem of sexual assault, while simultaneously taking anti-criminalization seriously. This balance is not an easy one, as adopting an anti-punitive disposition sometimes necessitates a more forgiving approach toward individuals who have nevertheless engaged in behavior one may find morally wrong or questionable. For instance, I still recall several months after my assaultive experience when I visited my hometown in the Midwest, where a local case involved a high school boy who had superimposed the face of one of his classmates—a teenage girl—onto a porn actress's body and then sent around this video to several of their classmates. Since the girl was under the age of consent, the boy was being charged for distributing child pornography, ultimately pleading to a prison sentence of several years.

When this occurred, I viewed the boy's punishment as justified, while now it seems unwise to me. Spending time in prison is more likely to result in this boy circling in and out of the criminal-legal system for much of the rest of his life—and, yes, continuing to enact harmful behavior due to the psychological harm caused by carceral settings—than it is to prevent him from committing a sexual violation again. To be clear, I am not justifying the boy's actions, as internet-based sexual harassment against girls and women remains a widespread problem.[91] However, from my perspective, criminalizing these actions does not improve matters.

In one of my classes, I have used this example as a point of discussion and I have noticed that my students have expressed more punitive attitudes toward the boy since #MeToo became widely known in 2017. A legitimate concern thus exists that some activism within #MeToo is strengthening punitive beliefs concerning sexual assault, even as others committed to this advocacy continue to challenge carceral frameworks.[92] I do not have all of the answers here in terms of how to approach every assaultive act, but generally believe that work attempting to reduce sexual assault should be anti-carceral. Adopting an anti-punitive approach may be particularly difficult in the context of sexual assault, given that the conclusion of media reporting on famous cases tends to link punishment of the assailant with justice for the survivor.

Pointing to survivors' negative police experiences, as I have done in this book, is one way to advance anti-carceral perspectives regarding sexual assault, yet other survivors' more positive police experiences may be used to construct criminalization as advantageous. As work devoted to reducing sexual assault further incorporates intersectionality, the criminal-legal system can be understood as an insufficient apparatus for achieving justice and reducing inequality. Understanding carceral institutions as producing large amounts of violence repositions them as counterproductive for ending sexual assault.

COMPLICATIONS WITH RESISTING MASS INCARCERATION AND POLICE PROFILING

At times, on the US left, I have seen assumptions that mass incarceration would largely end by releasing inmates who have been imprisoned on drug-related charges. Although the criminalizing of drug offenses remains a significant problem, most individuals are incarcerated for other reasons, as four out of five people in US jails and prisons are currently locked up on a different charge.[93] Thus, it is a myth that solely releasing prisoners for drug offenses would end mass incarceration, as doing so would not return the United States to incarceration rates that existed prior to Nixon's and then Reagan's declaration of a "war on drugs."[94] Instead, deeper changes remain necessary. Given high rates of sexual assault in the United States, incarceration would expand dramatically, potentially to over 20 percent of the population, if every assaultive experience led to imprisonment.[95] Such an approach seems untenable to me, and incarcerating millions more people represents the opposite of an intersectional social justice framework that I am advancing in this text.

In relation to police profiling, media frameworks have often adopted this dichotomous framing, "Are you with the police or Black Lives Matter?" That framework may be used to facilitate greater allegiance with the latter, but these binaries frequently seem designed to stake out a "sensible middle ground," in which the question is asked to characterize both sides of the debate as extreme or wrongheaded. A more aggressive defense of the status quo may involve questions such as, "do you dislike the police?" or "do you think most cops are 'bad people'?" These questions construct the most measured response as one that falls somewhere in the middle of a dichotomous "police versus Black Lives Matter" framework.

This measured or implicitly idealized response is positioned as something akin to, "Some police officers need to be fired or punished, but not all of them are bad people." From my perspective, this framework is unhelpful because it relies on an individualistic framework of "bad people" rather than focusing on structures of inequality, as "good people" may nevertheless have biases of which they are unaware. Moving forward, it would be beneficial if anti-carceral work continued to tie police profiling practices with structures of inequality, rather than individualizing this behavior by focusing on the particular motivations or prejudices of individual officers.

BROADER HISTORICAL CHANGES OVER TIME IN UNDERSTANDINGS OF ANTI-LGBTQ VIOLENCE

Beyond criminalization and sexual assault, thinking more broadly about anti-LGBTQ violence provides an opportunity for examining historical changes and future possibilities. Only a short time ago, as recently as 2015, when I spoke about the phrase "hate crime" in my courses, students did not know what this term meant. At that time, students knew about cases in which anti-LGBTQ violence was implicitly and problematically understood as involving a Black male assailant attacking a white gay male victim. Then, in large part because of the election of Donald Trump in 2016, I began to notice a fairly abrupt shift. Suddenly, almost all of my students knew what the phrase "hate crime" meant and those previous understandings that focused on white gay men's violent experiences felt outdated to them. Transgender women of color were now understood as the prototypical survivor of anti-LGBTQ violence, and a focus on Black male assailants became understood as something that only conservatives would do.[96]

While many of these changes are steps in the right direction—focusing on the violent experiences of transgender women of color rather than white gay men is an improvement in advancing a more intersectional understanding of anti-LGBTQ violence—these changes also bring some of their own challenges. I do not view the greater understanding of "hate crime" as an improvement, as I have argued that this discourse, as well as the legislation that accompanies it, largely reinforces social inequalities; for example, passage of hate crime laws typically grants considerably more funding to the criminal-legal system.[97] Previously, since my students were unaware of the meaning of "hate crime," they were typically open to leftist critiques of the legislation. Now, this discourse has largely been accepted in liberal social circles as beneficial, making it more difficult to challenge in these arenas. Further, focusing on Black transgender women's violent experiences may reproduce stereotypes of a "dangerous" Black male assailant who is on the DL. Even these representations of violence against transgender women of color may do some similar work as previous narratives focusing on white gay men, as the focal point in both narratives may reinforce associations of Blackness with danger.

In addition, while drawing attention to transgender women of color's violent experiences may usefully highlight persistent racism and transphobia in the United States, this emphasis can become a problem when it serves as a check mark of sorts, without furthering intersectional engagement. Similar to how I have sometimes seen groups and individuals use "Black Lives Matter" in this way—to convey an enlightened racial sensibility that nevertheless does not involve anything beyond the articulation of this phrase—it is vital to remain attuned to how transgender women of color's violent experiences may be used in a way that prevents rather than facilitates further involvement in intersectional politics. To be clear, the problem is not with Black Lives Matter or a focus on transgender women of color's violent experiences, but with how some individuals have used these points of emphasis in a way that shields them from having to engage in racial or transgender social justice work. These points of emphasis may certainly be an entry into leftist or intersectional politics for many individuals, yet it also remains important not to use them as buzzwords that are supported by little else.

Another recent social change I have noticed is that many of these representations of violence against LGBTQ people and racial minorities involve a portrayal of assailants as white cisgender men. Media have focused on this violence in a way that reflects the current US political landscape, where a racist, homophobic, or transphobic person, perhaps associated with the far-right or positioned as a Trump supporter, commits the attack. These representations have typically been stranger attacks, which is a problem, given that most violence does not occur in this way and given that this emphasis is one of the ways that the criminal-legal system sustains itself: by constructing "safety" from strangers as paramount. Thus, what I would like to see more of moving forward is a focus not only on the violent experiences of multiply marginalized individuals but also on more routine forms of violence. The entire structure of focusing on stranger abductions or random attacks in a public setting is part of what needs to change, as it should not be understood as a progressive emphasis simply because the assailant belongs to the US political right.

The current cultural narrative of an individual on the right attacking an LGBTQ individual or a person of color aligns quite nicely with a media-generated, for-profit business model designed to attract audiences across the political spectrum. These narratives can reinforce punitive sensibilities, as the feeling this reporting tends to evoke is one of indignation, in which the individual on the right may be presented as psychologically disturbed or extraordinarily hateful. I make this argument not to defend prejudiced people on the right, but to advance a leftist critique of these more mainstream approaches.[98]

An additional concern is that this media coverage often, either implicitly or explicitly, positions the assailant as belonging to the white working class. This point of emphasis not only fits in with contemporary US politics but also reinforces class inequality. These representations may reinforce the biases of a middle-class audience, allowing this group to feel above, rather than implicated in, unequal power relations. For leftist and intersectional work, it remains important to address the needs of working-class people, including those who are white, as neoliberal reforms over the last several decades have deepened class inequality and eroded worker protections.[99] In relation to sexual assault, a history of presenting white low-income men as assailants exists, including in relation to sexual assault against men, as exemplified by a famous scene in the 1972 film *Deliverance*; a white man who is coded as low income rapes one of the male characters in the "back-woods" of northern Georgia, famously telling him to "squeal like a pig."[100]

Current understandings of social class and anti-queer violence also need to be contextualized historically, as perceptions have not always been as they are now. Throughout at least much of the first half of the twentieth century, homosexuality was associated with groups such as the white working class, and white people with class privilege expressed their dislike of same-gender sexuality to demonstrate their cultural sophistication.[101] Upper-class white heterosexual people engaged in anti-queer discrimination to shore up their class privilege, while linking homosexuality with more marginalized groups such as racial minorities and the white working class.[102] In this sense, while the white working class were once linked with homosexuality, that perception has altered considerably, where they are now figured into stereotypes of assailants of anti-queer violence. While historical change is certainly messy and does not follow a straight line of progress, it would be beneficial to challenge the values of the US upper class rather than continuing to facilitate their privilege through representations of anti-LGBTQ violence that deepen class inequality.[103]

CONCLUDING REMARKS: SEXUAL ASSAULT AND POWER RELATIONS

Narrowing in on sexual assault more specifically, a problematic understanding of this violence, as I have argued, involves an exclusive focus on the survivor's behavior prior to the violation. This emphasis may include a construction of survivors who engaged in consensual sexual activity as deserving some blame for their assaultive experience.[104] In moving away from individualistic and sex-negative approaches that demand "responsibility" through the avoidance of casual sexual encounters, a queer and feminist politics that centers notions of self-determination and bodily autonomy has a considerable amount of potential here. A rich history of LGBTQ activism, as well as reproductive justice work, has pointed to the importance of self-determination in terms of gender and sexuality, and approaches for combatting sexual assault would benefit by building on these traditions.[105]

Media representations of sexual assault tend to individualize the assailant's and survivor's actions, decontextualizing what happened from power relations based on race, gender, and sexuality. To use but one example of the importance of these power relations, gender inequality clearly remains implicated in sexual scripts and social understandings of consent.[106] That is, forms of sexual assault may occur due to gender expectations that a masculine partner's sexual pleasure is predominant and that these individuals are supposed to push for what they want, while the other person serves as the "gatekeeper" to refuse or accept those advances. A masculine partner may then assume that a "more feminine" partner secretly desires sex even when indicating otherwise.

These gendered and heteronormative scripts do not structure some queer relations, yet they are also not exclusive to heterosexual people, as participants at times thought that their assailants had privileged their own sexual needs due to an investment in dominant forms of masculinity. Problematizing cultural aspects that enable unpleasant sexual experiences would help with reducing rates of sexual assault and with making sexual relations more rewarding.[107] Joseph Fischel has referred to this approach as the politicizing of "bad sex."[108] If "bad sex" is further politicized, it helps with improving a wide range of unpleasant sexual experiences rather than focusing on a narrow set of assaultive experiences that appear more unambiguously horrific.

Some dominant frameworks for addressing sexual assault such as a "yes means yes" approach to sexual relations do not exactly help advance more complexity, as the straightforwardness of the phrase implies that the articulation of the word "yes" means exactly what it is intended to mean. Comprehensive sex education that includes instruction on consent has often failed in a US context, which suggests that these "yes means yes" approaches are even controversial in many locations. In such cases, this type of consent education is better than nothing, yet for institutions that already have education on consent, these forms of instruction would benefit by bringing in even more nuanced understandings. For example, even though many individuals may be silent during sexual relations or may not be able to speak for a range of reasons—how does one say "yes" or "no" with something in their mouth?—sexual assault has usually been understood by examining what the survivor said during the encounter. Instead, in accepting that assaults can and do occur without the articulation of any verbal discourse, sexual assault advocacy can help with focusing on more complex forms of assault and with understanding a survivor's silence in relation to broader structures of inequality.

My argument here is that understandings of sexual violence would benefit by continuing to become less definitive or clear-cut, as stereotypical constructions of rape define sexual victimization in narrow terms. That is, traditional approaches establish sexual assault not only as a stranger attack that perhaps occurs at night in a public space but also as an extreme act of force that may involve a weapon or include a brutal beating. These understandings exclude many survivors and can be used to dismiss many assaultive experiences. In short, they remain an impossible standard for many survivors to measure up to, also helping to protect more privileged assailants. Stranger attacks have long been linked with marginalized race and class groups, which means that as long as sexual assault remains defined in these narrow terms, it will be understood as an act that primarily marginalized assailants commit.

Throughout this book, I have argued that a variety of concepts—such as emasculation, police profiling and harassment, and even sexual assault itself—should be reimagined in more intersectional ways. Sexual assault scholarship has focused on gender and masculinity for a considerable amount of time now, and it is not that these aspects are unimportant or that they should be overlooked, but that other power relations—such as race and sexuality, as I have shown—are also integral and shape how gender operates as well. Focusing solely on gender or masculinity may reinforce perspectives that are disproportionately linked with whiteness or heterosexuality. In contrast, as challenges to multiple power relations become even more deeply integrated into work devoted to reducing sexual assault, this advocacy and scholarship can benefit a wider range of survivors and reveal the limitations of frameworks that privilege one form of inequality over other systems of oppression.

APPENDIX   Methods

I interviewed sixty queer men from July 2016 to August 2017, recruiting participants from a wide range of organizations in Atlanta and New York City, many of
which provide services for LGBTQ people of color. These two cities were chosen
for recruitment to attract a diverse group of respondents and a high percentage
of Black queer men. At the organizations, recruitment flyers were typically placed
on a bulletin board or in a waiting room; a few of these places posted the flyer on
their website, which helped with attracting individuals who would not visit the
organization in person. Most of these organizations focused on LGBTQ issues,
while a few others were devoted to survivors. The recruitment flyer read: "Do you
Identify as a Gay, Bisexual, or Queer Man, and Have You Experienced Rape or
Sexual Assault Since You've Been 18?" Emphasis was placed on adult experiences
of sexual assault to avoid recruiting men who had only encountered childhood
sexual abuse, although participants were asked about these experiences as well.[1]

Individuals interested in participating contacted me via phone or email. All
of the interviews took place in person, not on the phone or online, at a location
of the interviewee's choice. Respondents received $50 for their participation.
With respondents' permission, the interviews were all tape-recorded. Given the
sensitive nature of this study—asking queer men to share their experiences of
sexual assault with a stranger—the recruitment process was relatively slow, as
I sometimes had to wait several weeks before someone would contact me. This
process made it difficult to interview a large number of people quickly, but it
also gave me plenty of time to sharpen and refine the questions I asked—what

qualitative researchers characterize as their "interview protocol"—and allowed me to analyze some of the data at the same time as I was interviewing people.

Of course, many survivors would not want to volunteer for a study in which they would be asked questions pertaining to their assaultive experiences. Thus, the data presented in this book must be viewed in relation to this context, as queer male survivors who have volunteered for an interview-based study may differ in some important ways from those who would not. For instance, participants were likely out to others regarding their assaultive experiences to a greater extent than most queer male survivors. Indeed, about one-third of the participants in this study reported an experience of sexual assault to the police, which is a considerably higher percentage than what other research has revealed regarding survivors more generally.[2]

In this sense, respondents may have been more forthcoming regarding their assaultive experiences than most survivors. At the same time, a significant percentage of the sample—over one-third of participants—had not told anyone else before me about any of their assaultive experiences, as these respondents appeared to use the interview as an opportunity to disclose an assault they had not yet been able to tell anyone about before that point in time. Consequently, respondents differed based on how forthcoming they were as well.

Although qualitative research is not usually generalizable, this type of scholarship is useful for providing in-depth, nuanced data and for revealing how individuals create meaning and perceive their experiences.[3] Qualitative studies of male sexual assault survivors have tended to rely on data obtained from federal, nonprofit, or criminal justice agencies.[4] Hlavka's interview data, for example, was acquired from forensic interviews at a nonprofit organization and Weiss's research involved open-ended narratives obtained from the US Department of Justice.[5] Such studies undoubtedly have considerable strengths as well, allowing for large sample sizes. Rather than relying on secondary data, however, I conducted my own research, enabling me to ask tailored questions and to collect in-depth data on a wide range of topics.

The interviews lasted from approximately one to three hours; the median interview was ninety-seven minutes. Fifteen of the interviews took place in Atlanta, whereas forty-five occurred in New York City. In accordance with the institutional review board of my university, I acquired written informed consent to ensure protection of participants' identities. During the interview, I conducted what qualitative social scientists refer to as "semi-structured interviews," which means that I had many questions prepared, while also asking some different follow-up questions depending on how the participant responded to my initial inquiry. I tend to be quite detailed and structured with the questions I plan on asking, yet because participants vary widely in their comfort level in terms of speaking about traumatic experiences, I was flexible and tailored my questions accordingly. While a number of specific questions were asked to every participant, these inquiries were often open enough to allow respondents to guide some of the discussion. One such example included questions regarding hierarchies of victimhood, which were general at first, as I was hoping not to invoke a particular type of hierarchy or a specific comparison group but to allow participants to explain how they felt on their own terms, as I asked many probes or follow-up questions during this time.

With studying violence or sexual assault, I have felt that my research works best when I ask about respondents' violent experiences early on, usually within the first minute or two, because otherwise the interaction feels as if a major topic is being avoided. During these first few minutes, some participants avoided going into detail or even described an assaultive experience they perceived as "less traumatic" and then later revealed the assault they viewed as more serious or harmful. These forms of avoidance can occur because participants may not yet feel comfortable with the interview process or may not yet view the researcher as a trustworthy person. I attempted to establish rapport by asking questions in such a way that respondents did not feel judged or interrogated but listened to and supported.

In comparison to the interview research I conducted for my first book, which focused on violence but not necessarily on sexual assault, the interviews I conducted for this study were considerably more emotionally difficult. The vast majority of participants were thankful for my research and the time I spent listening to them—I received considerably more praise and thanks after these interviews than after the interviews conducted for my first book—yet I also had more respondents become very emotional and occasionally even angry during the interviews. Participants' sadness typically arose from recounting traumatic experiences and their anger was directed at others they knew, yet researchers who study traumatic topics may sometimes feel as if this anger is directed toward us.[6]

A gap exists between what participants may want out of an interview—such as emotional or psychological benefits from being able to speak about their experiences—and what the researcher may want, such as good data for their project. This disjuncture is an ethical concern, and a particularly important one for researchers to account for when studying topics such as sexual assault, since survivors may feel as if their assailant had violated their sense of boundaries. Interviewers risk reproducing these dynamics if they appear intrusive. To reduce the possibility of harm, I asked a lot of questions, especially early during the interview, that could be characterized as therapeutic, focusing on survivors' feelings. This approach likely not only helped with making participants feel more comfortable but also provided them with greater emotional or psychological benefits than if I had not asked these questions. When thinking about ethical considerations, I also limited harm through my construction of the interview protocol, building to more specific questions about what had happened during the assault and scaffolding the questions in such a way that the interview generally moved from simpler to more complex topics.

Given these ethical concerns, most of the issues I cared about most deeply arose after some trust had been established, meaning that I usually asked about them after a fair amount of time. For example, I asked my emasculation questions during the latter half of the interview because I worried that asking these questions early on might result in some participants hesitating to share feelings that elicit shame, such as those related to emasculation.[7] Similarly, I did not want to convey an assumption that participants should have called the police if they did not, and thus, I did not ask questions about contacting and interacting with the police until late in the interview.

Toward the end of the interview, participants were asked whether their assailants were the same race or ethnicity as them, if such information had not already been divulged, to ascertain whether the violence was intra-racial or interracial; perceptions of the assailant's gender were also asked at this time. Evaluating aspects such as racial or ethnic status based on appearance is undoubtedly a troubling practice, as such an approach can reinforce the essentializing of racial difference, yet I had to rely on respondents' perceptions given the interview-based nature of this study. Participants often knew their assailants prior to the assault, as well as where they lived, and none of the respondents hesitated in answering this question.

When collecting these data, my positionality as a white cisgender gay man undoubtedly shaped what was shared with me. Although I have tried not to reinforce social hierarchies in this book, the interview process, as well as my analysis of the data, are inevitably immersed in power relations and cannot be decontextualized from broader systems of inequality. Queer men of color likely spent a considerable amount of time explaining their particular challenges to someone, a white academic, they probably viewed as not encountering those same challenges. Age, in addition to race and gender, also shaped the data I gathered. Since I was in my mid-to-late thirties when conducting these interviews, white queer men around that age appeared particularly forthcoming about some of their perceptions and experiences. Queer men of color, in contrast, sometimes appeared to feel apprehensive about how their experiences would be represented by a white gay man, yet I attempted to develop rapport by showing interest in learning as much as possible about their perceptions.

For data analysis, I examined transcripts of the interviews using the qualitative coding software program ATLAS.ti.[8] Grounded theory methods were used to analyze the transcripts, with open, axial, and selective coding processes.[9] A grounded theory approach offers detailed procedural steps for generating categories inductively from the data.[10] Following Abrahamson's guidelines for inductive analyses to begin with researchers "immersing" themselves in the documents, I first read and took notes on all of the transcripts to gain a sense of each individual narrative.[11] This process is especially useful for understanding each transcript on its own terms and for viewing it in relation to the broader sample. At times, particularly memorable interviews, especially those conducted toward the end, will make a disproportionately strong impression, while this process of examining each interview consecutively helps with providing a sense of the specificity of an individual participant as well as a better understanding of the respondents overall. After reading and taking notes on each transcript, I then employed open coding to identify initial concepts, with line-by-line analysis of the transcripts.[12] This process of "breaking down" the data yielded many concepts related to participants' meaning-making processes, generating initial codes through close examination.[13]

Adhering to Corbin and Strauss's suggestion for axial coding, whereby connections, categories, and relationships are made among the concepts generated from open coding, I then created axial codes.[14] Some of these codes were quite broad at first—for example, I had one called "racialized narratives and concerns"—while others were more specific, such as "emasculation and whiteness" or "differences among participants of color in their reporting to the police." Regardless of how specific the codes were initially, they were usually refined during this time, as I continued to examine them in relation to the data, narrowing the set of codes to those that appeared most frequent and important.

This axial coding process also involved evaluating the adequacy of the codes, some of which were reworked to improve their fit with the data. The code "differences among participants of color in their reporting to the police" became framed around gender expression, as my examination of that code revealed this relationship. Thus, I split that axial code into more specific ones titled "Black participants, surprised by the negative police response" and "participants of color, not surprised by the negative police response." This split then allowed for each of these codes to be enhanced, tested against the data, and fleshed out on their own terms rather than remaining overly broad.

Additional examples of the codes include "Black participants' descriptions of 'troublemaker' discourse" and "younger white participants' surprise at an unsupportive police response." Other codes became broadened into a category. For example, I created a category titled, "outing—multiple identities" from several axial codes such as "outing in relation to HIV" and "outing in relation to BDSM," since many of the codes that focused on outing revealed multiple and simultaneous forms of nonconsensual disclosure.

Through the process of selective coding, in which I analyzed the axial codes and wrote theoretical memos, core categories emerged.[15] For instance, at this time, I created a core category titled "emasculation as a racialized response," in which multiple axial codes related to emasculation became subcategories of this larger category. At this point, I also created a core category titled "structural marginalization," in which several of the codes and categories were connected or integrated into this larger one.

After creating these core categories, I analyzed the transcripts again, selectively coding any data related to the categories, in addition to refining and validating the relationships that had been established through the constant comparative method utilized throughout the coding process.[16] This process of reexamining my codes and categories with the data involved a rigorous process of interrogating their trustworthiness by asking questions such as "does this finding make sense?" and "can I trust it?"[17] Overall, I employed a constant comparative method at multiple stages of analysis, testing the emerging results against further data until patterns were revealed.

As data analysis progressed, I also revised codes that were overly broad or specific. One of the important parts of data analysis is to have codes that are not overly broad in that they should cohere around a narrow enough finding, issue, or pattern. Alternatively, it can become a problem when codes are overly specific to the point that few quotes appear within them, making it difficult to identify trends. Instead, my codes were specific enough that they cohered around a particular finding or pattern, while also being broad enough that they revealed a trend in the overall sample. In general, these codes and categories form the basis of this book, as I have used them to write the chapters presented here.

Part of the data analysis process involved calculating some quantifiable information to determine the extent of a pattern. This process, in which I used methods related to content analysis more than grounded theory, revealed the extent of the emerging patterns and enabled me to document trends in the sample.[18] During this time, I also tabulated respondents' demographic characteristics, which are presented in a table after this methods section. This demographic information comes from a short questionnaire that participants completed after the interview; thus, it reflects their self-identification. In total, thirty-nine respondents self-identified as gay, twelve as bisexual, seven as queer, and two as pansexual. In terms of gender identity, fifty-five of the participants identified as cisgender, while five identified as transgender. Moreover, two participants identified as "nonbinary men" (one as cisgender and one as transgender). All but two of the respondents were born in the United States. Participants ranged from eighteen to seventy-seven years old, with the greatest percentage of the sample in their thirties; the median age was thirty-eight.

With regard to race and ethnicity, thirty-seven participants self-identified as Black or African American, fourteen as white, nine as Latino or Latinx, three as Asian or South Asian, and one as Native American. These numerical totals for race and ethnicity exceed sixty, given that four participants identified as belonging to two of these categories. In terms of gender expression, I first asked respondents a series of open-ended questions during the interview and then posed a more close-ended one, asking participants to classify their gender expression along a continuum, to make categorization easier. On this measurement, ten participants identified as feminine, fifteen as more feminine than masculine, twenty-one as in-between feminine and masculine, eleven as more masculine than feminine, and three as masculine. Sixteen of the participants also identified as gender nonconforming. Participants of color and white respondents identified at similar rates in terms of gender expression, as nineteen of forty-six, or 41.3 percent, of the participants of color identified on the more feminine side of the gender expression measurement and six of fourteen, or 42.9 percent, of the white respondents did so. For determining social class positions, I asked about respondents' employment and educational history and their experiences with homelessness, if applicable, as well as where they grew up and what their parents did for a living.

Participants generally described multiple experiences of sexual assault, as a majority had experienced adult anal rape, as well as childhood sexual abuse, at least once. Of course, sexual assault during adulthood includes acts beyond anal rape; most participants also described such experiences. All of the participants had one or more assaultive experience in which the assailant was a man. Additionally, one respondent had an assaultive experience as an adult in which the assailant was a woman, and four participants experienced childhood sexual abuse from a woman. Geographic differences existed in the sample, as respondents in Atlanta were the most likely to experience an assault in the context of a relationship, while participants in New York City, although also the most likely to experience an assault in this context, were sexually victimized more frequently during a hookup. Thus, the frequency of the hookup and relationship contexts may vary for queer male survivors depending on their geographic location.

AUTHOR BACKGROUND

I have written one book about violence already, although I have never written about any of my own experiences.[19] I grew up in a violent home, in which I both experienced and committed violence as a teenager. Sexual assault was not part of this environment, at least to my knowledge, although violent relations between multiple family members were present. As an adult, I have sometimes found it hard to forgive myself for the physical violence I committed when I was young. For this reason, instead of thinking and speaking about assailants as "out there," I find it more useful to frame these matters as something that most humans are capable of justifying and committing. Otherwise, it remains difficult to explain high rates of this violence. This understanding also helps with avoiding a self-righteous sort of attitude in which individuals construct themselves as "above" or "beyond" these issues. Not everyone commits violence, of course, but most are capable of it under particular conditions, and systems of oppression such as institutional racism and sexism are also not "out there," entirely independent of us, but part of us and sometimes inform what we do.

Much later than these adolescent experiences, when I was in my late twenties, I was also sexually assaulted. Similar to some of the men I interviewed, my assaultive experience occurred in the context of a hookup. Grindr and other phone apps were not around at this time, but chat rooms were. The assault occurred one night when I was drunk and invited a man over to my apartment to have consensual sex. When I was performing oral sex on him, he pressed forcefully on the back of my head to the point where his penis hurt my mouth. My memory is that I started to push against his pelvis to signal that I wanted it to stop, although I cannot be sure exactly what happened at this time, since I became scared and the entire incident happened relatively quickly. Regardless, he continued to push against the back of my head, and then I started to gag or choke, quickly vomiting thereafter. At this point, he stopped and stepped back. I apologized, saying, "sorry," for vomiting in part on him.

I find it important not to undermine this experience, but I have also been uncomfortable with labeling or thinking of myself as a "survivor." Certainly, I can recognize that taking on this label may be helpful for students of mine who have been sexually assaulted. Through writing this book, I have also questioned my resistance to this term, as I have only recently even begun to speak about myself as someone who was sexually assaulted. Is this resistance about masculinity, and not wanting to admit that I was a man who was sexually violated? Since some definitions of rape do not include oral penetration, is it simply easier for me to think, "Well, I was not anally raped, so I'm not really a survivor"? Is it because this man was the same race as me, white, and, as my results in this text would suggest, I may have recognized it as an assault a long time ago if he had been a man of color? Is it all of the reasons above? I do not have definitive answers here, but through this research I have come to see that this resistance to understanding oneself as a survivor is by no means exclusive to me.

Additionally, I understood on many levels that my homosexuality or my desire to have consensual sex did not cause this assault to happen, but I also began to question aspects of my life, and yes, blame myself to an extent. I had been dating my current spouse for less than a year at the time, and we had recently decided to be in an open relationship before the assault had occurred. When I was violated, it led me to wonder if it was a mistake to be in an open relationship. It sounds silly or wrongheaded to me now—"open relationships lead to sexual assault"—but the reality is that I had those thoughts. I also felt dirty after this man left my apartment, and sometimes even now when I say the word "sorry," I am reminded of how bad I felt for saying that word then, when he should have been the one apologizing.

My assaultive experience reveals the importance of having nuanced discussions about sexual assault. I believe that the man who assaulted me was aware that I was in pain and was not enjoying what he was doing—and that he either did not care or found my pain sexually arousing—but I cannot be absolutely certain of this belief. It is also possible that he simply did not see my pain or fear, or that he mistakenly thought I was enjoying these emotional reactions. Such uncertainty can be difficult for survivors to experience, as I have questioned his thought process repeatedly and replayed what happened in my mind countless times. Rape apologists may use these complexities or possibilities to dismiss survivors' experiences. However, I also think these complexities need to be discussed, as it becomes a problem for survivors who have these experiences when representations of rape and sexual assault are continually presented as unambiguous rather than complex.[20] In the spirit that I have written this book, I do not wish carceral or punitive approaches toward the man who assaulted me, yet I would also like to see sexual assault scholarship and advocacy continue to draw attention to complexities around many forms of assault.

Although I still do not like talking about the assault, this research project has made me more comfortable doing so and more aware of the reasons why speaking about it may be hard for many queer male survivors. The first talk I ever gave on this topic took place at my university, and I invited students in one of my courses. While this talk focused on sexual assault more generally against LGBTQ people and I did not reveal anything personal—I certainly did not speak about my assaultive experience—it changed some dynamics in the class moving forward. Students began to approach me more carefully. For instance, rather than students simply asking me a question after class, they would preface the question with something akin to, "Is it OK for me to ask you a question?"

I do not know what they were thinking, but it felt as if some of them now entered the classroom believing, "Wow, our professor has been raped," and suddenly became more cautious about participating. The change felt odd to me—after all, I felt like exactly the same person and professor before giving the talk—but it made me think more deeply about how survivors are perceived. Indeed, as detailed in this book, participants often thought that others began to perceive them more negatively after disclosing their assaultive experience. I have written this book in part to draw attention to queer male survivors' struggles in this regard—in particular, how survivors experience these challenges differently based on their social position.

Respondents' Demographic Characteristics Organized by Gender, Sexuality, and Gender Identity (N = 60)

Pseudonym	Age	Race/Ethnicity	Gender Expression, in Relation to Masculinity and Femininity, and Gender Nonconformity
		Cisgender gay men	
David	18	Black	more feminine than masculine ("more feminine" hereafter)
Brandon	21	Black	more feminine
Jeremiah	22	Black	in between, gender nonconforming ("GNC" hereafter)
Jalen	24	Black	in between
Marcel	27	Black	feminine, GNC
Donald	28	Black	more masculine than feminine ("more masculine" hereafter)
Vondell	29	Black	more masculine
Tyrice	30	Black	in between
Clayton	32	Black	in between
Herman	36	Black	feminine, GNC
Kemal	37	Black	feminine
Marcus	37	Black	masculine
Ornell	37	Black	feminine, GNC
Kenneth	42	Black	more feminine
Jayden	45	Black	masculine
Latrelle	49	Black	in between
Gene	50	Black	more feminine
Sherman	53	Black	feminine
Kyle	54	Black	more masculine
Yamen	55	Black	masculine
Antonne	58	Black	in between
Jontray	58	Black	in between
Anthony	59	Black	more feminine
Marteese	60	Black	more feminine
Justin	62	Black	more feminine, GNC
Elijah	63	Black	in between
Brian	19	Latino	more feminine, GNC
Juan	47	Latino	feminine, GNC
Tario	47	Latino	in between
Mateo	56	Latino	more feminine
Joel	30	South Asian	in between
Danny	31	White	more masculine
Allen	38	White	feminine
Norman	38	White	in between
Chad	48	White	feminine, GNC
Shane	49	White	more feminine, GNC

Pseudonym	Age	Race/Ethnicity	Gender Expression, in Relation to Masculinity and Femininity, and Gender Nonconformity
Sean	53	White	in between
Melvin	59	White	in between
Paul	77	White	more masculine

Cisgender bisexual men

Damon	26	Black	in between
Xavier	26	Black	more masculine
Darius	34	Black	in between
Dannell	41	Black	more masculine
Reymond	53	Black	more feminine, GNC
Emerson	24	Black and Latino	in between
Mendez	27	Black and Latino	feminine
Kamar	40	Black and Latino	in between, GNC
Lee	38	Asian	more feminine
Tyler	44	Asian	more masculine
William	36	White	more feminine, GNC
Zachary	44	White	feminine

Cisgender queer men

Charlie	26	White	more feminine
Francis	27	White	in between

Cisgender nonbinary pansexual man

Sergio	22	Latinx	in between, GNC

Cisgender pansexual man

Samuel	37	Black	more masculine, GNC

Transgender queer men

Leonard	55	Black	more feminine
Santiago	49	Latino	more masculine
Grey	35	White	in between
Jude	39	White	more masculine, GNC

Transgender nonbinary queer man

Clyde	33	Black and Native American	in between, GNC

Notes

INTRODUCTION

1. Abdullah-Khan, *Male Rape*; Javaid, *Male Rape, Masculinities, and Sexualities*; Stemple, Flores, and Meyer, "Sexual Victimization"; Tillapaugh, "The Wounds of Our Experience."

2. Crenshaw, "Mapping the Margins"; Curry, "Expendables for Whom"; Ralston, "An Intersectional Approach."

3. Coulter et al., "Prevalence of Past-Year Sexual Assault"; Stemple and Meyer, "The Sexual Victimization"; Terwiel, "What Is Carceral Feminism?"; Wooten, "Revealing a Hidden Curriculum." *Latinx* is used throughout to be inclusive of nonbinary, intersex, and transgender people, or others who may not view themselves according to a strict gender binary, which is implied in constructions such as Latino/a. I use this term when referring to participants in general because one of the respondents in this study identified as Latinx. I use the term *Latino* when referring to participants who identified in this way. The use of *Latinx* is not without its concerns, as it can be used by those in the Global North and then applied to individuals in the Global South who are entirely unfamiliar with it, yet I have settled on this imperfect term to be as inclusive as possible.

4. Curry, "Expendables for Whom," 289.

5. See Foster, *Rethinking Rufus*, for a historical account of Black men's assaultive experiences in the context of slavery, including a chapter that focuses on same-gender relations among Black men.

6. P. H. Collins, *Black Feminist Thought*; Crenshaw, "Mapping the Margins"; Zinn and Dill, "Theorizing Difference."

7. Choo and Ferree, "Practicing Intersectionality"; May, *Pursuing Intersectionality*; McCall, "The Complexity of Intersectionality."

8. Cho, Crenshaw, and McCall, "Toward a Field"; Crenshaw, "Demarginalizing the Intersection"; Hancock, *Intersectionality*.

9. C. Connell, "Contesting Racialized Discourses"; Han, *Geisha of a Different Kind*; Hunter, "All the Gays Are White"; Muñoz, *Disidentifications*; Ocampo, "Making Masculinity."

10. Armstrong, Gleckman-Krut, and Johnson, "Silence, Power, and Inequality"; Freedman, *Redefining Rape*; Pascoe and Hollander, "Good Guys Don't Rape." White men have also historically and continually committed sexual violence against Black women to reinforce racialized gender hierarchies—see Feinstein, *When Rape Was Legal*, for an analysis of rape perpetrated against enslaved Black women by white men, including an examination of how white women often enabled this violence.

11. An. Davis, *Women, Race and Class*, 172.

12. Curry, "Expendables for Whom"; Pascoe and Hollander, "Good Guys Don't Rape."

13. Crenshaw, "Mapping the Margins"; McGuire, *At the Dark End of the Street*; Pierce-Baker, *Surviving the Silence*; Ritchie, *Invisible No More*; Wooten, "Revealing a Hidden Curriculum." For an anthology of readings, see INCITE!, *Color of Violence*.

14. Crenshaw, "Mapping the Margins."

15. For more recent analysis of how this marginalization operates, see P. H. Collins, "On Violence."

16. Curry, "Expendables for Whom"; Phipps, "Every Woman Knows a Weinstein."

17. González-López, *Family Secrets*; McGuffey, "Saving Masculinity"; Menjívar, *Enduring Violence*; Powell, Hlavka, and Mulla, "Intersectionality and Credibility"; Ralston, "An Intersectional Approach."

18. Curry, "Expendables for Whom"; Garvey, Hitchins, and McDonald, "Queer-Spectrum Student Sexual Violence"; Javaid, "Poison Ivy"; Patterson, *Queering Sexual Violence*; Tillapaugh, "The Wounds of Our Experience."

19. Dick, *The Hunting Ground*.

20. Ford and Soto-Marquez, "Sexual Assault Victimization"; Lowe and Rogers, "The Scope of Male Rape"; Messinger and Koon-Magnin, "Sexual Violence"; Rothman, Exner, and Baughman, "The Prevalence of Sexual Assault"; Schulze, Koon-Magnin, and Bryan, *Gender Identity, Sexual Orientation, and Sexual Assault*.

21. Rothman, Exner, and Baughman, "The Prevalence of Sexual Assault."

22. Rothman, Exner, and Baughman, 55.

23. Coulter and Rankin, "College Sexual Assault and Campus Climate."

24. Féron, *Wartime Sexual Violence against Men*; Madriz, *Nothing Bad Happens to Good Girls*; Messner, "Bad Men, Good Men, Bystanders"; Pascoe and Hollander, "Good Guys Don't Rape."

25. *Heteronormativity* is used throughout to refer to the assumption that heterosexuality is natural, normal, and preferred, as well as the systematic privileging of heterosexuality over other sexualities based on this assumption.

26. Pseudonyms are used throughout to ensure participants' confidentiality.

27. *Gender expression* is used to refer to the way a person views and conveys their gender in relation to categories such as femininity or masculinity and through aspects such as behavior or appearance. It should be understood not as static but as varying based on social context. During the interview, participants were asked if they perceived their gender expression as "feminine," "more feminine than masculine," "in between feminine and masculine," "more masculine than feminine," or "masculine." The breakdown in terms of how participants answered this question is shown in a table at the end of the appendix. Throughout this text, for the sake of brevity, I refer to participants who described their gender expression as "more feminine than masculine" as "feminine" and those who identified as "more masculine than feminine" as "masculine." Those participants who described their gender expression as "in between feminine and masculine" are identified as neither feminine nor masculine.

28. Ferrales, Brehm, and McElrath, "Gender-Based Violence," 572. See also: Funk, "Queer Men and Sexual Assault"; Tillapaugh, "The Wounds of Our Experience"; K. Weiss, "Too Ashamed to Report."

29. *Gender expansive* is used throughout this text to refer to individuals who view their gender expression in ways that do not conform to traditional gender roles, such as masculinity for men.

30. Curry, "Expendables for Whom"; Garfield, *Knowing What We Know*; Richie, *Arrested Justice*.

31. C. Donovan and coauthors, in *Comparing Domestic Abuse in Same Sex and Heterosexual Relationships*, have noted that LGBTQ people's lack of embeddedness in LGBTQ friendship and community networks is one of the conditions that makes intimate partner violence especially likely to occur. For more on the privileging of whiteness in LGBTQ communities, see C. Connell, "Contesting Racialized Discourses"; Hinkson, "The Colorblind Rainbow"; Robinson, "Personal Preference."

32. P. H. Collins, *Intersectionality as Critical Social Theory*. See Carbado, "Colorblind Intersectionality" for a list of common critiques of intersectionality, including this idea that the theory has "run its course," and for responses to such criticisms. Jennifer Nash, in *Black Feminism Reimagined*, further details the various ways that intersectionality may be dismissed or cast as a "threat," including sometimes even within feminist movements, which has led to a Black

feminist defensiveness over policing its boundaries that Nash wants to move beyond.

33. Scholarship generally indicates that a deeper, more intersectional, understanding of hierarchies among men remains needed, with conceptualizations that account for contextual variation and conceive of such hierarchies in expansive ways—see, S. Barnes, "Becoming a Man"; Ralston, "An Intersectional Approach"; Schippers, "Recovering the Feminine Other"; Wingfield, "Are Some Emotions Marked 'Whites Only'?"

34. Puar, *Terrorist Assemblages*. See Carbado, "Colorblind Intersectionality," for a response to these critiques.

35. *Cisgender* is used to refer to individuals whose gender aligns with their sex assigned at birth. For example, someone who identifies as a man and was assigned male at birth is a cisgender man.

36. Wiley and Bottoms, "Attitudinal and Individual Differences."

37. Beauchamp, *Going Stealth*; Al. Davis, *Bathroom Battlegrounds*; Stone, "Gender Panics." These discourses may also affect others' perceptions of sexual abuse or assault. For example, a transgender teacher accused of sexual violence may be viewed more negatively than a cisgender one, given that transphobic stereotypes associate the former with sexually assaultive behavior. Sex panics have also disproportionately been imposed on LGB people and racial minorities, with false accusations being believed when the accused is perceived as an outsider by the larger community—see Barnard, *Sex Panic Rhetorics, Queer Interventions*; Halperin and Hoppe, *The War on Sex*; Lancaster, *Sex Panic and the Punitive State*; Meiners, *For the Children?* For further complications and critiques of some of the emphasis on "sex panics," and for more on the social problem of sexual abuse, see Cheit, *The Witch-Hunt Narrative*, and Whittier, *Frenemies*.

38. See Guadalupe-Diaz, *Transgressed*, for detailed analysis of transgender people's experiences of sexual assault and intimate partner violence.

39. Garvey, Hitchins, and McDonald, "Queer-Spectrum Student Sexual Violence"; Javaid, "Poison Ivy"; Messinger and Koon-Magnin, "Sexual Violence"; Patterson, *Queering Sexual Violence*.

40. Xu and Zheng, "Does Sexual Orientation Precede Childhood Sexual Abuse?"

41. Fanghanel, "Asking for It"; Gavey, *Just Sex?*; Harding, *Asking for It*; Harris, *Beyond the Rapist*; Hlavka, "Normalizing Sexual Violence."

42. Davies and Hudson, "Judgments toward Male and Transgendered Victims"; P. Dunn, "Men as Victims"; Lowe and Rogers, "The Scope of Male Rape."

43. Alcoff, *Rape and Resistance*; Gilson, "Vulnerability and Victimization"; Madriz, *Nothing Bad Happens to Good Girls*.

44. Bost, *Evidence of Being*; Kilty and Bogosavljevic, "Emotional Storytelling"; Mumford, *Not Straight, Not White*; Stockton, *Beautiful Bottom, Beautiful Shame*. For more on how notions of toxicity and disgust affect Black queer women as well, see J. Nash, "Black Anality."

45. Darabont, *The Shawshank Redemption*.

46. Donaldson, "A Million Jockers, Punks, and Queens"; Eigenberg, "Male Rape."

47. Fleisher and Krienert, *The Myth of Prison Rape*; J. L. Jackson, "Sexual Necropolitics and Prison Rape Elimination." See Kunzel, *Criminal Intimacy*, for more on the history of prisoners' sex practices behind bars and public interpretations of this sex, as well as an emphasis on the pleasure, rather than the danger, that exists in these spaces.

48. Bridges, "A Very Gay Straight?"; Bridges and Pascoe, "Hybrid Masculinities"; Messner, "Bad Men, Good Men, Bystanders"; Schippers, "Recovering the Feminine Other."

49. R. Connell, *Gender and Power*; R. Connell, *Masculinities*.

50. R. Connell, *Masculinities*; R. Connell and Messerschmidt, "Hegemonic Masculinity."

51. McCune, *Sexual Discretion*; Ocampo, "Making Masculinity"; Winder, "Shouting It Out."

52. P. H. Collins, *Black Sexual Politics*; Hunter, "All the Gays Are White"; Ocampo, "Making Masculinity."

53. Han, *Geisha of a Different Kind*; Muñoz, *Disidentifications*; Stockton, *Beautiful Bottom, Beautiful Shame*.

54. S. Barnes, "Becoming a Man"; Hunter, "All the Gays Are White"; McCune, *Sexual Discretion*; McGuffey, "Saving Masculinity"; Reid-Pharr, *Black Gay Man*; Pitt, "Still Looking for My Jonathan"; Winder, "Shouting It Out."

55. Christie, "The Ideal Victim."

56. Crenshaw, "Mapping the Margins"; DeFilippis and Anderson-Nathe, "Embodying Margin to Center."

57. P. H. Collins, *Black Feminist Thought*; May, *Pursuing Intersectionality*; Spade, *Normal Life*.

58. Choo and Ferree, "Practicing Intersectionality"; Cho, Crenshaw, and McCall, "Toward a Field"; Hancock, *Intersectionality*; Moraga and Anzaldúa, *This Bridge Called My Back*.

59. Mumford, *Not Straight, Not White*; Reid-Pharr, *Black Gay Man*; Ward, *Respectably Queer*.

60. Curry, in "Expendables for Whom," makes this point regarding the #MeToo movement and the literature on sexual assault. In *Male Survivors of Wartime Sexual Violence*, Schulz points out that traditional scholarly analyses of wartime violence, situated in international relations, have frequently ignored gender entirely; meanwhile, research in this field of study addressing gender has not typically explored wartime sexual violence against boys and men, equating "gender" with "women."

61. Garvey, Hitchins, and McDonald, "Queer-Spectrum Student Sexual Violence"; Javaid, "Poison Ivy"; Messinger and Koon-Magnin, "Sexual Violence"; Patterson, *Queering Sexual Violence*.

62. Phipps, "Every Woman Knows a Weinstein." Westbrook, in *Unlivable Lives*, extends this argument to many forms of anti-violence activism more

broadly, as activists focusing on identity may unintentionally leave members of the identity group feeling resigned to violence or as if it is inevitable.

63. See Muehlenhard et al., "The Complexities of Sexual Consent," for a review.

64. This line of work has contended that consent needs to be understood as a socially contingent process that cannot be separated from power relations; see Barker, "Consent Is a Grey Area?"; Fischel, *Screw Consent*; Harris, "Yes Means Yes." Making this argument does not mean that survivors' perceptions should be dismissed as inauthentic, but that consent needs to be rethought as dynamic and as implicated in social processes. Speaking to survivors, the variability in perceptions of consent becomes fairly apparent, given that one person will understand an act as consensual, while another will view a similar act as nonconsensual.

65. Muehlenhard et al., "Evaluating the One-in-Five Statistic," 551.

66. For more on these debates regarding definitions of sexual assault, see Alcoff, *Rape and Resistance*; Hlavka, "Normalizing Sexual Violence"; Khan et al., "The Social Organization of Sexual Assault"; Mardorossian, *Framing the Rape Victim*.

67. Mouilso, Fischer, and Calhoun, "A Prospective Study." See Muehlenhard et al., "Evaluating the One-in-Five Statistic," for further discussion of various working definitions. In "Understanding How University Students," Hills et al. outline some potential problems with conflating wantedness with consent and pleasureableness with wantedness.

68. Alcoff, *Rape and Resistance*; Harris, *Beyond the Rapist*; Muehlenhard et al., "The Complexities of Sexual Consent."

69. Fanghanel, "Asking for It"; Harris, *Beyond the Rapist*.

70. This matter differed somewhat based on age, as older participants were more likely than younger ones to have assaultive experiences that had taken place more than five years prior to the interview. The participation of men with experiences of anal rape occurred in part because of the language used on my recruitment flyer: "Do You Identify as a Gay, Bisexual, or Queer Man, and Have You Experienced Rape or Sexual Assault Since You've Been 18?" I included the word *rape* on the recruitment flyer to clarify the scope of the project, as I worried that omitting it would lead to greater confusion or ambiguity for some individuals who saw the flyer.

71. Abdullah-Khan, *Male Rape*; Alcoff, *Rape and Resistance*; Graham, "Male Rape and the Careful Construction."

72. Dwyer and Tomsen, "The Past Is the Past?"; Hanhardt, *Safe Space*; Stewart-Winter, *Queer Clout*.

73. Bernstein, *Brokered Subjects*; Russell, "Queer Penalties"; Spade, *Normal Life*.

74. Harris, *Beyond the Rapist*; Messner, "Bad Men, Good Men, Bystanders"; Pascoe and Hollander, "Good Guys Don't Rape."

CHAPTER 1. "WHY DIDN'T YOU FIGHT BACK?"

1. This process has been increasingly referred to as "gaslighting"—see P. Sweet, "The Sociology of Gaslighting."

2. Lewis et al., "Sexistential Crisis"; Nguyen, *A View from the Bottom*; Schippers, "Recovering the Feminine Other."

3. Messinger, in *LGBTQ Intimate Partner Violence*, makes the important point that LGBTQ people may not be out with regard to their sexuality or gender identity and therefore in the context of intimate partner violence may avoid reaching out to others for help because they have not disclosed the relationship itself. Participants in this study were disproportionately out regarding their sexuality or gender identity when experiencing sexual assault in a relationship, although they had sometimes not disclosed other aspects of their identity, which I examine in chapter 6.

4. DeKeseredy, Dragiewicz, and Schwartz, *Abusive Endings*; A. Jones, *Next Time, She'll Be Dead*.

5. For further analysis of LGBTQ people's experiences of multiple victimization, see DeKeseredy et al., "Polyvictimization," in which the authors show that LGBTQ students experience high rates of sexual harassment, sexual assault, intimate partner violence, and stalking, often simultaneously. See also: Messinger, *LGBTQ Intimate Partner Violence*; B. Weiss, "Who Can We Tell." More generally, in addition to "polyvictimization," other researchers have used a range of concepts to encapsulate these multiple and interrelated forms of violence, including Kelly's "continuum of violence," in *Surviving Sexual Violence*, and Hamby and Grynch's "web of violence," in their book of the same name. These concepts are useful not only for showing the concurrent degradation of survivors that may occur through multiple forms of abuse but also for revealing the many injurious behaviors that may nevertheless be trivialized by outsiders given their legality. For more on assailants' controlling behaviors, which are not necessarily accompanied by physically violent or injurious actions, see Stark, *Coercive Control*.

6. M. Brown and Groscup, "Perceptions of Same-Sex Domestic Violence"; Messinger, *LGBTQ Intimate Partner Violence*; Stanziani, Cox, and Coffey, "Adding Insult to Injury." Messinger, in *LGBTQ Intimate Partner Violence*, outlines the five myths of LGBTQ intimate partner violence, including that it is rare, less severe, and the same as all other forms. Police also appear to view incidents with same-gender couples as less severe—see Hirschel and McCormack, "Same-Sex Couples and the Police."

7. See the table in the appendix.

8. These numbers only apply to participants who referred to strength in relation to themselves; over half of the participants, which included many white respondents, characterized their assailant as strong, likely as a way of

underscoring that it would have been difficult or impossible for them to physically resist the assailant.

9. Javaid, "The Dark Side of Men"; McGuffey, "Saving Masculinity"; Messerschmidt, *Hegemonic Masculinity*; Sumerau, *Violent Manhood*.

10. R. Donovan and Williams, "Living at the Intersection"; McGuffey, "Rape and Racial Appraisals"; S. Nash, "Through Black Eyes."

11. P. H. Collins, "The Tie that Binds"; R. Donovan and Williams, "Living at the Intersection"; Hine, "Rape and the Inner Lives"; McGuffey, "Rape and Racial Appraisals"; S. Nash, "Through Black Eyes."

12. Hunter, "All the Gays Are White"; Moore, *Invisible Families*; Pitt, "Still Looking for My Jonathan"; Winder, "Shouting It Out."

13. P. H. Collins, *Black Sexual Politics*; E. P. Johnson, *Appropriating Blackness*; B. Smith, "Blacks and Gays."

14. P. H. Collins, *Black Sexual Politics*; D. Meyer, "An Intersectional Analysis"; E. P. Johnson, *Appropriating Blackness*.

15. P. H. Collins, *Black Sexual Politics*; D. Meyer, "An Intersectional Analysis."

16. Han, *Geisha of a Different Kind*; Hunter, "All the Gays Are White"; Ocampo, "Making Masculinity."

17. P. H. Collins, *Black Sexual Politics*; McCune, *Sexual Discretion*; D. Meyer, *Violence against Queer People*.

18. Hunter, "All the Gays Are White"; E. P. Johnson, *Sweet Tea*; Ocampo, "Making Masculinity"; Stockton, *Beautiful Bottom, Beautiful Shame*. For more on how these dynamics operate for Muslim queer men, see Pérez, *A Taste for Brown Bodies*, in which the author examines how cosmopolitan white gay male desire for racialized others may be used to shore up the US nation-state, including processes of imperialism and neoliberalism.

19. Hinkson, "The Colorblind Rainbow"; Reid-Pharr, *Black Gay Man*; Robinson, "Personal Preference."

20. Bassichis and Spade, "Queer Politics and Anti-Blackness"; Carbado, "Black Rights, Gay Rights, Civil Rights." I use the term *sexual minorities* throughout to refer to people who do not identify as heterosexual.

21. Nguyen, *A View from the Bottom*; Reid-Pharr, *Black Gay Man*; Ward, *Respectably Queer*.

22. Alcoff, *Rape and Resistance*.

23. Petrosky et al., "Racial and Ethnic Differences"; Stacey, "Macrostructural Opportunity."

24. Cannon, Ferreira, and Buttell, "Critical Race Theory"; Potter, *Battle Cries*.

25. R. Connell, *Masculinities*; Hoskin, "Femmephobia"; Richardson, "Whether You Are Gay or Straight."

26. Little, "Who's the Victim Here?"; Messner, "Forks in the Road."

27. Larance et al., "Understanding and Addressing"; Myhill, "Measuring Domestic Violence."

28. Renzetti, "The Challenge to Feminism."

29. Curry, "Expendables for Whom"; Rios, *Punished*; Suddler, *Presumed Criminal*.

30. Nguyen, *A View from the Bottom*; Schippers, "Recovering the Feminine Other."

31. Curry, "Expendables for Whom."

32. D. Meyer, *Violence against Queer People*, 44–63.

33. P. H. Collins, *Black Sexual Politics*; Suddler, *Presumed Criminal*.

34. Estrich, *Real Rape*; Harris, *Beyond the Rapist*.

35. McCune, *Sexual Discretion*; Snorton, *Nobody Is Supposed to Know*. See Somerville, *Queering the Color Line*, for further analysis of the historical overlap of race and sexuality, including how the Black/white "color line" in the late nineteenth century shaped the development of homosexuality as a sexual identity.

36. Boykin, *Beyond the Down Low*; McCune, *Sexual Discretion*; Snorton, *Nobody Is Supposed to Know*.

37. Chapin, "Writing a Love Letter"; J. Jordan, *Serial Survivors*.

38. Garfield, *Through Our Eyes*, 2. Further, Garfield states, "Today, as in the past, African American men are ever-confronted with an imposing image—the violent-black-male. This disfiguring image is accompanied by an equally disfiguring narrative that marginalizes the value of their lives and calls into question their humanity, for they are socially and cultural positioned in our society as inferior beings" (2).

39. Javaid, "Poison Ivy"; Ralston, "An Intersectional Approach."

CHAPTER 2. QUEER MALE SURVIVORS AND POLICE INTERACTIONS

1. Abdullah-Khan, *Male Rape*; M. Jackson et al., "Secondary Victimization"; Javaid, *Male Rape, Masculinities, and Sexualities*.

2. Abdullah-Khan, *Male Rape*, 134; Rumney, "Gay Male Rape Victims," 238.

3. M. Jackson et al., "Secondary Victimization"; Javaid, *Male Rape, Masculinities, and Sexualities*.

4. Javaid, "Poison Ivy," 762.

5. M. Jackson et al., "Secondary Victimization"; Lowe and Rogers, "The Scope of Male Rape"; Rumney, "Policing Male Rape."

6. P. Dunn, "Men as Victims"; Lowe and Rogers, "The Scope of Male Rape"; Tillapaugh, "The Wounds of Our Experience."

7. Braga, Brunson, and Drakulich, "Race, Place, and Effective Policing"; Brunson, "Police Don't Like Black People"; Epp, Maynard-Moody, and Haider-Markel, *Pulled Over*.

8. Dwyer, "Policing Lesbian, Gay, Bisexual, and Transgender Young People"; Gonzalez, "Making It Home"; Ritchie, "Crimes against Nature."

9. Dwyer, "Policing Lesbian, Gay, Bisexual, and Transgender Young People"; D. Meyer, *Violence against Queer People*; Mogul, Ritchie, and Whitlock, *Queer (In)Justice*; Ritchie, "Crimes against Nature."

10. Ball, "Queer Criminology as Activism"; Panfil, *The Gang's All Queer*; Woods, "Queer Contestations."

11. Buist and Lenning, *Queer Criminology*; Dwyer and Tomsen, "The Past Is the Past?"; Ritchie, "Crimes against Nature."

12. Gonzalez, "Making It Home"; Ransby, *Making All Black Lives Matter*; K.-Y. Taylor, *From #BlackLivesMatter to Black Liberation*.

13. Dwyer, "Policing Lesbian, Gay, Bisexual, and Transgender Young People"; Spade, *Normal Life*; Steele, Collier, and Sumerau, "Lesbian, Gay, and Bisexual Contact with Police."

14. Buist and Stone, "Transgender Victims and Offenders"; K. Gibson, *Street Kids*; Stotzer, "Law Enforcement and Criminal Justice Personnel."

15. I. Meyer et al., "Incarceration Rates."

16. Exploring differences across racial lines remains important, yet examining intra-racial variation is also necessary given that a growing body of scholarship indicates significant differences within racial groups; see J. Gibson and Nelson, *Black and Blue*; Unnever, Gabbidon, and Chouhy, *Building a Black Criminology*.

17. See D. Meyer, "So Much for Protect and Serve," for a table showing the twenty-one participants who had negative reporting experiences of a sexual assault. Although the larger sample of participants includes five transgender men and two pansexual men, these respondents did not report any of their assaultive experiences to the police.

18. K. Gibson, *Street Kids*; Spade, *Normal Life*; White and Fradella, *Stop and Frisk*.

19. Browne, *Dark Matters*; Flores, *Caught Up*; K. Gibson, *Street Kids*.

20. Gregory and Lees, *Policing Sexual Assault*; Lowe and Rogers, "The Scope of Male Rape"; K. Weiss, "Too Ashamed to Report."

21. Pedulla, in "The Positive Consequences," found that Black queer men experience less employment discrimination in some contexts than their heterosexual counterparts, since employers may apply negative stereotypes of Black men more to the latter than to the former. A similar process may operate in some contexts regarding police profiling. That is, a police officer may racially profile a Black man the officer sees as heterosexual and masculine because this man is perceived as threatening or dangerous, while not profiling a Black queer or feminine man. That is, queerness or femininity may mute the effects of stereotypes that link Black men with criminality. In other contexts, however, officers' perceptions of queerness may intensify or produce forms of policing that Black, heterosexual men would not confront.

22. Hirschel and McCormack, "Same-Sex Couples and the Police." This ten-year study also shows that queer couples of color and individuals are more likely to be arrested for intimate partner violence than their white counterparts.

23. F. Edwards, Lee, and Esposito, "Risk of Being Killed"; Hinton, *From the War on Poverty to the War on Crime*; Legewie, "Racial Profiling"; Rios, *Punished*.

24. Gelman, Fagan, and Kiss, "An Analysis of the New York City Police"; Legewie, "Racial Profiling"; Cl. Taylor, *Fight the Power*.

25. Daum, "The War on Solicitation"; K. Gibson, *Street Kids*; Mogul, Ritchie, and Whitlock, *Queer (In)Justice*.

26. For more on how these practices affect marginalized LGBTQ people, see K. Gibson, *Street Kids*; Robinson, *Coming Out to the Streets*.

27. Epp, Maynard-Moody, and Haider-Markel, *Pulled Over*; Ransby, *Making All Black Lives Matter*; K.-Y. Taylor, *From #BlackLivesMatter to Black Liberation*.

28. K. Gibson, *Street Kids*; Mogul, Ritchie, and Whitlock, *Queer (In)Justice*; Spade, *Normal Life*.

29. Mogul, Ritchie, and Whitlock, *Queer (In)Justice*; Ritchie, "Crimes against Nature."

30. Buist and Stone, "Transgender Victims and Offenders"; K. Gibson, *Street Kids*; Robinson, *Coming Out to the Streets*.

31. Critical criminology, a theoretical perspective concerned with understanding and critiquing the ways in which the criminal-legal system reinforces social inequalities, has increasingly been employed in studies involving queer populations—see Ball, "Queer Criminology as Activism"; Buist and Lenning, *Queer Criminology*.

32. Beauchamp, *Going Stealth*; Berlant, "Slow Death"; Mbembe, *Necropolitics*; Puar, *The Right to Maim*.

33. Armenta, *Protect, Serve, and Deport*; Gottschalk, *Caught*; Kilgore, "Mass Incarceration."

34. "Detention Statistics"; Miroff, "Nearly 1 Million Migrants Arrested."

35. For more on intersections of queerness and immigration, and Latinx LGBTQ people more generally, see Carrillo, *Pathways of Desire*; Chávez, *Queer Migration Politics*; Quesada, Gomez, and Vidal-Ortiz, *Queer Brown Voices*.

36. Two participants said that they had previously taken a date rape drug for recreational purposes.

37. Epp, Maynard-Moody, and Haider-Markel, *Pulled Over*. Consistent with my results here, Guadalupe-Diaz, in "Disclosure," found that nonwhite LGB survivors of intimate partner violence are less likely than their white counterparts to report such forms of abuse to the police.

38. Buist and Lenning, *Queer Criminology*; D. Meyer, "Omar Mateen as U.S. Citizen"; Stewart-Winter, *Queer Clout*.

39. Daum, "The War on Solicitation"; Dwyer and Tomsen "The Past Is the Past?"; Mogul, Ritchie, and Whitlock, *Queer (In)Justice*.

40. R. Ferguson, *One-Dimensional Queer*; Hanhardt, *Safe Space*.

41. Daum, "The War on Solicitation"; Mogul, Ritchie, and Whitlock, *Queer (In)Justice*; Spade, *Normal Life*.

42. Dwyer and Tomsen, "The Past Is the Past?"; Hanhardt, *Safe Space*; Haritaworn, *Queer Lovers and Hateful Others*.

43. Hanhardt, *Safe Space*; Reddy, *Freedom with Violence*; Stewart-Winter, *Queer Clout*.

44. K. Gibson, *Street Kids*; Mogul, Ritchie, and Whitlock, *Queer (In)Justice*; Ritchie, "Crimes against Nature."

45. For more on police officers' perceptions of a survivor's credibility, see O'Neal, "Victim Is Not Credible," in which the author outlines the factors, including indicators of "real rape" and judgments of "character flaws," that affect the likelihood of officers questioning a female survivor's credibility.

46. Hanhardt, *Safe Space*; Judge, *Blackwashing Homophobia*; Spade, *Normal Life*.

47. D. Meyer, *Violence against Queer People*.

48. Carruthers, *Unapologetic*; Ransby, *Making All Black Lives Matter*; K.-Y. Taylor, *From #BlackLivesMatter to Black Liberation*.

49. Ritchie, *Invisible No More*; Salamon, *The Life and Death of Latisha King*.

50. "A Few Quick Statistics"; J. L. Jackson, "Sexual Necropolitics and Prison Rape Elimination"; Ritchie, *Invisible No More*; "Responding to Transgender Victims of Sexual Assault."

51. Daum, "The War on Solicitation"; Dwyer and Tomsen "The Past Is the Past?"; Epp, Maynard-Moody, and Haider-Markel, *Pulled Over*; Mogul, Ritchie, and Whitlock, *Queer (In)Justice*.

52. Dwyer and Tomsen "The Past Is the Past?"; Epp, Maynard-Moody, and Haider-Markel, *Pulled Over*.

CHAPTER 3. SURVIVORS' SELF-BLAME AND DIFFERENCES WITHIN THE QUEER UMBRELLA

1. For analyses of survivors' self-blame from a psychological perspective and reviews of this body of literature, see Binion and Gray, "Minority Stress Theory"; Kennedy and Prock, "I Still Feel Like I Am Not Normal."

2. Gasper et al., in "You're Gay, It's Just What Happens," found similar results among sexual minority men in Canada. Jennifer Nash, in "Black Anality," has argued that Black women's sexuality is frequently imagined to be dirty, toxic, or wasteful. In this study, I did not find racial differences in the percentage of participants who described feelings of dirtiness, yet the high percentage of Black queer men in the sample may have informed the extent to which respondents mentioned this emotional response.

3. Alcoff, *Rape and Resistance*; Harding, *Asking for It*; O'Neal, "Victim Is Not Credible"; Stubbs-Richardson, Rader, and Cosby, "Tweeting Rape Culture." For more on how these dynamics operate in other contexts, see William Ryan's classic text, *Blaming the Victim*.

4. Estrich, *Real Rape*; Madriz, *Nothing Bad Happens to Good Girls*; Pascoe and Hollander, "Good Guys Don't Rape." There are some exceptions to this trend in media, such as the recent HBO show, *I May Destroy You*.

5. Gavey, *Just Sex?*; Harris, *Beyond the Rapist*; Soss, Fording, and Schram, *Disciplining the Poor*.

6. Callis, "Playing with Butler and Foucault"; Garber, *Vice Versa*; Toft and Yip, "Intimacy Negotiated."

7. Diamond, *Sexual Fluidity*; Fahs, "Compulsory Bisexuality?"

8. Bermea, Eeden-Moorefield, and Khaw, "A Systematic Review"; Turell, Brown, and Herrmann, "Disproportionately High." While these "cheater" stereotypes are undoubtedly problematic, bisexual people also remain active in polyamorous communities, as attempts to distance bisexual people from such stereotypes can institute a conservative politics in which monogamy becomes privileged over non-monogamy—see Toft and Yip, "Intimacy Negotiated." For more on the regulation of sexual normativity in relation to compulsory monogamy, see Schippers, *Beyond Monogamy*.

9. Belous and Bauman, "What's in a Name?"; Callis, "Bisexual, Pansexual, Queer." In *A History of Bisexuality*, Angelides outlines a theory of bisexuality that points to how bisexual people historically understood their sexualities in a similar way to modern notions of pansexuality, even though the discourse of pansexuality had not yet developed.

10. Further, positioning bisexuality as "less evolved" than pansexuality depends on a construction of bisexual people as not doing enough to resist the gender binary. Asking primarily bisexual and pansexual people whether they are challenging binary notions of gender and sexuality remains unhelpful in that it relegates this task to, and places additional pressures on, these groups. Alternatively, heterosexual and homosexual people also need to engage in work that helps to destabilize binary understandings of gender and sexuality.

11. Callis, "Playing with Butler and Foucault"; Foucault, *The History of Sexuality*; Katz, *The Invention of Heterosexuality*.

12. Canaday, *The Straight State*; Chauncey, *Gay New York*.

13. Butler, *Gender Trouble*; Fausto-Sterling, *Sexing the Body*; Stryker, *Transgender History*; West and Zimmerman, "Doing Gender."

14. The recruitment flyer read: "Do You Identify as a Gay, Bisexual, or Queer Man, and Have You Experienced Rape or Sexual Assault Since You've Been 18?"

15. Hlavka, "Speaking of Stigma"; McGuffey "Saving Masculinity"; Powell, Hlavka, and Mulla "Intersectionality and Credibility."

16. Elliot, "Engaging Trans Debates"; A. Johnson, "Transnormativity"; B. Rogers, *Trans Men in the South*. For more on how transnormativity often relies on whiteness and negates Blackness, see Snorton, *Black on Both Sides*.

17. Several of the transgender men in Schilt's study, as documented in *Just One of the Guys?* experienced employment discrimination in which employers had characterized transgender men as visually unappealing to a cisgender audience and then fired a transgender man from his job.

18. Guadalupe-Diaz, in *Transgressed*, similarly found that many transgender survivors relied on their friends as a main avenue of support. Guadalupe-Diaz connects this violence with a larger anti-transgender social environment that emboldens abusive partners and causes greater emotional harm to the survivor. In particular, the author states, "Trans people live in what can be described as a 'trans-antagonistic' culture, an overtly hostile and oppositional social environment that regulates, polices, and maintains recognition of only two genders" (27). These structural conditions then make it more likely that transgender people will stay in abusive relationships and that violence against them will be justified or condoned. For more on how dominant constructions of masculinity may contribute to this violence, see Sumerau, *Violent Manhood*.

19. For more on transgender people's experiences of intimate partner violence, see Guadalupe-Diaz, *Transgressed*; Messinger and Guadalupe-Diaz, *Transgender Intimate Partner Violence*; M. Rogers, "Challenging Cisgenderism."

20. Daum, "The War on Solicitation"; Safer et al., "Barriers to Health Care"; Spade, *Normal Life*.

21. Abelson, *Men in Place*; Safer et al., "Barriers to Health Care"; Stein, *Unbound*.

22. Lee, "The Trans Panic Defense Revisited"; Salamon, *The Life and Death of Latisha King*; Schilt and Westbrook, "Doing Gender, Doing Heteronormativity."

23. See Pfeffer's *Queering Families* for an analysis of cisgender women's emotional labor in their partnerships with transgender men.

24. Buist and Stone, "Transgender Victims and Offenders"; Dwyer, "Policing Lesbian, Gay, Bisexual, and Transgender Young People"; Robinson, *Coming Out to the Streets*.

25. Daum, "The War on Solicitation"; Easterbrook-Smith, "Not on the Street"; Mogul, Ritchie, and Whitlock, *Queer (In)Justice*.

26. K. Gibson, *Street Kids*; Spade, *Normal Life*; Stotzer, "Law Enforcement and Criminal Justice Personnel."

27. Meadow, *Trans Kids*; Spade, *Normal Life*.

28. Sprankle et al., "The Role of Sex Work Stigma"; Weitzer, "Resistance to Sex Work Stigma."

29. Shepp et al., "Sexual Assault Survivors"; Sprankle et al., "The Role of Sex Work Stigma."

30. Hirsch and Khan, *Sexual Citizens*; Ringrose and Renold, "Slut-Shaming"; K. Weiss, "Male Sexual Victimization."

CHAPTER 4. RACIAL DIFFERENCES
REGARDING EMASCULATION

1. Funk, "Queer Men and Sexual Assault"; Hlavka, "Speaking of Stigma"; Stanko and Hobdell, "Assault on Men"; K. Weiss, "Too Ashamed to Report."

2. Ferrales, Brehm, and McElrath, "Gender-Based Violence," 572.

3. Coxell and King, "Gender, Sexual Orientation, and Sexual Assault"; P. Dunn, "Men as Victims"; Funk, "Queer Men and Sexual Assault"; Tillapaugh, "The Wounds of Our Experience."

4. Javaid, "The Dark Side of Men," 275.

5. Ferrales, Brehm, and McElrath, "Gender-Based Violence," 566.

6. See D. Meyer, "Racializing Emasculation," for the protocol of the emasculation questions asked during the interview and for a table with a more specific numerical breakdown by race/ethnicity and by intra-racial/interracial assault.

7. P. H. Collins, *Black Sexual Politics*; Deska et al., "Black Racial Phenotypicality"; Hoberman, *Black and Blue*.

8. Messerschmidt, *Masculinities in the Making*.

9. McCune, *Sexual Discretion*; Muñoz, *Disidentifications*; Ocampo, "Making Masculinity."

10. Higginbotham, *Righteous Discontent*.

11. P. H. Collins, "The Tie That Binds"; Grundy, "Lifting the Veil"; McGuffey, "Blacks and Racial Appraisals."

12. In this chapter, with gender expression, I have collapsed participants who resisted dominant constructions of masculinity and identified as "in between feminine and masculine" with those who identified as "feminine" and "more feminine than masculine." In this sense, respondents are divided based on a masculine/non-masculine divide in this chapter. Gender expression is obviously more complex than this masculine/non-masculine binary would suggest, yet the most salient intra-racial differences I found in terms of emasculation were between participants who identified as masculine and those who did not.

13. Ferrales, Brehm, and McElrath, "Gender-Based Violence"; Hlavka, "Speaking of Stigma"; Oeur, *Black Boys Apart*.

14. McGuffey, "Blacks and Racial Appraisals," 288.

15. Badour et al., "Disgust, Mental Contamination, and Posttraumatic Stress"; Hirsch and Khan, *Sexual Citizens*; Ringrose and Renold, "Slut-Shaming."

16. Sjoberg, *Women as Wartime Rapists*; K. Weiss, "Male Sexual Victimization."

17. Qu and Dumay, "The Qualitative Research Interview."

18. E. P. Johnson, *Appropriating Blackness*; D. Meyer, *Violence against Queer People*; Pascoe, *Dude, You're a Fag*; Ocampo, "Making Masculinity."

19. See Hlavka, "Speaking of Stigma," and K. Weiss, "Too Ashamed to Report," for analyses of how young men and boys may feel emasculated.

20. Allen, "Male Victims of Rape"; Javaid, "The Dark Side of Men"; Walker, Archer, and Davies, "Effects of Rape on Men."

21. Mathers, Sumerau, and Cragun, "The Limits of Homonormativity"; Walters, *The Tolerance Trap*. These social changes arguably began several decades ago—see Duggan, "The New Homonormativity," Conrad, *Against Equality*, and Warner, *The Trouble with Normal*, for analyses of "homonormativity" and for how these processes operated in the 1990s. For a critique of "homonormativity" as a concept, see G. Brown, "Homonormativity."

22. Hlavka, "Speaking of Stigma"; K. Weiss, "Too Ashamed to Report."

23. McGuffey "Saving Masculinity"; Powell, Hlavka, and Mulla, "Intersectionality and Credibility."

24. Messinger and Koon-Magnin, "Sexual Violence."

25. P. H. Collins, *Black Sexual Politics*; A. Ferguson, *Bad Boys*; Hoberman, *Black and Blue*.

26. R. Donovan and Williams, "Living at the Intersection"; Grundy, "Lifting the Veil"; McGuffey, "Rape and Racial Appraisals"; S. Nash, "Through Black Eyes."

27. D. Meyer, *Violence against Queer People*.

28. Khan et al., "The Social Organization of Sexual Assault."

29. Ferrales, Brehm, and McElrath, "Gender-Based Violence"; K. Weiss, "Too Ashamed to Report."

30. McCune, *Sexual Discretion*; Muñoz, *Disidentifications*.

CHAPTER 5. CONSTRUCTING HIERARCHIES
OF VICTIMHOOD

1. Henry, "Theorizing Wartime Rape"; Javaid, "Poison Ivy"; Tillapaugh, "The Wounds of Our Experience."

2. Estrich, *Real Rape*.

3. Pascoe and Hollander, "Good Guys Don't Rape," 74.

4. Freedman, *Redefining Rape*; Gilson, "Vulnerability and Victimization"; Messner, "Bad Men, Good Men, Bystanders."

5. Hlavka, "Speaking of Stigma," 498–499.

6. Hlavka, , "Speaking of Stigma," 499.

7. I quote Linda Martín Alcoff, in *Rape and Resistance*, later in this chapter for a specific example.

8. Alcoff, *Rape and Resistance*; Fanghanel, *Disrupting Rape Culture*; Harris, *Beyond the Rapist*; Mulla, *The Violence of Care*; O'Neal, "Victim Is Not Credible";

Venema, "Police Officer Schema." As Corrigan documents, in *Up Against a Wall*, an additional problem beyond the mistreatment of survivors is that community institutions frequently fail to take rape seriously, as organizations that advocate for survivors often remain institutionally marginalized from the larger political and cultural environment in which they are located.

9. Cl. Cohen, *Male Rape Is a Feminist Issue*; Henry, "Theorizing Wartime Rape"; Jenness and Fenstermaker, "Forty Years after Brownmiller"; McLean, "The Male Victim of Sexual Assault."

10. Through 2012, the federal definition of rape for data collection purposes was framed entirely around women, effectively excluding men as survivors. For a more detailed discussion, see S. Jordan, Mehrotra, and Fujikawa, "Mandating Inclusion"; Messinger and Koon-Magnin, "Sexual Violence."

11. For the interview protocol of how I asked these questions, see D. Meyer, "Constructing Hierarchies of Victimhood."

12. Some studies involving women survivors have revealed considerably higher percentages in terms of those who knew other survivors—for example, DeKeseredy and colleagues, in "Thinking Critically," point out that 81 percent of the women survivors in their study knew other women who were sexually assaulted. This difference points to the possibility that participants did not have discussions about sexual assault with others they knew, which likely intensified their feelings of social isolation after experiencing the violation.

13. P. H. Collins, *Black Sexual Politics*; E. P. Johnson, *Appropriating Blackness*; McCune, *Sexual Discretion*. For more on the effects, both positive and negative, of race-based community norms, see N. Jones, *The Chosen Ones*, in which the author shows that police interactions, violent experiences, and conservative gender ideologies affect Black men's perceptions of themselves regarding harmful behavior they may have enacted.

14. Armstrong, Gleckman-Krut, and Johnson, "Silence, Power, and Inequality"; Curry, "Expendables for Whom."

15. Hancock, *Solidarity Politics for Millennials*.

16. Blumell and Rodriguez, "Ambivalent Sexism and Gay Men"; T. Edwards, *Erotics and Politics*; Hale and Ojeda, "Acceptable Femininity?"; Ward, "Queer Sexism."

17. For more on how this operates in gay male communities, see T. Edwards, *Erotics and Politics*; Hale and Ojeda, "Acceptable Femininity?"; Ward, "Dyke Methods."

18. Hlavka, "Speaking of Stigma"; Martin, "The Rape Prone Culture"; Small, "Constructing Sexual Harm"; K. Weiss, "Too Ashamed to Report."

19. Fanghanel, *Disrupting Rape Culture*; Harris, *Beyond the Rapist*; Messinger and Koon-Magnin, "Sexual Violence."

20. Alcoff, *Rape and Resistance*; Hlavka, "Normalizing Sexual Violence"; Pascoe and Hollander, "Good Guys Don't Rape."

21. Alcoff, *Rape and Resistance*; Harris, *Beyond the Rapist*.

22. J. Dunn, *Judging Victims*; Ricciardelli, Spencer, and Dodge, "Society Wants to See a True Victim."

23. Hoskin, "Femmephobia"; Richardson, "Whether You Are Gay or Straight."

24. Schwalbe et al., "Generic Processes."

25. Madriz, *Nothing Bad Happens to Good Girls*; Messner, "Bad Men, Good Men, Bystanders."

26. Fahs, Plante, and McClelland, "Working at the Crossroads"; Harris, *Beyond the Rapist*.

27. Bauer, *Queer BDSM Intimacies*; Fahs and McClelland, "When Sex and Power Collide."

28. Bauer, *Queer BDSM Intimacies*; Fahs, Plante, and McClelland, "Working at the Crossroads"; Fischel, *Screw Consent*.

29. Barker, "Consent Is a Grey Area?"; Harris, *Beyond the Rapist*; Pascoe and Hollander, "Good Guys Don't Rape."

30. Javaid, "Poison Ivy."

31. Hookup cultures may of course contribute to forms of sexual assault—for more on these effects on college campuses, see Wade, *American Hookup*.

32. Hills et al., "Understanding How University Students"; Hindes and Fileborn, "Reporting on Sexual Violence."

33. Brownmiller, *Against Our Will*; see Cahill, *Rethinking Rape*, for a summary and critique of these arguments.

34. Dworkin, *Intercourse*; MacKinnon, *Toward a Feminist Theory of the State*.

35. Alcoff, *Rape and Resistance*; Gavey, *Just Sex?*

36. Gilson, "Vulnerability and Victimization"; Henry, "Theorizing Wartime Rape." In *Rethinking Rape*, Cahill critiques both the "rape as violence" and the "rape as an expression of sexuality" perspectives. See Mardorossian, *Framing the Rape Victim* for a critique of Cahill's argument and a consideration of agency that does not rely on notions of autonomous subjectivity.

37. Estrich, *Real Rape*; Harris, *Beyond the Rapist*; Messinger and Koon-Magnin, "Sexual Violence." For more on the extent to which individuals on hookup apps may be strangers, or not, see M. Davis et al., "Location, Safety, and (Non) Strangers," in which the authors argue against monolithic understandings of queer men's sexual lives on digital media.

38. Clark, "The Vulnerability of the Penis"; K. Weiss, "Too Ashamed to Report."

39. Nguyen, *A View from the Bottom*; Ravenhill and de Visser, "It Takes a Man."

40. Fahs and McClelland, "When Sex and Power Collide"; Gavey, *Just Sex?*; Harris, "Yes Means Yes."

41. Mason, *The Spectacle of Violence*; Perry, *In the Name of Hate*; Tomsen, *Violence, Prejudice, and Sexuality*.

42. D. Meyer, *Violence against Queer People*; Perry, *In the Name of Hate*.

43. Foucault, *The History of Sexuality*; Sullivan, *A Critical Introduction to Queer Theory*.

44. Butler, *Gender Trouble*; Sullivan, *A Critical Introduction to Queer Theory*.

45. Alcoff, *Rape and Resistance*, 2. Brison, in *Aftermath*, argues that survivors are often urged to forget about their traumatic experiences and contends that this response from others arises out an active fear of believing that a similar experience could happen to oneself.

CHAPTER 6. OUTING, DISCLOSING MARGINALIZED IDENTITIES, AND NAVIGATING MULTIPLE STIGMAS

1. de Heer and Jones, "Measuring Sexual Violence"; Garvey, Hitchins, and McDonald, "Queer-Spectrum Student Sexual Violence"; Patterson, *Queering Sexual Violence*.

2. de Heer and Jones, "Measuring Sexual Violence"; Garvey, Hitchins, and McDonald, "Queer-Spectrum Student Sexual Violence"; Patterson, *Queering Sexual Violence*. For more on how closeting and outing remain intersectional processes, see McDonald, Harris, and Ramirez, "Revealing and Concealing Difference."

3. Saguy, in *Come Out, Come Out, Whoever You Are*, examines how a wide range of groups and activists disclose aspects of their identity to resist stigma and advocate for social change, including but not limited to #MeToo activists. She also explores these processes for more conservative movements that may mock or undermine an LGBTQ coming out process.

4. Halperin and Hoppe, *The War on Sex*; Hoppe, *Punishing Disease*; Niedt, "PrEP Talk."

5. Crimp, *Melancholia and Moralism*; McKay, *Patient Zero*.

6. P. H. Collins, *Black Sexual Politics*; Ghaziani, *The Dividends of Dissent*.

7. Ghaziani, *The Dividends of Dissent*. See Bost, *Evidence of Being*, for more on how Black queer men during the 1980s resisted their marginalization in mainstream culture and LGBTQ communities, including through media, poetry, and performance. Mumford, in *Not Straight, Not White*, explores Black queer men's historical marginalization, as well as their resistance to structural inequalities, in an even larger historical context, from the 1950s to the 1990s. For more on how the marginalization experienced by Black LGBTQ people who are HIV positive continued into the 1990s and beyond, see Ca. Cohen, *The Boundaries of Blackness*.

8. Halperin and Hoppe, *The War on Sex*; Hoppe, *Punishing Disease*; O'Byrne and Holmes, "Public Health STI/HIV Surveillance."

9. See Cheng, "How to Survive," for an analysis of how white gay men have typically featured most centrally in films and documentaries focusing on

HIV-positive people and groups such as ACT UP. Kilty and Bogosavljevic, in "Emotional Storytelling," emphasize how these portrayals are often more pathologizing when Black queer men are represented as HIV positive.

10. Barker, "Consent Is a Grey Area?"; Fanghanel, "Asking for It"; M. Weiss, *Techniques of Pleasure.*

11. Barker, "Consent Is a Grey Area?"

12. Bauer, *Queer BDSM Intimacies*; Dunkley and Brotto, "The Role of Consent"; M. Weiss, *Techniques of Pleasure.*

13. Fanghanel, "Asking for It."

14. Barker, Iantaffi, and Gupta, "Kinky Clients"; Dunkley and Brotto, "The Role of Consent."

15. Barker, "Consent Is a Grey Area?"

16. Fanghanel, "Asking for It"; M. Weiss, *Techniques of Pleasure.*

17. For more on how whiteness operates in BDSM spaces, see Martinez, "Overwhelming Whiteness of BDSM."

18. Hasinoff, *Sexting Panic*; McGlynn, Rackeley, and Houghton, "Beyond 'Revenge Porn.'" For analyses that include queer people, see Hall and Hearn, *Revenge Pornography*, and Waldman, "Law, Privacy, and Online Dating."

CONCLUSION

1. P. H. Collins, "On Violence"; Fanghanel, *Disrupting Rape Culture*; Harris, *Beyond the Rapist*; Pascoe and Hollander, "Good Guys Don't Rape"; Price, *Structural Violence*. In *Gender Identity, Sexual Orientation, and Sexual Assault*, Schulze, Koon-Magnin, and Bryan found that including sexual orientation into studies predicted higher levels of rape myth acceptance than traditional analyses that have presumed a heterosexual encounter. This finding points to the importance of considering sexuality and anti-queer prejudice in studies of attitudes toward sexual assault, in addition to the significance of destabilizing heteronormative assumptions in this line of research.

2. MacKinnon, *Toward a Feminist Theory of the State*; Messner, "Bad Men, Good Men, Bystanders"; Russo, *Feminist Accountability.*

3. Cahill, *Rethinking Rape*; Messner, "Bad Men, Good Men, Bystanders"; Pascoe and Hollander, "Good Guys Don't Rape."

4. Ehrlich, *Representing Rape*; Fanghanel, *Disrupting Rape Culture*; Hlavka, "Normalizing Sexual Violence"; Hills et al., "Understanding How University Students"; Walfield, "Men Cannot Be Raped."

5. J. Jordan, *Serial Survivors*; Kennedy and Prock, "I Still Feel Like I Am Not Normal."

6. Alcoff, *Rape and Resistance*; Harris, *Beyond the Rapist*; O'Neal, "Victim Is Not Credible"; Pascoe and Hollander, "Good Guys Don't Rape."

7. Walfield, "Men Cannot Be Raped"; K. Weiss, "Too Ashamed to Report." Some studies indicate that this blame may be directed at men who have been sexually assaulted by women the most, due to gendered understandings that men should be able to prevent women's violence—see Hlavka, "Speaking of Stigma"; K. Weiss, "Too Ashamed to Report."

8. Coulter et al., "Prevalence of Past-Year Sexual Assault"; Coulter and Rankin, "College Sexual Assault and Campus Climate"; Curry, "Expendables for Whom"; Hine, "Rape and the Inner Lives"; Wooten, "Revealing a Hidden Curriculum."

9. Alcoff, *Rape and Resistance*; Estrich, *Real Rape*; Harris, *Beyond the Rapist*.

10. Colburn and Melander, "Beyond Black and White"; Muhammad, *The Condemnation of Blackness*; Russell-Brown, *The Color of Crime*; Suddler, *Presumed Criminal*.

11. An. Davis, *Women, Race and Class*; Curry, "Expendables for Whom"; Ralston, "An Intersectional Approach"; Slakoff and Brennan, "The Differential Representation."

12. Curry, "Expendables for Whom"; Ralston, "An Intersectional Approach."

13. Bost, *Evidence of Being*; Mumford, *Not Straight, Not White*; Reid-Pharr, *Black Gay Man*; Stockton, *Beautiful Bottom, Beautiful Shame*; Wingfield, "Are Some Emotions Marked 'Whites Only'?"

14. Bourke, "Foreword," ix. See also, Bedera and Nordmeyer, "An Inherently Masculine Practice"; Fahlberg and Pepper, "Masculinity and Sexual Violence."

15. Henry, "Theorizing Wartime Rape"; Phipps, "Every Woman Knows a Weinstein"; Sjoberg, *Women as Wartime Rapists*.

16. Gilson, "Vulnerability and Victimization"; Henry, "Theorizing Wartime Rape."

17. Larance et al., "Understanding and Addressing"; Little, "Who's the Victim Here?"; Messner, "Forks in the Road." While this history of false equivalency exists, research also suggests that many violent relationships involve both partners using violence—see Bates, "Current Controversies."

18. For example, Michael Messner, in "Bad Men, Good Men, Bystanders," has argued that women "are still the major victims of gender-based violence and are still also the major source of activist response to it" (61).

19. Curry, "Expendables for Whom."

20. Coulter et al., "Prevalence of Past-Year Sexual Assault"; Curry, "Expendables for Whom"; Stemple and Meyer, "The Sexual Victimization."

21. Coulter et al., "Prevalence of Past-Year Sexual Assault"; Stemple, Flores, and Meyer, "Sexual Victimization"; Terwiel, "What Is Carceral Feminism?"; Wooten, "Revealing a Hidden Curriculum." Dean Spade, in *Mutual Aid*, argues for an expansion of solidarity with individuals on the US political left, through the advancement of mutual aid projects, collective action, and movement building. He characterizes a "deservingness" hierarchy as a potential pitfall of mutual aid projects, given that such hierarchies may prevent collective mobilization and

establish more individuals as "undeserving" of mutual aid—a designation that has historically and continually been associated with racial minorities.

22. Graham, "Male Rape and the Careful Construction"; Tillapaugh, "The Wounds of Our Experience."

23. Doherty and Anderson, "Making Sense of Male Rape"; Donaldson, "A Million Jockers, Punks, and Queens"; Tillapaugh, "The Wounds of Our Experience."

24. Graham, "Male Rape and the Careful Construction." See also, Hindes and Fileborn, "Reporting on Sexual Violence," who found that news media frame gay men's advances on heterosexual men as violence, while conversely constructing heterosexual men's advances on women as nonviolence.

25. Davies and Hudson, "Judgments toward Male and Transgendered Victims"; Lowe and Rogers, "The Scope of Male Rape"; Rumney, "Gay Male Rape Victims."

26. Goldscheid, "Sexual Assault by Federal Actors"; Parent and Ferriter, "The Co-occurrence of Asexuality"; Ritchie, *Invisible No More*.

27. An. Davis and Shaylor, "Race, Gender, and the Prison Industrial Complex"; "A Few Quick Statistics"; J. L. Jackson, "Sexual Necropolitics and Prison Rape Elimination"; Ritchie, *Invisible No More*. For more on the many harsh conditions facing women prisoners, as well as the strategies employed by these women to navigate gendered violence, see Owen, Wells, and Pollock, *In Search of Safety*.

28. Goldscheid, "Sexual Assault by Federal Actors"; O'Leary, "Addressing the Epidemic."

29. Messinger and Koon-Magnin, "Sexual Violence"; Rosenberg and Oswin, "Trans Embodiment"; Spade, *Normal Life*.

30. I. Meyer et al., "Incarceration Rates."

31. Karlsson and Zielinski, "Sexual Victimization."

32. Deer and Barefoot, "The Limits of the State Law"; Terwiel, "What Is Carceral Feminism?"; Thuma, *All Our Trials*.

33. Bracewell, "Sex Wars"; Gruber, *The Feminist War on Crime*; Musto, "Transing Critical Criminology"; Seigel, *Violence Work*.

34. Goodmark, "Reimagining VAWA"; Schenwar and Law, *Prison by Any Other Name*; Thuma, *All Our Trials*.

35. Sawyer and Wagner, "Mass Incarceration."

36. McCrea et al., "Understanding Violence"; Seigel, *Violence Work*; Spade, *Normal Life*; Wacquant, *Prisons of Poverty*; Wang, *Carceral Capitalism*.

37. Best, *Random Violence*; R. Collins, *Violence*.

38. R. Brown, "Policing in American History"; Spruill, "Slave Patrols"; Williams, *Our Enemies in Blue*. See Haley, *No Mercy Here*, for how forms of racialized gender violence continued after the Civil War against Black women, as they were imprisoned and subjected to brutal convict labor systems. Police forces were also instrumental in regulating Jim Crow laws mandating separate public

facilities, and mass incarceration over the past fifty years has affected Black Americans to a great extent—see Alexander, *The New Jim Crow*; Hinton, *From the War on Poverty to the War on Crime*; Kilgore, "Mass Incarceration"; Schoenfeld, *Building the Prison State*.

39. H. E. Barnes, "Historical Origin of the Prison System"; Foucault, *Discipline and Punish*.

40. H. E. Barnes, "Historical Origin of the Prison System"; Foucault, *Discipline and Punish*.

41. An. Davis, *Are Prisons Obsolete?*; Gotell, "Reassessing"; Musto, "Transing Critical Criminology." See Schenwar and Law, *Prison by Any Other Name*, for an analysis of how "alternatives" to imprisonment are often framed in ways that actually expand punitiveness.

42. Law, "Against Carceral Feminism"; Ch. Taylor, "Anti-Carceral Feminism"; Terwiel, "What Is Carceral Feminism?"

43. Ptacek, *Restorative Justice and Violence against Women*; Rodriguez, Ben-Moshe, and Rakes, "Carceral Protectionism"; Terwiel, "What Is Carceral Feminism?"

44. Deer and Barefoot, "The Limits of the State Law"; Kim, "From Carceral Feminism"; Zinsstag and Keenan, *Restorative Responses to Sexual Violence*.

45. Goodmark, "Reimagining VAWA"; Schenwar and Law, *Prison by Any Other Name*; Spade, *Mutual Aid*.

46. Goodmark, "Reimagining VAWA"; Ch. Taylor, *Foucault, Feminism, and Sex Crimes*; Thuma, *All Our Trials*.

47. Johnstone, *Restorative Justice*; Ptacek, *Restorative Justice and Violence against Women*; Zinsstag and Keenan, *Restorative Responses to Sexual Violence*.

48. Sherman and Strang, *Restorative Justice*.

49. Kim, "Anti-Carceral Feminism"; Schenwar and Law, *Prison by Any Other Name*; Ch. Taylor, "Anti-Carceral Feminism."

50. Sherman and Strang, *Restorative Justice*. See also, Goodmark, "Reimagining VAWA," 12; Kim, "Anti-Carceral Feminism," 316.

51. Kim, "From Carceral Feminism"; Rodriguez, Ben-Moshe, and Rakes, "Carceral Protectionism"; Ch. Taylor, *Foucault, Feminism, and Sex Crimes*.

52. Law, "Against Carceral Feminism"; Russo, *Feminist Accountability*; Schenwar and Law, *Prison by Any Other Name*; Thuma, *All Our Trials*.

53. Kim, "Anti-Carceral Feminism," 313; see also, Spade, *Mutual Aid*.

54. Mingus, "Transformative Justice."

55. Mingus, "Transformative Justice."

56. INCITE! Women of Color against Violence, "Community Accountability"; Mingus, "Transformative Justice."

57. Kim, "Anti-Carceral Feminism"; Rodriguez, Ben-Moshe, and Rakes, "Carceral Protectionism"; Ch. Taylor, *Foucault, Feminism, and Sex Crimes*. For more on the history of how antiracist activists have resisted the carceral state,

see Dillon, *Fugitive Life*. Antiracist activists during the 1970s were frequently involved in, or linked with, movements combatting US imperialism and global capitalism. Roderick Ferguson, in *One-Dimensional Queer*, further shows that this history of gay liberation activism in the 1970s and beyond was never a singular focus on sexual freedom, but placed radical critiques of colonization, incarceration, and capitalism central to their fight for social change. For more on this leftist activism, see Carroll, *Mobilizing New York*, and Hobson, *Lavender and Red*. For more recent resistance in transgender movements, see Stanley and Smith, *Captive Genders*.

58. Musto, *Control and Protect*; Russo, *Feminist Accountability*; Ch. Taylor, "Anti-Carceral Feminism"; Terwiel, "What Is Carceral Feminism?"

59. Gotell, "Reassessing"; Spade, *Mutual Aid*; E. Sweet, "Carceral Feminism."

60. Law, "Against Carceral Feminism"; Musto, *Control and Protect*; Rodriguez, Ben-Moshe, and Rakes, "Carceral Protectionism."

61. Bracewell, "Sex Wars"; An. Davis, *Are Prisons Obsolete?*; Gotell, "Reassessing"; Musto, "Transing Critical Criminology."

62. Gotell, "Reassessing"; Gruber, *The Feminist War on Crime*; Press, "#MeToo"; Vitale, *The End of Policing*.

63. Schenwar and Law, *Prison by Any Other Name*; E. Sweet, "Carceral Feminism"; Thuma, *All Our Trials*.

64. Goodmark, "Reimagining VAWA"; Law, "Against Carceral Feminism"; Stark, *Coercive Control*.

65. Goodmark, *Decriminalizing Domestic Violence*, "Reimagining VAWA."

66. DeKeseredy et al., "Thinking Critically."

67. Goodmark, "Reimagining VAWA"; Gruber, *The Feminist War on Crime*; Law, "Against Carceral Feminism."

68. Goodmark, "Reimagining VAWA," 8. For more, see Deer and Barefoot, "The Limits of the State Law."

69. Goodmark, "Reimagining VAWA"; Soss, Fording, and Schram, *Disciplining the Poor*; Wacquant, *Prisons of Poverty*.

70. Gottschalk, *Caught*; Musto, "Transing Critical Criminology"; Soss, Fording, and Schram, *Disciplining the Poor*; Thuma, *All Our Trials*.

71. Moran, in "Homophobic Violence," has argued that traditional accounts of violence reduce its enactment to the effects of social class, while many feminists have pointed out that relatively privileged groups of men, such as middle-class college students, enact some forms of violence, such as sexual assault, at rates comparable to more marginalized men. In response, Moran argues that while many feminists have emphasized the important effects of gender inequality, she worries that social class has too frequently been ignored in feminist analyses and points to the need for examining the overlap of gender and class. For more on the complex relationship between sexual assault and social class, see Phipps, "Rape and Respectability."

72. Goodmark, "Reimagining VAWA," 10.

73. de Heer et al., "Sexual Consent and Communication"; DeKeseredy et al., "Polyvictimization"; Ford and Soto-Marquez, "Sexual Assault Victimization"; Messinger and Koon-Magnin, "Sexual Violence."

74. Coulter et al., "Prevalence of Past-Year Sexual Assault"; Guadalupe-Diaz, *Transgressed*; Messinger and Koon-Magnin, "Sexual Violence."

75. Law, "Against Carceral Feminism"; Press, "#MeToo"; Thuma, *All Our Trials*.

76. Deer and Barefoot, "The Limits of the State Law"; Goodmark, "Reimagining VAWA"; Gruber, *The Feminist War on Crime*; Musto, *Control and Protect*.

77. Flores, *Caught Up*; Kilgore, "Mass Incarceration"; Sawyer and Wagner, "Mass Incarceration."

78. Browne, *Dark Matters*; Flores, *Caught Up*; K. Gibson, *Street Kids*.

79. Kilgore, "Mass Incarceration"; Sawyer and Wagner, "Mass Incarceration"; Schenwar and Law, *Prison by Any Other Name*. For more on how movements designed to reduce sexual violence have sometimes expanded the surveillance powers of social service agencies, see Bumiller, *In an Abusive State*. Terwiel, in "What Is Carceral Feminism?" argues that the carceral state did not arise out of feminism but distorted the work that feminists were doing. For more on this complex history, see Gottschalk, *The Prison and the Gallows*.

80. Law, "Against Carceral Feminism"; Thuma, *All Our Trials*; Whittier, "Carceral and Intersectional Feminism."

81. Goodmark, "Reimagining VAWA"; Whittier, "Carceral and Intersectional Feminism."

82. Goodmark, *Decriminalizing Domestic Violence*; Goodmark, "Reimagining VAWA."

83. Goodmark, "Reimagining VAWA."

84. INCITE! Women of Color Against Violence, "Community Accountability."

85. GenerationFIVE, "Transformative Justice Handbook."

86. Terwiel, "What Is Carceral Feminism?," 434. See also Deer, "Decolonizing Rape Law"; Deer and Barefoot, "The Limits of the State Law"; A. Smith, "Decolonizing Anti-Rape Law."

87. DeKeseredy et al., "Thinking Critically."

88. Alcoff, *Rape and Resistance*; Fanghanel, *Disrupting Rape Culture*; Hlavka, "Normalizing Sexual Violence."

89. Hannon, "Judge Ruled."

90. M. Miller, "A Steep Price to Pay."

91. See Hasinoff, *Sexting Panic*, for an analysis of the ways to deal with this social problem in non-carceral ways. See Bernstein, "Militarized Humanitarianism Meets Carceral Feminism," and Musto, *Control and Protect*, for further analyses of how criminalization occurs in campaigns constructed around "sex trafficking."

92. For more on feminist complicities with the carceral state, see Bernstein, *Brokered Subjects*; Bumiller, *In an Abusive State*; Press, "#MeToo Must Avoid 'Carceral Feminism'"; Ch. Taylor, "Anti-Carceral Feminism." I have argued that a similar approach operates in some LGBTQ communities and forms of advocacy—see D. Meyer, "Resisting Hate Crime Discourse." See Russell, *Queer Histories and the Politics of Policing*, for more on this matter. For an example of how sexual assault activism may reinforce carceral feminism or penal populism, see Phillips and Chagnon, "Six Months Is a Joke." More broadly, for a review of some critiques of #MeToo, see Gill and Orgad, "The Shifting Terrain."

93. Sawyer and Wagner, "Mass Incarceration."

94. Alexander, *The New Jim Crow*; Garland, *The Culture of Control*; Kilgore, "Mass Incarceration."

95. Goodmark, "Reimagining VAWA"; Gruber, *The Feminist War on Crime*; Ch. Taylor, *Foucault, Feminism, and Sex Crimes*.

96. Guadalupe-Diaz, in *Transgressed*, states that "violence against trans people of color is disproportionately documented in the limited available reports on violence in the LGBTQ community" and that "the vast majority of trans victims of homicide are people of color, more narrowly, women of color" (57). See Coulter et al., "Prevalence of Past-Year Sexual Assault," for macro-level evidence of these trends on college campuses, where Black transgender people had the highest rates of sexual assault victimization. Etaugh, in "Prevalence of Intimate Partner Violence," argues that much of the work on LGBTQ people's experiences of intimate partner violence would benefit from incorporating more intersectionality.

97. D. Meyer, "Resisting Hate Crime Discourse"; Spade, *Normal Life*. For more on how the discourse and legislation of hate crime contributes to understandings of an "ideal" victimhood, see Mason, "The Symbolic Purpose."

98. Wang, in *Carceral Capitalism*, argues that the moral framework of "innocence" is often central to liberal and mainstream antiracist narratives, but that this framework continues the dichotomous approach of "proper" and "improper" victims, which has been racialized. This framing also then delegitimizes more militant or radical forms of rebellion against white supremacy—as "improper"—and decouples the lives of white people from the structural oppression of Black Americans. For more on the construction of "innocence" in relation to the carceral state, see Meiners, *For the Children?*

99. Harvey, *A Brief History of Neoliberalism*; Soss, Fording, and Schram, *Disciplining the Poor*; Wacquant, *Prisons of Poverty*.

100. Boorman, *Deliverance*.

101. Chauncey, *Gay New York*; Faderman, *Odd Girls and Twilight Lovers*.

102. Of course, the reverse is also true—racial minorities and members of the working class were instrumental during this time in LGBTQ activism. As Robinson states in *Coming Out to the Streets*, "The history of LGBTQ people in the

United States is a story about LGBTQ youth homelessness. Street kids comprised an essential part of the Stonewall riots. They were a central part of the LGBTQ movement" (16). Low-income queer youth, many of whom were Black, Latinx, gender expansive, and what would now be considered transgender, have been involved in LGBTQ activism from the beginning. For more on the historical participation of these groups in LGBTQ activism, see Porter, "A Rainbow in Black"; Pulido, *Black, Brown, Yellow, and Left*; Stryker, *Transgender History*. LGBTQ activism has roots in Black and working-class communities, overlapping in the 1960s with the labor movement and groups such as the Black Panther Party.

103. Brim, *Poor Queer Studies*; Floyd, *The Reification of Desire*; Sears, "Queer Anti-Capitalism."

104. Cahill, *Rethinking Rape*; Gavey, *Just Sex?*; Madriz, *Nothing Bad Happens to Good Girls*.

105. Carroll, *Mobilizing New York*; Gould, *Moving Politics*; Hobson, *Lavender and Red*.

106. Alcoff, *Rape and Resistance*; Harris, *Beyond the Rapist*; Pascoe and Hollander, "Good Guys Don't Rape."

107. Fanghanel, "Asking For It"; Fischel, *Screw Consent*.

108. Fischel, *Screw Consent*, 20.

1. As mentioned in an endnote for the introduction to this book, I included "rape" on the recruitment flyer to clarify the scope of the project, as I worried that omitting it would lead to greater confusion or ambiguity for some individuals who saw the flyer. Nevertheless, using this word likely resulted in a greater share of participants who had experiences of anal rape than if I had omitted it.

2. Goodmark, "Reimagining VAWA"; Harris, *Beyond the Rapist*; Rumney, "Gay Male Rape Victims."

3. Holstein and Gubrium, *The Active Interview*; Miles, Huberman, and Saldaña, *Qualitative Data Analysis*.

4. Javaid, "Poison Ivy."

5. Hlavka, "Speaking of Stigma"; K. Weiss, "Too Ashamed to Report."

6. Campbell, in *Emotionally Involved*, has detailed the emotional effects that studying sexual assault can have on researchers themselves.

7. A more detailed description of the questions I asked related to emasculation can be found in D. Meyer, "Racializing Emasculation," and more detail on the questions related to the police can be found in D. Meyer, "So Much for Protect and Serve."

8. Mayring, "Qualitative Content Analysis"; Miles, Huberman, and Saldaña, *Qualitative Data Analysis*.

9. Böhm, "Theoretical Coding"; Charmaz, *Constructing Grounded Theory*; Corbin and Strauss, *Basics of Qualitative Research.*

10. Charmaz, *Constructing Grounded Theory*; Giles, de Lacey, and Muir-Cochrane, "Coding, Constant Comparisons"; Glaser, *Theoretical Sensitivity.*

11. Abrahamson, *Social Research Methods*, 286.

12. Charmaz, *Constructing Grounded Theory*; Giles, de Lacey, and Muir-Cochrane, "Coding, Constant Comparisons"; Schreier, *Qualitative Content.*

13. Glaser and Strauss, *Discovery of Grounded Theory*; Mayring, "Qualitative Content Analysis"; Miles, Huberman, and Saldaña, *Qualitative Data Analysis.*

14. Corbin and Strauss, *Basics of Qualitative Research.*

15. Böhm, "Theoretical Coding"; Miles, Huberman, and Saldaña, *Qualitative Data Analysis.*

16. Corbin and Strauss, *Basics of Qualitative Research*; Giles, de Lacey, and Muir-Cochrane, "Coding, Constant Comparisons"; Schreier, *Qualitative Content.*

17. Abrahamson, *Social Research Methods*; Golafshani, "Understanding Reliability"; Miles, Huberman, and Saldaña, *Qualitative Data Analysis.*

18. Mayring, "Qualitative Content Analysis"; Schreier, *Qualitative Content.*

19. D. Meyer, *Violence against Queer People.*

20. See Alcoff, *Rape and Resistance*, for a further exploration of this argument.

References

Abdullah-Khan, Noreen. 2008. *Male Rape: The Emergence of a Social and Legal Issue*. New York, NY: Palgrave Macmillan.

Abelson, Miriam. 2019. *Men in Place: Trans Masculinity, Race, and Sexuality in America*. Minneapolis: University of Minnesota Press.

Abrahamson, Mark. 1983. S*ocial Research Methods*. Englewood Cliffs, NJ: Prentice Hall.

Alcoff, Linda Martín. 2018. *Rape and Resistance: Understanding the Complexities of Sexual Violation*. Medford, MA: Polity.

Alexander, Michelle. 2010. *The New Jim Crow: Mass Incarceration in the Age of Colorblindness*. New York, NY: New Press.

Allen, Stephanie. 2002. "Male Victims of Rape: Responses to a Perceived Threat to Masculinity." In *New Visions of Crime Victims*, edited by Carolyn Hoyle and Richard Young, pp. 23–48. Portland, OR: Hart.

Angelides, Steven. 2001. *A History of Bisexuality*. Chicago, IL: University of Chicago Press.

Armenta, Amada. 2017. *Protect, Serve, and Deport: The Rise of Policing as Immigration Enforcement*. Oakland: University of California Press.

Armstrong, Elizabeth, Miriam Gleckman-Krut, and Lanora Johnson. 2018. "Silence, Power, and Inequality: An Intersectional Approach to Sexual Violence." *Annual Review of Sociology* 44:99–122.

Badour, Christal, Matthew Feldner, Kimberly Babson, Heidemarie Blumenthal, and Courtney Dutton. 2013. "Disgust, Mental Contamination, and

Posttraumatic Stress: Unique Relations Following Sexual Versus Non-Sexual Assault." *Journal of Anxiety Disorders* 27(1):155–162.

Ball, Matthew. 2016. "Queer Criminology as Activism." *Critical Criminology* 24(4):473–487.

Barker, Meg. 2013. "Consent Is a Grey Area? A Comparison of Understandings of Consent in *Fifty Shades of Grey* and on the BDSM Blogosphere." *Sexualities* 16(8):896–914.

Barker, Meg, Alessandra Iantaffi, and Camel Gupta. 2007. "Kinky Clients, Kinky Counselling? The Challenges and Potentials of BDSM." In *Feeling Queer or Queer Feelings*, edited by Lindsey Moon, pp. 106–124. London, UK: Routledge.

Barnard, Ian. 2020. *Sex Panic Rhetorics, Queer Interventions*. Tuscaloosa: University of Alabama Press.

Barnes, Harry Elmer. 1921. "Historical Origin of the Prison System in America." *Journal of Criminal Law and Criminology* 12(1):35–60.

Barnes, Sandra. 2021. "Becoming a Man: A Duboisian Examination of the Experiences of Black Men Who Have Sex with Men." *Social Problems* 68(2):207–225.

Bassichis, Morgan, and Dean Spade. 2014. "Queer Politics and Anti-Blackness." In *Queer Necropolitics*, edited by Jin Haritaworn, Adi Kuntsman, and Silvia Posocco, pp. 191–210. New York, NY: Routledge.

Bates, Elizabeth. 2016. "Current Controversies within Intimate Partner Violence: Overlooking Bidirectional Violence." *Journal of Family Violence* 31(8):937–940.

Bauer, Robin. 2014. *Queer BDSM Intimacies: Critical Consent and Pushing Boundaries*. London, UK: Palgrave Macmillan.

Beauchamp, Toby. 2019. *Going Stealth: Transgender Politics and U.S. Surveillance Practices*. Durham, NC: Duke University Press.

Bedera, Nicole, and Kristjane Nordmeyer. 2021. "An Inherently Masculine Practice: Understanding the Sexual Victimization of Queer Women." *Journal of Interpersonal Violence* 36(23–24):11188–11211.

Belous, Christopher, and Melissa Bauman. 2017. "What's in a Name? Exploring Pansexuality Online." *Journal of Bisexuality* 17(1):58–72.

Berlant, Lauren. 2007. "Slow Death (Sovereignty, Obesity, Lateral Agency)." *Critical Inquiry* 33(4):754–780.

Bermea, Autumn, Brad van Eeden-Moorefield, and Lyndal Khaw. 2018. "A Systematic Review of Research on Intimate Partner Violence among Bisexual Women." *Journal of Bisexuality* 18(4):399–424.

Bernstein, Elizabeth. 2010. "Militarized Humanitarianism Meets Carceral Feminism: The Politics of Sex, Rights, and Freedom in Contemporary Antitrafficking Campaigns." *Signs* 36(1):45–71.

———. 2018. *Brokered Subjects: Sex, Trafficking, and the Politics of Freedom*. Chicago, IL: University of Chicago Press.

Best, Joel. 1999. *Random Violence: How We Talk about New Crimes and New Victims*. Berkeley: University of California Press.

Binion, Kendal, and Matt Gray. 2020. "Minority Stress Theory and Internalized Homophobia among LGB Sexual Assault Survivors: Implications for Posttraumatic Adjustment." *Journal of Loss and Trauma* 25(5):454–471.

Blumell, Lindsey, and Nathian Shae Rodriguez. 2020. "Ambivalent Sexism and Gay Men in the US and UK." *Sexuality & Culture* 24(1):209–229.

Böhm, Andreas. 2004. "Theoretical Coding: Text Analysis in Grounded Theory." In *A Companion to Qualitative Research*, edited by Uwe Flick, Ernst von Kardoff, and Ines Steink, pp. 270–275. Thousand Oaks, CA: Sage.

Boorman, John, dir. 1972. *Deliverance*. Warner Brothers.

Bost, Darius. 2018. *Evidence of Being: The Black Gay Cultural Renaissance and the Politics of Violence*. Chicago, IL: University of Chicago Press.

Bourke, Joanna. 2009. "Foreword." In *Theorizing Sexual Violence*, edited by Renée J. Heberle and Victoria Grace, pp. ix–xiv. New York, NY: Routledge.

Boykin, Keith. 2006. *Beyond the Down Low: Sex, Lies, and Denial in Black America*. New York, NY: Da Capo.

Bracewell, Lorna. 2020. "Sex Wars, SlutWalks, and Carceral Feminism." *Contemporary Political Theory* 19(1):61–82.

Braga, Anthony, Rod Brunson, and Kevin Drakulich. 2019. "Race, Place, and Effective Policing." *Annual Review of Sociology* 45:535–555.

Bridges, Tristan. 2014. "A Very 'Gay' Straight? Hybrid Masculinities, Sexual Aesthetics, and the Changing Relationship between Masculinity and Homophobia." *Gender & Society* 28(1):58–82.

Bridges, Tristan, and C. J. Pascoe. 2014. "Hybrid Masculinities: New Directions in the Sociology of Men and Masculinities." *Sociology Compass* 8(3):246–58.

Brim, Matt. 2020. *Poor Queer Studies: Confronting Elitism in the University*. Durham, NC: Duke University Press.

Brison, Susan. 2002. *Aftermath: Violence and the Remaking of a Self*. Princeton, NJ: Princeton University Press.

Brown, Gavin. 2012. "Homonormativity: A Metropolitan Concept That Denigrates 'Ordinary' Gay Lives." *Journal of Homosexuality* 59(7):1065–1072.

Brown, Michael, and Jennifer Groscup. 2009. "Perceptions of Same-Sex Domestic Violence among Crisis Center Staff." *Journal of Family Violence* 24(2):87–93.

Brown, Robert. 2019. "Policing in American History." *Du Bois Review* 16(1):189–195.

Browne, Simone. 2015. *Dark Matters: On the Surveillance of Blackness*. Durham, NC: Duke University Press.

Brownmiller, Susan. 1975. *Against Our Will: Men, Women, and Rape*. New York, NY: Fawcett.

Brunson, Rod. 2007. "'Police Don't Like Black People': African-American Young Men's Accumulated Police Experiences." *Criminology & Public Policy* 6(1):71–101.

Buist, Carrie, and Emily Lenning. 2016. *Queer Criminology*. New York, NY: Routledge.

Buist, Carrie, and Codie Stone. 2014. "Transgender Victims and Offenders: Failures of the United States Criminal Justice System and the Necessity of Queer Criminology." *Critical Criminology* 22(1):35–47.

Bumiller, Kristin. 2008. *In an Abusive State: How Neoliberalism Appropriated the Feminist Movement against Sexual Violence*. Durham, NC: Duke University Press.

Butler, Judith. 1990. *Gender Trouble: Feminism and the Subversion of Identity*. New York, NY: Routledge.

Cahill, Ann. 2001. *Rethinking Rape*. Ithica, NY: Cornell University Press.

Callis, April. 2009. "Playing with Butler and Foucault: Bisexuality and Queer Theory." *Journal of Bisexuality* 9(3–4):213–233.

———. 2014. "Bisexual, Pansexual, Queer: Non-Binary Identities and the Sexual Borderlands." *Sexualities* 17(1–2):63–80.

Canaday, Margot. 2009. *The Straight State: Sexuality and Citizenship in Twentieth-Century America*. Princeton, NJ: Princeton University Press.

Campbell, Rebecca. 2002. *Emotionally Involved: The Impact of Researching Rape*. New York, NY: Routledge.

Cannon, Clare, Regardt Ferreira, and Fred Buttell. 2020. "Critical Race Theory, Parenting, and Intimate Partner Violence: Analyzing Race and Gender." *Research on Social Work Practice* 30(1):122–134.

Carbado, Devon. 2013. "Colorblind Intersectionality." *Signs* 38(4):811–845.

———. 2017. "Black Rights, Gay Rights, Civil Rights." In *Sexuality and Equality Law*, edited by Suzanna Goldberg, pp. 305–328. New York, NY: Routledge.

Carrillo, Héctor. 2018. *Pathways of Desire: The Sexual Migration of Mexican Gay Men*. Chicago, IL: University of Chicago Press.

Carroll, Tamar. 2015. *Mobilizing New York: AIDS, Antipoverty, and Feminist Activism*. Chapel Hill: University of North Carolina Press.

Carruthers, Charlene. 2018. *Unapologetic: A Black, Queer, and Feminist Mandate for Radical Movements*. Boston, MA: Beacon.

Chapin, Angelina. 2016. "Writing a Love Letter Instead of a Police Report: Why Victims Contact Sex Attackers." *The Guardian*, February 13. Available at: https://www.theguardian.com/world/2016/feb/13/jian-ghomeshi-trial-sexual -assault-victims-response (accessed October 13, 2020).

Charmaz, Kathy. 2014. *Constructing Grounded Theory*. Thousand Oaks, CA: Sage.

Chauncey, George. 1994. *Gay New York: Gender, Urban Culture, and the Making of the Gay Male World*. New York, NY: Basic.

Chávez, Karma. 2013. *Queer Migration Politics: Activist Rhetoric and Coalitional Possibilities*. Urbana: University of Illinois Press.

Cheit, Ross. 2014. *The Witch-Hunt Narrative: Politics, Psychology, and the Sexual Abuse of Children*. New York, NY: Oxford University Press.

Cheng, Jih-Fei. 2016. "How to Survive: AIDS and Its Afterlives in Popular Media." *Women's Studies Quarterly* 44(1/2):73–92.

Cho, Sumi, Kimberlé Williams Crenshaw, and Leslie McCall. 2013. "Toward a Field of Intersectionality Studies: Theory, Applications, and Praxis." *Signs* 38(4):785–810.

Choo, Hae Yeon, and Myra Marx Ferree. 2010. "Practicing Intersectionality in Sociological Research: A Critical Analysis of Inclusions, Interactions, and Institutions in the Study of Inequalities." *Sociological Theory* 28(2):129–149.

Christie, Nils. 1986. "The Ideal Victim." In *From Crime Policy to Victim Policy*, edited by Fattah Ezzat, pp. 17–30. Basingstoke, UK: Palgrave Macmillan.

Clark, Janine Natalya. 2019. "The Vulnerability of the Penis: Sexual Violence against Men in Conflict and Security Frames." *Men and Masculinities* 22(5):778–800.

Cohen, Cathy. 1999. *The Boundaries of Blackness: AIDS and the Breakdown of Black Politics*. Chicago, IL: University of Chicago Press.

Cohen, Claire. 2014. *Male Rape Is a Feminist Issue: Feminism, Governmentality and Male Rape*. New York, NY: Palgrave Macmillan.

Colburn, Alayna, and Lisa Melander. 2018. "Beyond Black and White: An Analysis of Newspaper Representations of Alleged Criminal Offenders Based on Race and Ethnicity." *Journal of Contemporary Criminal Justice* 34(4):383–398.

Collins, Patricia Hill. 1998. "The Tie That Binds: Race, Gender and US Violence." *Ethnic and Racial Studies* 21(5):917–938.

———. 2000. *Black Feminist Thought: Knowledge, Consciousness and the Politics of Empowerment*. 2nd ed. New York, NY: Routledge.

———. 2004. *Black Sexual Politics: African Americans, Gender, and the New Racism*. New York, NY: Routledge.

———. 2017. "On Violence, Intersectionality and Transversal Politics." *Ethnic and Racial Studies* 40(9):1460–1473.

———. 2019. *Intersectionality as Critical Social Theory*. Durham, NC: Duke University Press.

Collins, Randall. 2009. *Violence: A Micro-Sociological Theory*. Princeton, NJ: Princeton University Press.

Connell, Catherine. 2016. "Contesting Racialized Discourses of Homophobia." *Sociological Forum* 31(3):599–618.

Connell, Raewyn. 1987. *Gender and Power: Society, the Person, and Sexual Politics*. Sydney, Australia: Allen and Unwin.

———. 1995. *Masculinities*. Sydney, Australia: Allen and Unwin.

Connell, Raewyn, and James Messerschmidt. 2005. "Hegemonic Masculinity: Rethinking the Concept." *Gender & Society* 19(6):829–859.

Conrad, Ryan, ed. 2010. *Against Equality: Queer Critiques of Gay Marriage*. Lewiston, ME: Against Equality Press.

Corbin, Juliet, and Anselm Strauss. 2015. *Basics of Qualitative Research: Techniques and Procedures for Developing Grounded Theory*. Thousand Oaks, CA: Sage.

Corrigan, Rose. 2013. *Up Against a Wall: Rape Reform and the Failure of Success*. New York: New York University Press.

Coulter, Robert, Christina Mair, Elizabeth Miller, John Blosnich, Derrick Matthews, and Heather McCauley. 2017. "Prevalence of Past-Year Sexual Assault Victimization among Undergraduate Students: Exploring Differences by and Intersections of Gender Identity, Sexual Identity, and Race/Ethnicity." *Prevention Science* 18(6):726–736.

Coulter, Robert, and Susan Rankin. 2020. "College Sexual Assault and Campus Climate for Sexual- and Gender-Minority Undergraduate Students." *Journal of Interpersonal Violence* 35(5–6):1351–1366.

Coxell, Adrian, and Michael King. 2002. "Gender, Sexual Orientation, and Sexual Assault." In *The Trauma of Sexual Assault*, edited by Jenny Petrak and Barbara Hedge, pp. 45–68. New York, NY: Wiley.

Crenshaw, Kimberlé. 1989. "Demarginalizing the Intersection of Race and Sex: A Black Feminist Critique of Antidiscrimination Doctrine, Feminist Theory and Antiracist Politics." *University of Chicago Legal Forum*:139–168.

———. 1991. "Mapping the Margins: Intersectionality, Identity Politics, and Violence against Women of Color." *Stanford Law Review* 43(6):1241–1299.

Crimp, Douglas. 2002. *Melancholia and Moralism: Essays on AIDS and Queer Politics*. Cambridge, MA: MIT Press.

Curry, Tommy. 2019. "Expendables for Whom: Terry Crews and the Erasure of Black Male Victims of Sexual Assault and Rape." *Women's Studies in Communication* 42(3):287–307.

Darabont, Frank, dir. 1994. *The Shawshank Redemption*. Castle Rock.

Daum, Courtenay. 2015. "The War on Solicitation and Intersectional Subjection: Quality-of-Life Policing as a Tool to Control Transgender Populations." *New Political Science* 37(4):562–581.

Davies, Michelle, and Jenefer Hudson. 2011. "Judgments toward Male and Transgendered Victims in a Depicted Stranger Rape." *Journal of Homosexuality* 58(2):237–247.

Davis, Alexander. 2020. *Bathroom Battlegrounds: How Public Restrooms Shape the Gender Order*. Oakland: University of California Press.

Davis, Angela. 1983. *Women, Race and Class*. New York, NY: Vintage.

———. 2003. *Are Prisons Obsolete?* New York, NY: Seven Stories.

Davis, Angela, and Cassandra Shaylor. 2001. "Race, Gender, and the Prison Industrial Complex: California and Beyond." *Meridians* 2(1):1–25.

Davis, Mark, Paul Flowers, Karen Lorimer, Jane Oakland, and Jamie Frankis. 2016. "Location, Safety and (Non) Strangers in Gay Men's Narratives on 'Hook-up' Apps." *Sexualities* 19(7):836–852.

Deer, Sarah. 2009. "Decolonizing Rape Law: A Native Feminist Synthesis of Safety and Sovereignty." *Wicazo Sa Review* 24(2):149–167.

Deer, Sarah, and Abigail Barefoot. 2018. "The Limits of the State: Feminist Perspectives on Carceral Logic, Restorative Justice and Sexual Violence." *Kansas Journal of Law & Public Policy* 28(3):505–526.

de Heer, Brooke, Meredith Brown, and Julianna Cheney. 2021. "Sexual Consent and Communication among the Sexual Minoritized: The Role of Heteronormative Sex Education, Trauma, and Dual Identities." *Feminist Criminology* 16(5):701–721.

de Heer, Brooke, and Lynn Jones. 2017. "Measuring Sexual Violence on Campus: Climate Surveys and Vulnerable Groups." *Journal of School Violence* 16(2):207–221.

DeKeseredy, Walter, Joseph Donnermeyer, Martin Schwartz, Kenneth Tunnell, and Mandy Hall. 2007. "Thinking Critically About Rural Gender Relations: Toward a Rural Masculinity Crisis/Male Peer Support Model of Separation/ Divorce Sexual Assault." *Critical Criminology* 15(4):295–311.

DeKeseredy, Walter, Martin Schwartz, Lindsay Kahle, and James Nolan. 2021. "Polyvictimization in a College Lesbian, Gay, Bisexual, Transgender, and Queer Community: The Influence of Negative Peer Support." *Violence and Gender* 8(1):14–20.

DeKeseredy, Walter, Molly Dragiewicz, and Martin Schwartz. 2017. *Abusive Endings: Separation and Divorce Violence against Women*. Oakland: University of California Press.

DeFilippis, Joseph, and Ben Anderson-Nathe. 2017. "Embodying Margin to Center: Intersectional Activism among Queer Liberation Organizations." In *LGBTQ Politics: A Critical Reader*, edited by Marla Brettschneider, Susan Burgess, and Christine Keating, pp. 110–133. New York: New York University Press.

Deska, Jason, Jonathan Kunstman, Michael Bernstein, Tejumola Ogungbadero, and Kurt Hugenberg. 2020. "Black Racial Phenotypicality Shapes Social Pain and Support Judgments." *Journal of Experimental Social Psychology*, Article 103998.

"Detention Statistics." 2020. *Freedom for Immigrants*. Available at: https://www .freedomforimmigrants.org/detention-statistics (accessed June 1, 2020).

Diamond, Lisa. 2008. *Sexual Fluidity: Understanding Women's Love and Desire*. Cambridge, MA: Harvard University Press.

Dick, Kirby, dir. 2015. *The Hunting Ground*. The Weinstein Company.

Dillon, Stephen. 2018. *Fugitive Life: The Queer Politics of the Prison State*. Durham, NC: Duke University Press.

Doherty, Kathy, and Irina Anderson. 2004. "Making Sense of Male Rape: Constructions of Gender, Sexuality and Experience of Rape Victims." *Journal of Community & Applied Social Psychology* 14(2):85–103.

Donaldson, Stephen "Donny." 2001. "A Million Jockers, Punks, and Queens." In *Prison Masculinities*, edited by Don Sabo, Terry Kupers, and Willie London, pp. 118–126. Philadelphia, PA: Temple University Press.

Donovan, Catherin, Marianne Hester, Jonathan Holmes, and Melanie McCarry. 2006. *Comparing Domestic Abuse in Same Sex and Heterosexual Relationships*. Swindon, UK: Economic and Social Research Council.

Donovan, Roxanne, and Michelle Williams. 2002. "Living at the Intersection." *Women & Therapy* 25(3–4):95–105.

Duggan, Lisa. 2002. "The New Homonormativity: The Sexual Politics of Neoliberalism." In *Materializing Democracy*, edited by Dana Nelson and Russ Castronovo, pp. 175–194. Durham, NC: Duke University Press.

Dunkley, Cara, and Lori Brotto. 2020. "The Role of Consent in the Context of BDSM." *Sexual Abuse* 32(6):657–678.

Dunn, Jennifer. 2010. *Judging Victims: Why We Stigmatize Survivors, and How They Reclaim Respect*. Boulder, CO: Lynne Rienner.

Dunn, Peter. 2012. "Men as Victims: 'Victim' Identities, Gay Identities, and Masculinities." *Journal of Interpersonal Violence* 27(17):3442–3467.

Dworkin, Andrea. 1987. *Intercourse*. New York, NY: Basic.

Dwyer, Angela. 2011. "Policing Lesbian, Gay, Bisexual and Transgender Young People: A Gap in the Research Literature." *Current Issues in Criminal Justice* 22(3):415–433.

Dwyer, Angela, and Stephen Tomsen. 2016. "The Past Is the Past? The Impossibility of Erasure of Historical LGBTIQ Policing." In *Queering Criminology*, edited by Angela Dwyer, Matthew Ball, and Thomas Crofts, pp. 36–53. New York, NY: Palgrave Macmillan.

Easterbrook-Smith, Gwyn. 2020. "'Not on the Street Where We Live': Walking While Trans Under a Model of Sex Work Decriminalisation." *Feminist Media Studies* 20(7):1013–1028.

Edwards, Frank, Hedwig Lee, and Michael Esposito. 2019. "Risk of Being Killed by Police Use of Force in the United States by Age, Race–Ethnicity, and Sex." *Proceedings of the National Academy of Sciences* 116(34):16793–16798.

Edwards, Tim. 1994. *Erotics and Politics: Gay Male Sexuality, Masculinity and Feminism*. New York, NY: Routledge.

Ehrlich, Susan. 2001. *Representing Rape: Language and Sexual Consent*. New York, NY: Routledge.

Eigenberg, Helen. 1989. "Male Rape: An Empirical Examination of Correctional Officers' Attitudes toward Rape in Prison." *The Prison Journal* 69(2):39–56.

Elliot, Patricia. 2009. "Engaging Trans Debates on Gender Variance: A Feminist Analysis." *Sexualities* 12(1):5–32.

Epp, Charles, Steven Maynard-Moody, and Donald Haider-Markel. 2014. *Pulled Over: How Police Stops Define Race and Citizenship*. Chicago, IL: University of Chicago Press.

Estrich, Susan. 1987. *Real Rape*. Cambridge, MA: Harvard University Press.

Etaugh, Claire. 2020. "Prevalence of Intimate Partner Violence in LGBTQ Individuals: An Intersectional Approach." In *Intimate Partner Violence and the LGBT+ Community*, edited by Brenda Russell, pp. 11–36. Cham, Switzerland: Springer.

Faderman, Lillian. 1991. *Odd Girls and Twilight Lovers: A History of Lesbian Life in Twentieth-Century America*. New York, NY: Columbia University Press.

Fahlberg, Anjuli and Mollie Pepper. 2016. "Masculinity and Sexual Violence: Assessing the State of the Field." *Sociology Compass* 10(8):673–683.

Fahs, Breanne. 2009. "Compulsory Bisexuality? The Challenges of Modern Sexual Fluidity." *Journal of Bisexuality* 9(3–4):431–449.

Fahs, Breanne, and Sara McClelland. 2016. "When Sex and Power Collide: An Argument for Critical Sexuality Studies." *Journal of Sex Research* 53(4–5):392–416.

Fahs, Breanne, Rebecca Plante, and Sara McClelland. 2018. "Working at the Crossroads of Pleasure and Danger: Feminist Perspectives on Doing Critical Sexuality Studies." *Sexualities* 21(4):503–519.

Fanghanel, Alexandra. 2020. "Asking for It: BDSM Sexual Practice and the Trouble of Consent." *Sexualities* 23(3):269–286.

———. 2020. *Disrupting Rape Culture: Public Space, Sexuality and Revolt*. Bristol, UK: Bristol University Press.

Fausto-Sterling, Anne. 2020. *Sexing the Body: Gender Politics and the Construction of Sexuality*. New York, NY: Basic.

Feinstein, Rachel. 2018. *When Rape Was Legal: The Untold History of Sexual Violence during Slavery*. New York, NY: Routledge.

Ferguson, Ann Arnett. 2001. *Bad Boys: Public Schools in the Making of Black Masculinity*. Ann Arbor: University of Michigan Press.

Ferguson, Roderick. 2019. *One-Dimensional Queer*. Medford, MA: Polity.

Féron, Élise. 2018. *Wartime Sexual Violence against Men: Masculinities and Power in Conflict Zones*. Lanham, MD: Rowman & Littlefield.

Ferrales, Gabrielle, Hollie Nyseth Brehm, and Suzy McElrath. 2016. "Gender-Based Violence against Men and Boys in Darfur: The Gender-Genocide Nexus." *Gender & Society* 30(4):565–589.

"A Few Quick Statistics." 2020. *Survived and Punished*. Available at: https://survivedandpunished.org/quick-statistics/ (accessed October 1, 2020).

Fischel, Joseph. 2019. *Screw Consent: A Better Politics of Sexual Justice*. Oakland: University of California Press.

Fleisher, Mark, and Jessie Krienert. 2009. *The Myth of Prison Rape: Sexual Culture in American Prisons*. Lanham, MD: Rowman & Littlefield.

Flores, Jerry. 2016. *Caught Up: Girls, Surveillance, and Wraparound Incarceration*. Oakland: University of California Press.

Floyd, Kevin. 2009. *The Reification of Desire: Toward a Queer Marxism*. Minneapolis: University of Minnesota Press.

Ford, Jessie, and José Soto-Marquez. 2016. "Sexual Assault Victimization among Straight, Gay/Lesbian, and Bisexual College Students." *Violence and Gender* 3(2):107–115.

Foster, Thomas. 2019. *Rethinking Rufus: Sexual Violations of Enslaved Men*. Athens: University of Georgia Press.

Foucault, Michel. 1977. *Discipline and Punish: The Birth of the Prison*. New York, NY: Pantheon.

———. 1978. *The History of Sexuality, Volume 1: An Introduction*. New York, NY: Pantheon.

Freedman, Estelle. 2013. *Redefining Rape*. Cambridge, MA: Harvard University Press.

Funk, Rus Ervin. 2012. "Queer Men and Sexual Assault: What Being Raped Says about Being a Man." In *Gendered Outcasts and Sexual Outlaws*, edited by Christopher Kendall and Wayne Martino, pp. 131–146. New York, NY: Routledge.

Garber, Marjorie. 1995. *Vice Versa: Bisexuality and the Eroticism of Everyday Life*. New York, NY: Simon & Schuster.

Garfield, Gail. 2005. *Knowing What We Know: African American Women's Experiences of Violence and Violation*. New Brunswick, NJ: Rutgers University Press.

———. 2010. *Through Our Eyes: African American Men's Experiences of Race, Gender, and Violence*. New Brunswick, NJ: Rutgers University Press.

Garland, David. 2001. *The Culture of Control: Crime and Social Order in Contemporary Society*. Chicago, IL: University of Chicago Press.

Garvey, Jason, Jessi Hitchins, and Elizabeth McDonald. 2017. "Queer-Spectrum Student Sexual Violence: Implications for Research, Policy, and Practice." In *Intersections of Identity and Sexual Violence on Campus*, edited by Jessica Harris and Chris Linder, pp. 155–172. Sterling, VA: Stylus.

Gaspar, Mark, Shayna Skakoon-Sparling, Barry Adam, David Brennan, Nathan Lachowsky, Joseph Cox, David Moore, Trevor Hart, and Daniel Grace. 2021. "'You're Gay, It's Just What Happens': Sexual Minority Men Recounting Experiences of Unwanted Sex in the Era of MeToo." *Journal of Sex Research* 58(9):1205–1214.

Gavey, Nicola. 2005. *Just Sex? The Cultural Scaffolding of Rape*. New York, NY: Routledge.

Gelman, Andrew, Jeffrey Fagan, and Alex Kiss. 2007. "An Analysis of the New York City Police Department's 'Stop-and-Frisk' Policy in the Context of Claims of Racial Bias." *Journal of the American Statistical Association* 102:813–823.

GenerationFIVE. 2017. "Transformative Justice Handbook." Available at: http://www.generationfive.org/resources/transformative-justice-documents/ (accessed November 9, 2020).

Ghaziani, Amin. 2008. *The Dividends of Dissent: How Conflict and Culture Work in Lesbian and Gay Marches on Washington*. Chicago, IL: University of Chicago Press.

Gibson, James, and Michael Nelson. 2018. *Black and Blue: How African Americans Judge the U.S. Legal System*. New York, NY: Oxford University Press.

Gibson, Kristina. 2011. *Street Kids: Homeless Youth, Outreach, and Policing New York's Streets*. New York: New York University Press.

Giles, Tracey, Sheryl de Lacey, and Eimear Muir-Cochrane. 2016. "Coding, Constant Comparisons, and Core Categories." *Advances in Nursing Science* 39(1):E29–44.

Gill, Rosalind, and Shani Orgad. 2018. "The Shifting Terrain of Sex and Power: From the 'Sexualization of Culture' to #MeToo." *Sexualities* 21(8):1313–1324.

Gilson, Erinn Cunniff. 2016. "Vulnerability and Victimization: Rethinking Key Concepts in Feminist Discourses on Sexual Violence." *Signs* 42(1):71–98.

Glaser, Barney. 1978. *Theoretical Sensitivity: Advances in the Methodology of Grounded Theory*. Mill Valley, CA: The Sociological Press.

Glaser, Barney, and Anselm Strauss. 2017. *Discovery of Grounded Theory: Strategies for Qualitative Research*. New York, NY: Routledge.

Golafshani, Nahid. 2003. "Understanding Reliability and Validity in Qualitative Research." *The Qualitative Report* 8(4):597–606.

Goldscheid, Julie. 2019. "Sexual Assault by Federal Actors, #MeToo, and Civil Rights." *Washington Law Review* 94(4):1639–1696.

Gonzalez, Shannon Malone. 2019. "Making It Home: An Intersectional Analysis of the Police Talk." *Gender & Society* 33(3):363–386.

González-López, Gloria. 2015. *Family Secrets: Stories of Incest and Sexual Violence in Mexico*. New York: New York University Press.

Goodmark, Leigh. 2018. *Decriminalizing Domestic Violence: A Balanced Policy Approach to Intimate Partner Violence*. Oakland: University of California Press.

———. 2021. "Reimagining VAWA: Why Criminalization Is a Failed Policy and What a Non-Carceral VAWA Could Look Like." *Violence Against Women* 27(1):84–101.

Gotell, Lise. 2015. "Reassessing the Place of Criminal Law Reform in the Struggle against Sexual Violence." In *Rape Justice*, edited by Anastasia Powell, Nicola Henry, and Asher Flynn, pp. 53–71. London, UK: Palgrave Macmillan.

Gottschalk, Marie. 2006. *The Prison and the Gallows: The Politics of Mass Incarceration in America*. New York, NY: Cambridge University Press.

———. 2016. *Caught: The Prison State and the Lockdown of American Politics*. Princeton, NJ: Princeton University Press.

Gould, Deborah. 2009. *Moving Politics: Emotion and ACT UP's Fight against AIDS*. Chicago, IL: University of Chicago Press.

Graham, Ruth. 2006. "Male Rape and the Careful Construction of the Male Victim." *Social & Legal Studies* 15(2):187–208.

Gregory, Jeanne, and Sue Lees. 1999. *Policing Sexual Assault.* New York, NY: Routledge.

Gruber, Aya. 2020. *The Feminist War on Crime: The Unexpected Role of Women's Liberation in Mass Incarceration.* Oakland: University of California Press.

Grundy, Saida. 2021. "Lifting the Veil on Campus Sexual Assault: Morehouse College, Hegemonic Masculinity, and Revealing Racialized Rape Culture through the Du Boisian Lens." *Social Problems* 68(2):226–249.

Guadalupe-Diaz, Xavier. 2016. "Disclosure of Same-Sex Intimate Partner Violence to Police among Lesbians, Gays, and Bisexuals." *Social Currents* 3(2):160–171.

———. 2019. *Transgressed: Intimate Partner Violence in Transgender Lives.* New York: New York University Press.

Hale, Sadie, and Tomás Ojeda. 2018. "Acceptable Femininity? Gay Male Misogyny and the Policing of Queer Femininities." *European Journal of Women's Studies* 25(3):310–324.

Haley, Sarah. 2016. *No Mercy Here: Gender, Punishment, and the Making of Jim Crow Modernity.* Chapel Hill: University of North Carolina Press.

Hall, Matthew, and Jeff Hearn. 2017. *Revenge Pornography: Gender, Sexuality and Motivations.* New York, NY: Routledge.

Halperin, David, and Trevor Hoppe, eds. 2017. *The War on Sex.* Durham, NC: Duke University Press.

Hamby, Sherry, and John Grych. 2013. *The Web of Violence: Exploring Connections among Different Forms of Interpersonal Violence and Abuse.* New York, NY: Springer.

Han, C. Winter. 2015. *Geisha of a Different Kind: Race and Sexuality in Gaysian America.* New York: New York University Press.

Hancock, Ange-Marie. 2011. *Solidarity Politics for Millennials: A Guide to Ending the Oppression Olympics.* New York, NY: Palgrave MacMillan.

———. 2016. *Intersectionality: An Intellectual History.* New York, NY: Oxford University Press.

Hanhardt, Christina. 2013. *Safe Space: Gay Neighborhood History and the Politics of Violence.* Durham, NC: Duke University Press.

Hannon, Elliot. 2019. "Judge Ruled Prosecutors Should Have Told 16-Year-Old Rape Victim Pressing Charges Would Destroy a Boy's life." *Slate,* July 3. Available at: https://slate.com/news-and-politics/2019/07/judge-new-jersey -16-year-old-rape-victim-good-family-college-scores-bias-privilege-destroy -life.html (accessed September 15, 2020).

Harding, Kate. 2015. *Asking for It: The Alarming Rise of Rape Culture—and What We Can Do about It.* Philadelphia, PA: De Capo.

Haritaworn, Jin. 2015. *Queer Lovers and Hateful Others: Regenerating Violent Times and Places*. London, UK: Pluto.

Harris, Kate Lockwood. 2018. "Yes Means Yes and No Means No, But Both These Mantras Need to Go: Communication Myths in Consent Education and Anti-Rape Activism." *Journal of Applied Communication Research* 46(2):155–178.

———. 2019. *Beyond the Rapist: Title IX and Sexual Violence on US Campuses*. New York, NY: Oxford University Press.

Harvey, David. 2005. *A Brief History of Neoliberalism*. New York, NY: Oxford University Press.

Hasinoff, Amy Adele. 2015. *Sexting Panic: Rethinking Criminalization, Privacy, and Consent*. Urbana: University of Illinois Press.

Henry, Nicola. 2016. "Theorizing Wartime Rape: Deconstructing Gender, Sexuality, and Violence." *Gender & Society* 30(1):44–56.

Higginbotham, Evelyn Brooks. 1994. *Righteous Discontent: The Women's Movement in the Black Baptist Church, 1880–1920*. Cambridge, MA: Harvard University Press.

Hills, Peter, Megan Pleva, Elisabeth Seib, and Terri Cole. 2021. "Understanding How University Students Use Perceptions of Consent, Wantedness, and Pleasure in Labeling Rape." *Archives of Sexual Behavior* 50(1):247–262.

Hindes, Sophie, and Bianca Fileborn. 2021. "Reporting on Sexual Violence 'Inside the Closet': Masculinity, Homosexuality and #MeToo." *Crime, Media, Culture* 17(2):163–184.

Hine, Darlene Clark. 1989. "Rape and the Inner Lives of Black Women in the Middle West: Preliminary Thoughts on the Culture of Dissemblance." *Signs* 14(4):912–920.

Hinkson, Kasia. 2021. "The Colorblind Rainbow: Whiteness in the Gay Rights Movement." *Journal of Homosexuality* 68(9):1393–1416.

Hinton, Elizabeth. 2016. *From the War on Poverty to the War on Crime: The Making of Mass Incarceration in America*. Cambridge, MA: Harvard University Press.

Hirsch, Jennifer, and Shamus Khan. 2020. *Sexual Citizens: A Landmark Study of Sex, Power, and Assault on Campus*. New York, NY: W. W. Norton & Company.

Hirschel, David and Philip McCormack. 2021. "Same-Sex Couples and the Police: A 10-Year Study of Arrest and Dual Arrest Rates in Responding to Incidents of Intimate Partner Violence." *Violence against Women* 27(9):1119–1149.

Hlavka, Heather. 2014. "Normalizing Sexual Violence: Young Women Account for Harassment and Abuse." *Gender & Society* 28(3):337–358.

———. 2017. "Speaking of Stigma and the Silence of Shame: Young Men and Sexual Victimization." *Men and Masculinities* 20(4):482–505.

Hoberman, John. 2012. *Black and Blue: The Origins and Consequences of Medical Racism*. Berkeley: University of California Press.

Hobson, Emily. 2016. *Lavender and Red: Liberation and Solidarity in the Gay and Lesbian Left*. Oakland: University of California Press.

Holstein, James, and Jaber Gubrium. 1995. *The Active Interview*. Thousand Oaks, CA: Sage.

hooks, bell. 2004. *We Real Cool: Black Men and Masculinity*. New York, NY: Routledge.

Hoppe, Trevor. 2018. *Punishing Disease: HIV and the Criminalization of Sickness*. Oakland: University of California Press.

Hoskin, Rhea Ashley. 2019. "Femmephobia: The Role of Anti-Femininity and Gender Policing in LGBTQ+ People's Experiences of Discrimination." *Sex Roles* 81(11):686–703.

Hunter, Marcus Anthony. 2010. "All the Gays Are White and All the Blacks Are Straight: Black Gay Men, Identity and Community." *Sexuality Research & Social Policy* 7(2):81–92.

INCITE! Women of Color Against Violence. 2003. "Community Accountability Working Document." Available at: https://incite-national.org/community-accountability-working-document/ (accessed November 9, 2020).

———, ed. 2016. *Color of Violence: The INCITE! Anthology*. Durham, NC: Duke University Press.

Jackson, Jessi Lee. 2013. "Sexual Necropolitics and Prison Rape Elimination." *Signs* 39(1):197–220.

Jackson, Michelle, Sarah Valentine, Eva Woodward, and David Pantalone. 2017. "Secondary Victimization of Sexual Minority Men Following Disclosure of Sexual Assault: 'Victimizing Me All Over Again . . .'" *Sexuality Research and Social Policy* 14(3):275–288.

Javaid, Aliraza. 2015. "The Dark Side of Men: The Nature of Masculinity and its Uneasy Relationship with Male Rape." *The Journal of Men's Studies* 23(3):271–292.

———. 2018. *Male Rape, Masculinities, and Sexualities: Understanding, Policing, and Overcoming Male Sexual Victimisation*. New York, NY: Palgrave Macmillan.

———. 2018. "'Poison Ivy': Queer Masculinities, Sexualities, Homophobia and Sexual Violence." *European Journal of Criminology* 15(6):748–766.

Jenness, Valerie, and Sarah Fenstermaker. 2016. "Forty Years after Brownmiller: Prisons for Men, Transgender Inmates, and the Rape of the Feminine." *Gender & Society* 30(1):14–29.

Johnson, Austin. 2016. "Transnormativity: A New Concept and Its Validation through Documentary Film about Transgender Men." *Sociological Inquiry* 86(4):465–491.

Johnson, E. Patrick. 2003. *Appropriating Blackness: Performance and the Politics of Authenticity*. Durham, NC: Duke University Press.

———. 2012. *Sweet Tea: Black Gay Men of the South: An Oral History*. Chapel Hill: University of North Carolina Press.

Johnstone, Gerry. 2013. *Restorative Justice: Ideas, Values, Debates*. New York, NY: Routledge.

Jones, Ann. 2000. *Next Time, She'll Be Dead: Battering and How to Stop It*. Boston, MA: Beacon.

Jones, Nikki. 2018. *The Chosen Ones: Black Men and the Politics of Redemption*. Oakland: University of California Press.

Jordan, Jan. 2008. *Serial Survivors: Women's Narratives of Surviving Rape*. Sydney, Australia: Federation Press.

Jordan, Sid, Gita Mehrotra, and Kiyomi Fujikawa. 2020. "Mandating Inclusion: Critical Trans Perspectives on Domestic and Sexual Violence Advocacy." *Violence Against Women* 26(6–7):531–554.

Judge, Melanie. 2017. *Blackwashing Homophobia: Violence and the Politics of Sexuality, Gender and Race*. New York, NY: Routledge.

Karlsson, Marie, and Melissa Zielinski. 2020. "Sexual Victimization and Mental Illness Prevalence Rates Among Incarcerated Women: A Literature Review." *Trauma, Violence, & Abuse* 21(2):326–349.

Katz, Jonathan Ned. 2007. *The Invention of Heterosexuality*. Chicago, IL: University of Chicago Press.

Kelly, Liz. 1988. *Surviving Sexual Violence*. Minneapolis: University of Minnesota Press.

Kennedy, Angie, and Kristen Prock. 2018. "'I Still Feel Like I Am Not Normal': A Review of the Role of Stigma and Stigmatization among Female Survivors of Child Sexual Abuse, Sexual Assault, and Intimate Partner Violence." *Trauma, Violence, & Abuse* 19(5):512–527.

Khan, Shamus, Joss Greene, Claude Ann Mellins, and Jennifer Hirsch. 2020. "The Social Organization of Sexual Assault." *Annual Review of Criminology* 3:139–163.

Kilgore, James. 2015. "Mass Incarceration: Examining and Moving beyond the New Jim Crow." *Critical Sociology* 41(2):283–295.

Kilty, Jennifer, and Katarina Bogosavljevic. 2019. "Emotional Storytelling: Sensational Media and the Creation of the HIV Sexual Predator." *Crime, Media, Culture* 15(2):279–299.

Kim, Mimi. 2018. "From Carceral Feminism to Transformative Justice: Women-of-Color Feminism and Alternatives to Incarceration." *Journal of Ethnic & Cultural Diversity in Social Work* 27(3):219–233.

———. 2020. "Anti-Carceral Feminism: The Contradictions of Progress and the Possibilities of Counter-Hegemonic Struggle." *Affilia* 35(3):309–326.

Kunzel, Regina. 2008. *Criminal Intimacy: Prison and the Uneven History of Modern American Sexuality*. Chicago, IL: University of Chicago Press.

Lancaster, Roger. 2011. *Sex Panic and the Punitive State*. Berkeley: University of California Press.

Larance, Lisa Young, Leigh Goodmark, Susan Miller, and Shamita Das Dasgupta. 2019. "Understanding and Addressing Women's Use of Force in Intimate Relationships: A Retrospective." *Violence Against Women* 25(1):56–80.

Law, Victoria. 2014. "Against Carceral Feminism." *Jacobin*, October 17. Available at: https://www.jacobinmag.com/2014/10/against-carceral-feminism/ (accessed November 6, 2020).

Lee, Cynthia. 2020. "The Trans Panic Defense Revisited." *American Criminal Law Review* 57(4):1411–1498.

Legewie, Joscha. 2016. "Racial Profiling and Use of Force in Police Stops: How Local Events Trigger Periods of Increased Discrimination." *American Journal of Sociology* 122(2):379–424.

Lewis, Brodie, Cassandra Hesse, Briana Cook, and Cory Pedersen. 2020. "Sexistential Crisis: An Intersectional Analysis of Gender Expression and Sexual Orientation in Masculine Overcompensation." *Journal of Homosexuality* 67(1):58–78.

Little, Betsi. 2020. "Who's the Victim Here? The Role of Gender, Social Norms, and Heteronormativity in the IPV Gender Symmetry Debate." In *Intimate Partner Violence and the LGBT+ Community*, edited by Brenda Russell, pp. 69–88. Cham, Switzerland: Springer.

Lowe, Michelle, and Paul Rogers. 2017. "The Scope of Male Rape: A Selective Review of Research, Policy and Practice." *Aggression and Violent Behavior* 35:38–43.

MacKinnon, Catharine. 1989. *Toward a Feminist Theory of the State*. Cambridge, MA: Harvard University Press.

Madriz, Esther. 1997. *Nothing Bad Happens to Good Girls: Fear of Crime in Women's Lives*. Berkeley: University of California Press.

Mardorossian, Carine. 2014. *Framing the Rape Victim: Gender and Agency Reconsidered*. New Brunswick, NJ: Rutgers University Press.

Martin, Patricia Yancey. 2016. "The Rape Prone Culture of Academic Contexts: Fraternities and Athletics." *Gender & Society* 30(1):30–43.

Martinez, Katherine. 2021. "Overwhelming Whiteness of BDSM: A Critical Discourse Analysis of Racialization in BDSM." *Sexualities* 24(5–6):733–748.

Mason, Gail. 2002. *The Spectacle of Violence: Homophobia, Gender and Knowledge*. New York, NY: Routledge.

———. 2014. "The Symbolic Purpose of Hate Crime Law: Ideal Victims and Emotion." *Theoretical Criminology* 18(1):75–92.

Mathers, Lain, J. E. Sumerau, and Ryan Cragun. 2018. "The Limits of Homonormativity: Constructions of Bisexual and Transgender People in the Post-Gay Era." *Sociological Perspectives* 61(6):934–952.

May, Vivian. 2015. *Pursuing Intersectionality, Unsettling Dominant Imaginaries*. New York, NY: Routledge.

Mayring, Philipp. 2004. "Qualitative Content Analysis." In *A Companion to Qualitative Research*, edited by Uwe Flick, Ernst von Kardoff, and Ines Steink, pp. 266–269. Thousand Oaks, CA: Sage.

Mbembe, Achille. 2019. *Necropolitics*. Durham, NC: Duke University Press.

McCall, Leslie. 2005. "The Complexity of Intersectionality." *Signs* 30(3):1771–1800.

McCrea, Katherine Tyson, Maryse Richards, Dakari Quimby, Darrick Scott, Lauren Davis, Sotonye Hart, Andre Thomas, and Symora Hopson. 2019. "Understanding Violence and Developing Resilience with African American Youth in High-Poverty, High-Crime Communities." *Children and Youth Services Review* 99:296–307.

McCune, Jeffrey. 2014. *Sexual Discretion: Black Masculinity and the Politics of Passing*. Chicago, IL: University of Chicago Press.

McDonald, James, Kate Lockwood Harris, and Jessica Ramirez. 2020. "Revealing and Concealing Difference: A Critical Approach to Disclosure and an Intersectional Theory of 'Closeting.'" *Communication Theory* 30(1):84–104.

McGlynn, Clare, Erika Rackley, and Ruth Houghton. 2017. "Beyond 'Revenge Porn': The Continuum of Image-Based Sexual Abuse." *Feminist Legal Studies* 25(1):25–46.

McGuffey, C. Shawn. 2008. "'Saving Masculinity:' Gender Reaffirmation, Sexuality, Race, and Parental Responses to Male Child Sexual Abuse." *Social Problems* 55(2):216–237.

———. 2010. "Blacks and Racial Appraisals: Gender, Race, and Intraracial Rape." In *Black Sexualities*, edited by Juan Battle and Sandra Barnes, pp. 273–298. New Brunswick, NJ: Rutgers University Press.

———. 2013. "Rape and Racial Appraisals: Culture, Intersectionality, and Black Women's Accounts of Sexual Assault." *Du Bois Review* 10(1):109–130.

McGuire, Danielle. 2010. *At the Dark End of the Street: Black Women, Rape, and Resistance: A New History of the Civil Rights Movement from Rosa Parks to the Rise of Black Power*. New York, NY: Vintage.

McKay, Richard. 2017. *Patient Zero and the Making of the AIDS Epidemic*. Chicago, IL: University of Chicago Press.

McLean, Iain. 2013. "The Male Victim of Sexual Assault." *Best Practice and Research Clinical and Gynaecology* 27(1):39–46.

Meiners, Erica. 2016. *For the Children? Protecting Innocence in a Carceral State*. Minneapolis: University of Minnesota Press.

Menjívar, Cecilia. 2011. *Enduring Violence: Ladina Women's Lives in Guatemala*. Berkeley: University of California Press.

Messerschmidt, James. 2016. *Masculinities in the Making: From the Local to the Global*. Lanham, MD: Rowman & Littlefield.

———. 2018. *Hegemonic Masculinity: Formulation, Reformulation, and Amplification*. Lanham, MD: Rowman & Littlefield.

Messinger, Adam. 2017. *LGBTQ Intimate Partner Violence: Lessons for Policy, Practice, and Research*. Oakland: University of California Press.

Messinger, Adam, and Xavier Guadalupe-Diaz, eds. 2020. *Transgender Intimate Partner Violence: A Comprehensive Introduction*. New York: New York University Press.

Messinger, Adam, and Sarah Koon-Magnin. 2019. "Sexual Violence in LGBTQ Communities." In *Handbook of Sexual Assault and Sexual Assault Prevention*, edited by William O'Donohue and Paul Schewe, pp. 661–674. Cham, Switzerland: Springer.

Messner, Michael. 2016. "Bad Men, Good Men, Bystanders: Who Is the Rapist?" *Gender & Society* 30(1):57–66.

———. 2016. "Forks in the Road of Men's Gender Politics: Men's Rights vs Feminist Allies." *International Journal for Crime, Justice and Social Democracy* 5(2):6–20.

Meyer, Doug. 2012. "An Intersectional Analysis of Lesbian, Gay, Bisexual, and Transgender (LGBT) People's Evaluations of Anti-Queer Violence." *Gender & Society* 26(6):849–873.

———. 2014. "Resisting Hate Crime Discourse: Queer and Intersectional Challenges to Neoliberal Hate Crime Laws." *Critical Criminology* 22(1):113–125.

———. 2015. *Violence against Queer People: Race, Class, Gender, and the Persistence of Anti-LGBT Discrimination*. New Brunswick, NJ: Rutgers University Press.

———. 2020. "Omar Mateen as U.S. Citizen, Not Foreign Threat: Homonationalism and LGBTQ Online Representations of the Pulse Nightclub Shooting." *Sexualities* 23(3):249–268.

———. 2020. "'So Much for Protect and Serve': Queer Male Survivors' Perceptions of Negative Police Experiences." *Journal of Contemporary Criminal Justice* 36(2):228–250.

———. 2022. "Racializing Emasculation: An Intersectional Analysis of Queer Men's Evaluations of Sexual Assault." *Social Problems* 69(1):39–57.

———. 2022. "Constructing Hierarchies of Victimhood: Queer Male Survivors' Evaluations of Sexual Assault Survivors." *Sexualities*. doi: 10.1177/13634607211060502.

Meyer, Ilan, Andrew Flores, Lara Stemple, Adam Romero, Bianca Wilson, and Jody Herman. 2017. "Incarceration Rates and Traits of Sexual Minorities in the United States: National Inmate Survey, 2011–2012." *American Journal of Public Health* 107(2):267–273.

Miles, Matthew, A. Michael Huberman, and Johnny Saldaña. 2019. *Qualitative Data Analysis: A Methods Sourcebook*. Thousand Oaks, CA: Sage.

Miller, Michael. 2016. "'A Steep Price to Pay for 20 Minutes of Action': Dad Defends Stanford Sex Offender." *Washington Post*, June 6. Available at:

https://www. Washingtonpost.com /news/morning-mix/wp/2016/06/06/a -steep-price-to-pay-for-20-minutes-of-action-dad-defends-stanford-sex-off ender/ (accessed October 6, 2020).

Mingus, Mia. 2019. "Transformative Justice; A Brief Description." *Leaving Evidence*, January 9. Available at: https://leavingevidence.wordpress.com /2019/01/09/transformative-justice-a-brief-description/ (accessed November 9, 2020).

Miroff, Nick. 2019. "Nearly 1 Million Migrants Arrested Along Mexico Border in Fiscal 2019, Most Since 2007." *Washington Post*, October 8. Available at: https://www.washingtonpost.com/immigration/nearly-1-million-migrants -arrested-along-mexico-border-in-fiscal-2019-most-since-2007/2019/10/08 /749413e4-e9d4-11e9-9306-47cb0324fd44_story.html (accessed June 1, 2020).

Mogul, Joey, Andrea Ritchie, and Kay Whitlock. 2011. *Queer (In)Justice: The Criminalization of LGBT People in the United States*. Boston, MA : Beacon.

Moore, Mignon. 2011. *Invisible Families: Gay Identities, Relationships, and Motherhood among Black Women*. Berkeley: University of California Press.

Moraga, Cherríe, and Gloria Anzaldúa, eds. 1981. *This Bridge Called My Back: Writings by Radical Women of Color*. Watertown, MA: Persephone.

Moran, Leslie. 2000. "Homophobic Violence: The Hidden Injuries of Class." In *Cultural Studies and the Working Class*, edited by Sally Munt, pp. 206–218. London, UK: Cassell.

Mouilso, Emily, Sarah Fischer, and Karen Calhoun. 2012. "A Prospective Study of Sexual Assault and Alcohol Use Among First-Year College Women." *Violence and Victims* 27(1):78–94.

Muhammad, Khalil Gibran. 2019. *The Condemnation of Blackness: Race, Crime, and the Making of Modern Urban America*. Cambridge, MA: Harvard University Press.

Muehlenhard, Charlene, Terry Humphreys, Kristen Jozkowski, and Zoë Peterson. 2016. "The Complexities of Sexual Consent Among College Students: A Conceptual and Empirical Review." *Journal of Sex Research* 53(4–5):457–487.

Muehlenhard, Charlene, Zoë Peterson, Terry Humphreys, and Kristen Jozkowski. 2017. "Evaluating the One-in-Five Statistic: Women's Risk of Sexual Assault While in College." *Journal of Sex Research* 54(4–5):549–576.

Mulla, Sameena. 2014. *The Violence of Care: Rape Victims, Forensic Nurses, and Sexual Assault Intervention*. New York: New York University Press.

Mumford, Kevin. 2016. *Not Straight, Not White: Black Gay Men from the March on Washington to the AIDS Crisis*. Chapel Hill: University of North Carolina Press.

Muñoz, José. 1999. *Disidentifications: Queers of Color and the Performance of Politics*. Minneapolis: University of Minnesota Press.

Musto, Jennifer. 2016. *Control and Protect: Collaboration, Carceral Protection, and Domestic Sex Trafficking in the United States.* Oakland: University of California Press.

———. 2019. "Transing Critical Criminology: A Critical Unsettling and Transformative Anti-Carceral Feminist Reframing." *Critical Criminology* 27(1):37–54.

Myhill, Andy. 2017. "Measuring Domestic Violence: Context Is Everything." *Journal of Gender-Based Violence* 1(1):33–44.

Nash, Jennifer. 2014. "Black Anality." *GLQ* 20(4):439–460.

———. 2019. *Black Feminism Reimagined: After Intersectionality.* Durham, NC: Duke University Press.

Nash, Shondrah. 2005. "Through Black Eyes: African American Women's Constructions of Their Experiences with Intimate Male Partner Violence." *Violence against Women* 11(11):1420–1440.

Nguyen, Tan Hoang. 2014. *A View from the Bottom: Asian American Masculinity and Sexual Representation.* Durham, NC: Duke University Press.

Niedt, Greg. 2020. "PrEP Talk: Media Narratives and the Terrifying Sublime." *Sexualities* 23(8):1378–1399.

O'Byrne, Patrick, and Dave Holmes. 2009. "Public Health STI/HIV Surveillance: Exploring the Society of Control." *Surveillance & Society* 7(1):58–70.

Ocampo, Anthony. 2012. "Making Masculinity: Negotiations of Gender Presentation among Latino Gay Men." *Latino Studies* 10(4):448–472.

Oeur, Freeden Blume. 2018. *Black Boys Apart: Racial Uplift and Respectability in All-Male Public Schools.* Minneapolis: University of Minnesota Press.

O'Leary, Cristina Hunter. 2020. "Addressing the Epidemic of Sexual Assault in California's Immigration Detention Centers." *Rethinking Policy on Gender, Sexuality, and Women's Issues, CSW Policy Brief* 25:1–4.

O'Neal, Eryn Nicole. 2019. "'Victim Is Not Credible': The Influence of Rape Culture on Police Perceptions of Sexual Assault Complainants." *Justice Quarterly* 36(1):127–160.

Owen, Barbara, James Wells, and Joycelyn Pollock. 2017. *In Search of Safety: Confronting Inequality in Women's Imprisonment.* Oakland: University of California Press.

Panfil, Vanessa. 2017. *The Gang's All Queer: The Lives of Gay Gang Members.* New York: New York University Press.

Parent, Mike and Kevin Ferriter. 2018. "The Co-occurrence of Asexuality and Self-Reported Post-Traumatic Stress Disorder Diagnosis and Sexual Trauma within the Past 12 Months among U.S. College Students." *Archives of Sexual Behavior* 47(4):1277–1282.

Pascoe, C. J. 2007. *Dude, You're a Fag: Masculinity and Sexuality in High School.* Berkeley: University of California Press.

Pascoe, C. J., and Jocelyn Hollander. 2016. "Good Guys Don't Rape: Gender, Domination, and Mobilizing Rape." *Gender & Society* 30(1):67–79.

Patterson, Jennifer, ed. 2016. *Queering Sexual Violence: Radical Voices from Within the Anti-Violence Movement.* Riverdale, NY: Riverdale Avenue Books.

Pedulla, David. 2014. "The Positive Consequences of Negative Stereotypes: Race, Sexual Orientation, and the Job Application Process." *Social Psychology Quarterly* 77(1):75–94.

Pérez, Hiram. 2015. *A Taste for Brown Bodies: Gay Modernity and Cosmopolitan Desire.* New York: New York University Press.

Perry, Barbara. 2001. *In the Name of Hate: Understanding Hate Crimes.* New York, NY: Routledge.

Petrosky, Emiko, Janet Blair, Carter Betz, Katherine Fowler, Shane Jack, and Bridget Lyons. 2017. "Racial and Ethnic Differences in Homicides of Adult Women and the Role of Intimate Partner Violence–United States, 2003–2014." *Morbidity and Mortality Weekly Report* 66(28):741–746.

Pfeffer, Carla. 2017. *Queering Families: The Postmodern Partnerships of Cisgender Women and Transgender Men.* New York, NY: Oxford University Press.

Phillips, Nickie, and Nicholas Chagnon. 2020. "'Six Months Is a Joke': Carceral Feminism and Penal Populism in the Wake of the Stanford Sexual Assault Case." *Feminist Criminology* 15(1):47–69.

Phipps, Alison. 2009. "Rape and Respectability: Ideas about Sexual Violence and Social Class." *Sociology* 43(4):667–683.

———. 2019. "'Every Woman Knows a Weinstein': Political Whiteness and White Woundedness in #MeToo and Public Feminisms around Sexual Violence." *Feminist Formations* 31(2):1–25.

Pierce-Baker, Charlotte. 2000. *Surviving the Silence: Black Women's Stories of Rape.* New York, NY: W. W. Norton & Company.

Pitt, Richard. 2009. "'Still Looking for My Jonathan': Gay Black Men's Management of Religious and Sexual Identity Conflicts." *Journal of Homosexuality* 57(1):39–53.

Porter, Ronald. 2012. "A Rainbow in Black: The Gay Politics of the Black Panther Party." *Counterpoints* 367:364–375.

Potter, Hillary. 2008. *Battle Cries: Black Women and Intimate Partner Abuse.* New York: New York University Press.

Powell, Amber Joy, Heather Hlavka, and Sameena Mulla. 2017. "Intersectionality and Credibility in Child Sexual Assault Trials." *Gender & Society* 31(4):457–480.

Press, Alex. 2018. "#MeToo Must Avoid 'Carceral Feminism.'" *Vox*, February 1. Available at: https://www.vox.com/the-big-idea/2018/2/1/16952744/me-too -larry-nassar-judge-aquilina-feminism (accessed October 25, 2020).

Price, Joshua. 2012. *Structural Violence: Hidden Brutality in the Lives of Women.* Albany: State University of New York Press.

Ptacek, James, ed. 2010. *Restorative Justice and Violence against Women.* New York, NY: Oxford University Press.

Puar, Jasbir. 2007. *Terrorist Assemblages: Homonationalism in Queer Times*. Durham, NC: Duke University Press.

———. 2017. *The Right to Maim: Debility, Capacity, Disability*. Durham, NC: Duke University Press.

Pulido, Laura. 2006. *Black, Brown, Yellow, and Left: Radical Activism in Los Angeles*. Berkeley: University of California Press.

Qu, Sandy, and John Dumay. 2011. "The Qualitative Research Interview." *Qualitative Research in Accounting and Management* 8(3):238–264.

Quesada, Uriel, Letitia Gomez, and Salvador Vidal-Ortiz. 2015. *Queer Brown Voices: Personal Narratives of Latina/o LGBT Activism*. Austin: University of Texas Press.

Ralston, Kevin. 2012. "An Intersectional Approach to Understanding Stigma Associated with Male Sexual Assault Victimization." *Sociology Compass* 6(4):283–292.

Ransby, Barbara. 2018. *Making All Black Lives Matter: Reimagining Freedom in the Twenty-First Century*. Oakland: University of California Press.

Ravenhill, James and Richard de Visser. 2018. "'It Takes a Man to Put Me on the Bottom': Gay Men's Experiences of Masculinity and Anal Intercourse." *Journal of Sex Research* 55(8):1033–1047.

Reddy, Chandan. 2011. *Freedom with Violence: Race, Sexuality, and the US State*. Durham, NC: Duke University Press.

Reid-Pharr, Robert. 2001. *Black Gay Man: Essays*. New York: New York University Press.

Renzetti, Claire. 1999. "The Challenge to Feminism Posed by Women's Use of Violence in Intimate Relationships." In *New Versions of Victims*, edited by Sharon Lamb, pp. 42–56. New York: New York University Press.

"Responding to Transgender Victims of Sexual Assault." 2014. Office of Justice Programs. Available at: https://ovc.ojp.gov/sites/g/files/xyckuh226/files/pubs /forge/ sexual_numbers.html (accessed October 1, 2020).

Ricciardelli, Rosemary, Dale Spencer, and Alexa Dodge. 2021. "'Society Wants to See a True Victim': Police Interpretations of Victims of Sexual Violence." *Feminist Criminology* 16(2):216–235.

Richardson, Niall. 2018. "'Whether You Are Gay or Straight, I Don't Like to See Effeminate Dancing': Effeminophobia in Performance-Level Ballroom Dance." *Journal of Gender Studies* 27(2):207–219.

Richie, Beth. 2012. *Arrested Justice: Black Women, Violence, and America's Prison Nation*. New York: New York University Press.

Ringrose, Jessica, and Emma Renold. 2012. "Slut-Shaming, Girl Power and 'Sexualisation': Thinking through the Politics of the International SlutWalks with Teen Girls." *Gender and Education* 24(3):333–343.

Rios, Victor. 2011. *Punished: Policing the Lives of Black and Latino Boys*. New York: New York University Press.

Ritchie, Andrea. 2013. "Crimes against Nature: Challenging Criminalization of Queerness and Black Women's Sexuality." *Loyola Journal of Public Interest Law* 14(2):355–374.

———. 2017. *Invisible No More: Police Violence against Black Women and Women of Color*. Boston, MA: Beacon.

Robinson, Brandon Andrew. 2015. "'Personal Preference' as the New Racism: Gay Desire and Racial Cleansing in Cyberspace." *Sociology of Race and Ethnicity* 1(2):317–330.

———. 2020. *Coming Out to the Streets: LGBTQ Youth Experiencing Homelessness*. Oakland: University of California Press.

Rodriguez, S. M., Liat Ben-Moshe, and H. Rakes. 2020. "Carceral Protectionism and the Perpetually (In)Vulnerable." *Criminology & Criminal Justice* 20(5):537–550.

Rogers, Baker. 2020. *Trans Men in the South: Becoming Men*. Lanham, MD: Lexington.

Rogers, Michaela. 2019. "Challenging Cisgenderism through Trans People's Narratives of Domestic Violence and Abuse." *Sexualities* 22(5–6):803–820.

Rosenberg, Rae, and Natalie Oswin. 2015. "Trans Embodiment in Carceral Space: Hypermasculinity and the US Prison Industrial Complex." *Gender, Place & Culture* 22(9):1269–1286.

Rothman, Emily, Deinera Exner, and Allyson Baughman. 2011. "The Prevalence of Sexual Assault against People Who Identify as Gay, Lesbian, or Bisexual in the United States: A Systematic Review." *Trauma, Violence, & Abuse* 12(2):55–66.

Rumney, Philip. 2008. "Policing Male Rape and Sexual Assault." *The Journal of Criminal Law* 72(1):67–86.

———. 2009. "Gay Male Rape Victims: Law Enforcement, Social Attitudes and Barriers to Recognition." *The International Journal of Human Rights* 13(2–3):233–250.

Russell, Emma. 2017. "Queer Penalties: The Criminal Justice Paradigm in Lesbian and Gay Anti-Violence Politics." *Critical Criminology* 25(1):21–35.

———. 2019. *Queer Histories and the Politics of Policing*. New York, NY: Routledge.

Russell-Brown, Katheryn. 2009. *The Color of Crime*. New York: New York University Press.

Russo, Ann. 2019. *Feminist Accountability: Disrupting Violence and Transforming Power*. New York: New York University Press.

Ryan, William. 1971. *Blaming the Victim*. New York, NY: Vintage.

Safer, Joshua, Eli Coleman, Jamie Feldman, Robert Garofalo, Wylie Hembree, Asa Radix, and Jae Sevelius. 2016. "Barriers to Health Care for Transgender Individuals." *Current Opinion in Endocrinology, Diabetes, and Obesity* 23(2):168–171.

Saguy, Abigail. 2020. *Come Out, Come Out, Whoever You Are*. New York, NY: Oxford University Press.

Salamon, Gayle. 2018. *The Life and Death of Latisha King: A Critical Phenomenology of Transphobia*. New York: New York University Press.

Sawyer, Wendy, and Peter Wagner. 2020. "Mass Incarceration: The Whole Pie 2020." Available at: https://www.prisonpolicy.org/reports/pie2020.html (accessed October 1, 2020).

Schenwar, Maya, and Victoria Law. 2020. *Prison by Any Other Name: The Harmful Consequences of Popular Reforms*. New York, NY: New Press.

Schilt, Kristen. 2010. *Just One of the Guys? Transgender Men and the Persistence of Gender Inequality*. Chicago, IL: University of Chicago Press.

Schilt, Kristen and Laurel Westbrook. 2009. "Doing Gender, Doing Heteronormativity: 'Gender Normals,' Transgender People, and the Social Maintenance of Heterosexuality." *Gender & Society* 23(4):440–464.

Schippers, Mimi. 2007. "Recovering the Feminine Other: Masculinity, Femininity, and Gender Hegemony." *Theory and Society* 36(1):85–102.

———. 2016. *Beyond Monogamy: Polyamory and the Future of Polyqueer Sexualities*. New York: New York University Press.

Schoenfeld, Heather. 2018. *Building the Prison State: Race and the Politics of Mass Incarceration*. Chicago, IL: University of Chicago Press.

Schreier, Margrit. 2012. *Qualitative Content Analysis in Practice*. Thousand Oaks, CA: Sage.

Schulz, Philipp. 2020. *Male Survivors of Wartime Sexual Violence: Perspectives from Northern Uganda*. Oakland: University of California Press.

Schulze, Corina, Sarah Koon-Magnin, and Valerie Bryan. 2019. *Gender Identity, Sexual Orientation, and Sexual Assault: Challenging the Myths*. Boulder, CO: Lynne Rienner.

Schwalbe, Michael, Daphne Holden, Douglas Schrock, Sandra Godwin, Shealy Thompson, and Michele Wolkomir. 2000. "Generic Processes in the Reproduction of Inequality: An Interactionist Analysis." *Social Forces* 79(2):419–452.

Sears, Alan. 2005. "Queer Anti-Capitalism: What's Left of Lesbian and Gay Liberation?" *Science & Society* 69(1):92–112.

Seigel, Micol. 2018. *Violence Work: State Power and the Limits of Police*. Durham, NC: Duke University Press.

Shepp, Veronica, Erin O'Callaghan, Anne Kirkner, Katherine Lorenz, and Sarah Ullman. 2020. "Sexual Assault Survivors Who Exchange Sex: Identity, Stigma, and Informal Responses from Support Providers." *Affilia* 35(1):105–128.

Sherman, Lawrence, and Heather Strang. 2007. *Restorative Justice: The Evidence*. London, UK: Smith Institute.

Sjoberg, Laura. 2016. *Women as Wartime Rapists: Beyond Sensation and Stereotyping*. New York: New York University Press.

Slakoff, Danielle, and Pauline Brennan. 2019. "The Differential Representation of Latina and Black Female Victims in Front-Page News Stories: A Qualitative Document Analysis." *Feminist Criminology* 14(4):488–516.

Small, Jamie. 2019. "Constructing Sexual Harm: Prosecutorial Narratives of Children, Abuse, and the Disruption of Heterosexuality." *Gender & Society* 33(4):560–582.

Smith, Andrea. 2011. "Decolonizing Anti-Rape Law and Strategizing Accountability in Native American Communities." *Social Justice* 37(4):36–43.

Smith, Barbara. 1999. "Blacks and Gays: Healing the Great Divide." In *Dangerous Liaisons*, edited by Eric Brandt, pp. 15–24. New York, NY: New Press.

Snorton, C. Riley. 2014. *Nobody Is Supposed to Know: Black Sexuality on the Down Low*. Minneapolis: University of Minnesota Press.

———. 2017. *Black on Both Sides: A Racial History of Trans Identity*. Minneapolis: University of Minnesota Press.

Somerville, Siobhan. 2000. *Queering the Color Line: Race and the Invention of Homosexuality in American Culture*. Durham, NC: Duke University Press.

Soss, Joe, Richard Fording, and Sanford Schram. 2011. *Disciplining the Poor: Neoliberal Paternalism and the Persistent Power of Race*. Chicago, IL: University of Chicago Press.

Spade, Dean. 2015. *Normal Life: Administrative Violence, Critical Trans Politics and the Limits of Law*. Durham, NC: Duke University Press.

———. 2020. *Mutual Aid: Building Solidarity during This Crisis (and the Next)*. Brooklyn, NY: Verso.

Sprankle, Eric, Katie Bloomquist, Cody Butcher, Neil Gleason, and Zoe Schaefer. 2018. "The Role of Sex Work Stigma in Victim Blaming and Empathy of Sexual Assault Survivors." *Sexuality Research and Social Policy* 15(3):242–248.

Spruill, Larry. 2016. "Slave Patrols, 'Packs of Negro Dogs' and Policing Black Communities." *Phylon* 53(1):42–66.

Stacey, Michele. 2019. "Macrostructural Opportunity and Violent Crime: The Impact of Social Structure on Inter- and Intra-Racial Violence." *American Journal of Criminal Justice* 44(1):125–145.

Stanko, Elizabeth, and Kathy Hobdell. 1993. "Assault on Men: Masculinity and Male Victimization." *The British Journal of Criminology* 33(3):400–415.

Stanley, Eric, and Nat Smith, eds. 2015. *Captive Genders: Trans Embodiment and the Prison Industrial Complex*. Oakland, CA: AK Press.

Stanziani, Marissa, Jennifer Cox, and C. Adam Coffey. 2018. "Adding Insult to Injury: Sex, Sexual Orientation, and Juror Decision-Making in a Case of Intimate Partner Violence." *Journal of Homosexuality* 65(10):1325–1350.

Stark, Evan. 2007. *Coercive Control: The Entrapment of Women in Personal Life*. New York, NY: Oxford University Press.

Steele, Sarah, Megan Collier, and J. E. Sumerau. 2018. "Lesbian, Gay, and Bisexual Contact with Police in Chicago: Disparities across Sexuality, Race, and Socioeconomic Status." *Social Currents* 5(4):328–349.

Stein, Arlene. 2018. *Unbound: Transgender Men and the Remaking of Identity.* New York, NY: Vintage.

Stemple, Lara, Andrew Flores, and Ilan Meyer. 2017. "Sexual Victimization Perpetrated by Women: Federal Data Reveal Surprising Prevalence." *Aggression and Violent Behavior* 34:302–311.

Stemple, Lara, and Ilan Meyer. 2014. "The Sexual Victimization of Men in America: New Data Challenge Old Assumptions." *American Journal of Public Health* 104(6): e19–e26.

Stewart-Winter, Timothy. 2016. *Queer Clout: Chicago and the Rise of Gay Politics.* Philadelphia: University of Pennsylvania Press.

Stockton, Kathryn Bond. 2006. *Beautiful Bottom, Beautiful Shame: Where "Black" Meets "Queer."* Durham, NC: Duke University Press.

Stone, Amy. 2018. "Gender Panics about Transgender Children in Religious Right Discourse." *Journal of LGBT Youth* 15(1):1–15.

Stotzer, Rebecca. 2014. "Law Enforcement and Criminal Justice Personnel Interactions with Transgender People in the United States: A Literature Review." *Aggression and Violent Behavior* 19(3):263–277.

Stryker, Susan. 2017. *Transgender History: The Roots of Today's Revolution.* New York, NY: Seal.

Stubbs-Richardson, Megan, Nicole Rader, and Arthur Cosby. 2018. "Tweeting Rape Culture: Examining Portrayals of Victim Blaming in Discussions of Sexual Assault Cases on Twitter." *Feminism & Psychology* 28(1):90–108.

Suddler, Carl. 2019. *Presumed Criminal: Black Youth and the Justice System in Postwar New York.* New York: New York University Press.

Sullivan, Nikki. 2003. *A Critical Introduction to Queer Theory.* New York: New York University Press.

Sumerau, J. E. 2020. *Violent Manhood.* Lanham, MD: Rowman & Littlefield.

Sweet, Elizabeth. 2016. "Carceral Feminism: Linking the State, Intersectional Bodies, and the Dichotomy of Place." *Dialogues in Human Geography* 6(2):202–205.

Sweet, Paige. 2019. "The Sociology of Gaslighting." *American Sociological Review* 84(5):851–75.

Taylor, Chloë. 2018. "Anti-Carceral Feminism and Sexual Assault—A Defense: A Critique of the Critique of the Critique of Carceral Feminism." *Social Philosophy Today* 34:29–49.

———. 2019. *Foucault, Feminism, and Sex Crimes: An Anti-Carceral Analysis.* New York, NY: Routledge.

Taylor, Clarence. 2018. *Fight the Power: African Americans and the Long History of Police Brutality in New York City.* New York: New York University Press.

Taylor, Keeanga-Yamahtta. 2016. *From #BlackLivesMatter to Black Liberation.* Chicago, IL: Haymarket.

Terwiel, Anna. 2020. "What Is Carceral Feminism?" *Political Theory* 48(4):421–442.

Thuma, Emily. 2019. *All Our Trials: Prisons, Policing, and the Feminist Fight to End Violence.* Urbana: University of Illinois Press.

Tillapaugh, Daniel. 2017. "'The Wounds of Our Experience': College Men Who Experienced Sexual Violence." In *Intersections of Identity and Sexual Violence on Campus*, edited by Jessica Harris and Chris Linder, pp. 101–118. Sterling, VA: Stylus.

Toft, Alex, and Andrew Kam-Tuck Yip. 2018. "Intimacy Negotiated: The Management of Relationships and the Construction of Personal Communities in the Lives of Bisexual Women and Men." *Sexualities* 21(1–2):233–250.

Tomsen, Stephen. 2009. *Violence, Prejudice and Sexuality.* New York, NY: Routledge.

Turell, Susan, Michael Brown, and Molly Herrmann. 2018. "Disproportionately High: An Exploration of Intimate Partner Violence Prevalence Rates for Bisexual People." *Sexual and Relationship Therapy* 33(1–2):113–131.

Unnever, James, Shaun Gabbidon, and Cecilia Chouhy, eds. 2019. *Building a Black Criminology: Race, Theory, and Crime.* New York, NY: Routledge.

Venema, Rachel. 2016. "Police Officer Schema of Sexual Assault Reports: Real Rape, Ambiguous Cases, and False Reports." *Journal of Interpersonal Violence* 31(5):872–899.

Vitale, Alex. 2017. *The End of Policing.* Brooklyn, NY: Verso.

Wacquant, Loïc. 2009. *Prisons of Poverty.* Minneapolis: University of Minnesota Press.

Wade, Lisa. 2017. *American Hookup: The New Culture of Sex on Campus.* New York, NY: W.W. Norton & Company.

Waldman, Ari Ezra. 2019. "Law, Privacy, and Online Dating: 'Revenge Porn' in Gay Online Communities." *Law & Social Inquiry* 44(4):987–1018.

Walfield, Scott. 2021. "'Men Cannot Be Raped': Correlates of Male Rape Myth Acceptance." *Journal of Interpersonal Violence* 36(13–14):6391–6417.

Walker, Jayne, John Archer, and Michelle Davies. 2005. "Effects of Rape on Men: A Descriptive Analysis." *Archives of Sexual Behavior* 34(1):69–80.

Walters, Suzanna Danuta. 2014. *The Tolerance Trap: How God, Genes, and Good Intentions Are Sabotaging Gay Equality.* New York: New York University Press.

Wang, Jackie. 2018. *Carceral Capitalism.* Cambridge, MA: MIT Press.

Ward, Jane. 2000. "Queer Sexism: Rethinking Gay Men and Masculinity." *Research on Men and Masculinities Series* 12:152–175.

———. 2008. *Respectably Queer: Diversity Culture in LGBT Activist Organizations.* Nashville, TN: Vanderbilt University Press.

———. 2016. "Dyke Methods: A Meditation on Queer Studies and the Gay Men Who Hate It." *Women's Studies Quarterly* 44(3/4):68–85.

Warner, Michael. 1999. *The Trouble with Normal: Sex, Politics, and the Ethics of Queer Life*. Cambridge, MA: Harvard University Press.

Weiss, Benjamin. 2020. "'Who Can We Tell Survivors to Call?' The Institutionalization of Criminal-Legal Interventions in a Domestic Violence Organization." *Social Problems* 67(2):270–285.

Weiss, Karen. 2010. "Male Sexual Victimization: Examining Men's Experiences of Rape and Sexual Assault." *Men and Masculinities* 12(3):275–298.

———. 2010. "Too Ashamed to Report: Deconstructing the Shame of Sexual Victimization." *Feminist Criminology* 5(3):286–310.

Weiss, Margot. 2011. *Techniques of Pleasure: BDSM and the Circuits of Sexuality*. Durham, NC: Duke University Press.

Weitzer, Ronald. 2018. "Resistance to Sex Work Stigma." *Sexualities* 21(5–6):717–729.

Westbrook, Laurel. 2020. *Unlivable Lives: Violence and Identity in Transgender Activism*. Oakland: University of California Press.

West, Candace, and Don Zimmerman. 1987. "Doing Gender." *Gender & Society* 1(2):125–151.

White, Michael, and Henry Fradella. 2019. *Stop and Frisk: The Use and Abuse of a Controversial Policing Tactic*. New York: New York University Press.

Whittier, Nancy. 2016. "Carceral and Intersectional Feminism in Congress: The Violence Against Women Act, Discourse, and Policy." *Gender & Society* 30(5):791–818.

———. 2018. *Frenemies: Feminists, Conservatives, and Sexual Violence*. New York, NY: Oxford University Press.

Wiley, Tisha and Bette Bottoms. 2013. "Attitudinal and Individual Differences Influence Perceptions of Mock Child Sexual Assault Cases Involving Gay Defendants." *Journal of Homosexuality* 60(5):734–749.

Williams, Kristian. 2015. *Our Enemies in Blue: Police and Power in America*. Oakland, CA: AK Press.

Winder, Terrell. 2015. "'Shouting It Out': Religion and the Development of Black Gay Identities." *Qualitative Sociology* 38(4):375–394.

Wingfield, Adia Harvey. 2010. "Are Some Emotions Marked 'Whites Only'? Racialized Feeling Rules in Professional Workplaces." *Social Problems* 57(2):251–268.

Woods, Jordan Blair. 2014. "Queer Contestations and the Future of a Critical 'Queer' Criminology." *Critical Criminology* 22(1):5–19.

Wooten, Sara Carrigan. 2017. "Revealing a Hidden Curriculum of Black Women's Erasure in Sexual Violence Prevention Policy." *Gender and Education* 29(3):405–417.

Xu, Yin, and Yong Zheng. 2017. "Does Sexual Orientation Precede Childhood Sexual Abuse? Childhood Gender Nonconformity as a Risk Factor and Instrumental Variable Analysis." *Sexual Abuse* 29(8):786–802.

Zinn, Maxine Baca, and Bonnie Thornton Dill. 1996. "Theorizing Difference from Multiracial Feminism." *Feminist Studies* 22(2):321–331.

Zinsstag, Estelle, and Marie Keenan, eds. 2017. *Restorative Responses to Sexual Violence: Legal, Social and Therapeutic Dimensions.* New York, NY: Routledge.

Index

Abdullah-Khan, Noreen, 45
Abrahamson, Mark, 184
AIDS crisis, 64, 66, 145–47, 211n9. *See also* HIV status
Alcoff, Linda Martín, 137
anal rape, 19–20, 131–35, 198n70
Angelides, Steven, 205n8
anti-carceral work, 162, 167–68, 172–73
anti-queer prejudice: comparisons with women survivors, 114–15, 117; patholo-gizing of survivors and, 121; police and, 45–46, 48, 54, 61, 64, 69; self-blame and, 73; sexual assault and, 11–12; social class and, 176; structural marginalization and, 7–8
anti-violence activism, 197n62
Asian queer men, 31–33
assailants: associated with white working class, 176; community-based accountabil-ity and, 164, 168; concern for well-being of, 170–71; controlling behaviors of, 26, 199n5; defining, 20; discourses of blame and, 26; hypermasculinity stereotypes and, 30; marginalization of, 156; mascu-linity and, 17–18, 36–37, 154; media dis-course on, 153–54; physical strength and, 30, 199n8; power relations and, 130;

psychological manipulation and, 26, 42; racialized discourses of, 3, 20, 30–31, 111, 113, 156; restorative justice and, 163–65; sexual desire motivations, 129–31; social class and, 108, 163, 216n71; social hierar-chies and, 155; transformative justice and, 163–65; valued masculine queerness and, 103–4; white men as, 108, 110, 175–76, 194n10; women, 81, 105–6, 159

bad sex, 177
BDSM (bondage, discipline, dominance and submission): association with sexual abuse, 149–50; concerns with outing, 22, 148–52; consent and, 149–50; racial differ-ences regarding, 150; revenge porn and, 151; risk aware consensual kink (RACK), 150; safe, sane, and consensual (SSC), 149; sexual assault and, 148–50; whiteness and, 212n17; white queer men and, 150–51
biphobia, 10, 66, 76–77, 151
bisexuality: cheating stereotypes and, 77, 205n8; intimate partner violence and, 77; pansexuality and, 78, 205n8, 206n10; perceptions of greediness and, 77; poly-amorous communities and, 205n8; privileging of heterosexual/homosexual

251

Founded in 1893,
UNIVERSITY OF CALIFORNIA PRESS
publishes bold, progressive books and journals
on topics in the arts, humanities, social sciences,
and natural sciences—with a focus on social
justice issues—that inspire thought and action
among readers worldwide.

The UC PRESS FOUNDATION
raises funds to uphold the press's vital role
as an independent, nonprofit publisher, and
receives philanthropic support from a wide
range of individuals and institutions—and from
committed readers like you. To learn more, visit
ucpress.edu/supportus.